Suddenly Jewish

The Life and Times of My Jewish Mother

by Joan Moran

Copyright © 2024 by Joan Moran

All rights reserved. Any trademarks, service marks, product names, or named features are assumed to be the property of their respective owners and are used only for reference. If any of these terms are used, no endorsement is implied. Except for review purposes, the reproduction of this book, in whole or part, electronically or mechanically, constitutes a copyright violation.

Editor: Katherine Moore, Cyndi Hughes
Cover & Book Design: Chesley Nassaney
Author Photo: David Daigle

Visit the author's website at www.joanfrancesmoran.com

Softcover ISBN: 978-0-9854375-6-5
Library of Congress Control Number: 2024916165

Printed in the United States of America.

TO MY BROTHER, LANCE,
WHOSE EYES ARE STILL ON ME.

CONTENTS

Lighting the Candles	xv
Rose	1
Rose & Jake	7
Test of Endurance	13
Esther	19
The City by the Bay	27
Commerce High School	41
Jake	53
Holidays	63
Diller's Kosher Restaurant	75
1927	85
Graduation	95
Work, Play, Love	103
The Jazz Age	115
Back Alleys	127
John	137
Meet The Family	145
Tying The Knot	157
To Life	165
Cracks in the Building	177
Daniel	187
The Winds of War	195
On the Home Front	205
A Different Kind of War	217
Joan	225
The Catholic Versus the Jew	235
Member of the Tribe	249

ACKNOWLEDGMENTS

Lance Moran
David Boucher
Rachel Martin
Soll Sussman
Pat Jackson
Carlos Format

INTRODUCTION

One spring afternoon, one of my closest friends, Sylvia, and I were having our usual monthly lunch at our favorite Mexican restaurant in Austin, Texas. Other than being about the same age, somewhere in our late sixties, the strongest connection we had was that we adored each other's sense of humor and intellect. Sylvia had spotted me years ago when I came to Austin to give a speech for Texas Women in Business. That weekend Sylvia heard of my memoir, 60, Sex & Tango: Confession of a Beatnik Boomer, and arranged a reading for me at a friend's home. After the reading, she asked me to speak again for the TWB. And the rest was history. Sylvia asked me to come back another time for a Mother's Day event and talk about my relationship with my mother. Years later, I moved to Austin, and my life took another direction.

Sylvia had a mind that encompassed vast quantities of information and minutiae. She was a crackerjack human resource administrator for over twenty years and was well respected in higher-up executive circles. It was like Sylvia ruled the world. At one of our lunches, we were talking about our divorces. I only knew she was divorced decades ago. She spoke little about her ex-husband, except to say he was Jewish and the father of her only daughter. Before I moved to Austin, I would come to the city to see my son and grandchildren and dance Argentine tango in Austin's tango festival. Sylvia insisted on coming to see me dance tango one afternoon. Sylvia walked into the second-floor dance area with a handsome man whose winning smile lit up the room.

"Joan, meet my friend, Richard. He wanted to come with me after the meeting to see you dance the tango. Richard and I used to work together at Dell. Not in the same department. He's a nerd engineer and I'm a hunter and gatherer."

"Richard is Jewish," Sylvia told me at our following meetup.

"Yes, like your first husband," I replied.

"Well, I'm Jewish. Why not?"

I looked at her as if she had lost her mind or had five heads. "Sylvia, you come from the border. You're from McAllen. I'm sure you've got this wrong. You're Catholic."

"I was raised Catholic, but when I was in my thirties, I found out that my mother was Jewish. There were many families in the Valley with Jewish roots, mostly Sephardic. They went to church on Sundays, but some of them still lit the candles on Shabbat in their basements."

The conversation continued as Sylvia drove me to the airport to return to Los Angeles.

"So you were Jewish when you married your first husband?" I asked.

"It's clear you don't know anything about the Rio Grande Valley in Texas," Sylvia said.

"It's a border town."

"It's more than that. Spain occupied the land now called Mexico and north through Texas for two centuries. During the beginning of the Spanish Inquisition, King Ferdinand and Queen Isabella wanted to consolidate power by expelling the Jewish population. A good number of the Jewish population converted to Catholicism. They were called conversos – Jews who practiced their rituals under the radar but pretended to be Catholic. Ferdinand and Isabella were cagey monarchs. They knew Jews controlled a fair amount of the Spanish wealth and possessed expertise in banking and finance, which could be used to the crown's advantage. They sent a cadre of Jews over to the Americas to manage a vast amount of territory where the Spanish military was engaged in keeping the lands for Spain. That's how the Jews came to Texas."

"Were you conflicted about being raised a Catholic and finding out you were Jewish?" I asked.

"Not too much," said Sylvia. Catholicism never got a stranglehold on me. Did it on you?"

"I was so Catholic that I wanted to be a nun. I was nineteen and dating a Jewish boy when my mother told me my Grandmother Rose was Jewish. I told my mother that being Jewish didn't skip a generation and that she was Jewish no matter how she protested. "I'm nothing," she said.

"And then, you were suddenly Jewish," said Sylvia.

"I suppose I already knew what being Jewish was about. I had more Jewish friends than any other group of people. Of course, I didn't know the rituals, the songs, prayers, stories nor the Hebrew language."

"But that wasn't the whole of being Jewish," said Sylvia. "There was a Jewish identity – as old as Moses."

"In time, with my new husband, the cycle of adhering to the teachings of the Catholic church began to fade into the deep recesses of my redundant mind. Other things like community and identity were more important."

"I know you, Joanie. I believe that you knew you were Jewish before you knew you were Jewish. You fell in love with a Jewish young man before your mother told you about your Grandma Rose. How do we know what we know?"

"We just know," we said in unison.

Sylvia was resilient and loving to the end of her life. I miss her every day.

Sylvia prompted me to remember all the stories I have heard through the years about people being told after decades that they were Jewish. Every story is different. I remember my friend Marc, whose father's side was German and his father's father was a rabbi. One day he told me that little known fact at the end of our conversation. Marc did not elaborate. Or there was a young lady I overheard talking to a friend at a honky-tonk bar in Austin who said that she found out her mother was Jewish by discovering that fact in a letter her mother wrote to her sister. Her mother told her sister she wanted nothing to do with her if she was going to be Jewish. When she asked her mother about that discovery, her mother told her to forget it. One Jew was enough in the family. However, her Jewish aunt stayed in her Jewish community, and the sisters never spoke again. But that young lady told me she spoke to her aunt regularly. There are hundreds, thousands of stories relating to the denial of Jewish identity.

In Tom Stoppard's stunning play, Leopoldstadt, he tells the story of a large, multi-generational Jewish family in Austria during the early stages of Hitler's rise to power. Its theme focuses on the destructive toll that antisemitism had on this particular family – almost every family member died in the Holocaust – and the playwright's subsequent escape with his parents from the Jewish neighborhood of Leopoldstadt in Vienna to London. Shortly thereafter, Mr. Stoppard's father, a doctor, was killed at sea by a Japanese bomber. Mr. Stoppard's mother remarried and changed her family name to Stoppard. She gave her son a new start while putting forever to rest the family history. The playwright lived a privileged life and became a well-known British playwright. He did not discover he was Jewish until his mid-fifties.

As I learned more about my mother's history, principally through the eyes of my brother, Lance, the idea that my mother had to hide her family secret began to make sense – it was the only way she could conceal her anger and fear about how the world treated Jews.

My mother, Estelle Moran, believed she was strong enough to relegate unwanted and often hateful innuendo to a hidden place in her brain – a hiding place that held the willfully forgotten. She believed it was better to know and be hurt than to forever suffer unquenched curiosity. She made no apologies for the way she lived her life hiding her Jewish identity. She displayed no guilt or shame for her belief in self rather than in a deity, a God. My mother valued change, movement, and success without fanfare.

My mother chose not to live with those who discriminated against the Jews. She was a friend to all and embraced everyone who was different. She made no apologies for the way she lived her life – hiding her secret was her business.

As I heard more and more stories from people who volunteered their personal relationship to Judaism, I began to feel the urge to write my mother's memoir. I also had a deeper understanding of the trope that having a Jewish identity made Jews foreigners in their own land. It's easier to think that antisemitism is a thing of the past. It is not the past. Antisemitism persists in time and carries over from one generation to another. It was almost incomprehensible to learn along my journey of writing this memoir that there resides a residue of antisemitism behind every gesture, last name, or association. It will always exist writ large as an existential condition, and to some it will always be an existential threat in the outside world.

The essence of my mother, Estelle Moran, is a constant in my life – she was a force of nature, an extraordinary being, an abiding presence who lived her life with grace and goodness, tenacity and curiosity, and always with great style. Although she did not place value in her Jewish identity, nor did she have a faith in a deity, she displayed no guilt or shame for her beliefs in the strength of her character. In time, I chose to believe that my mother carried within herself the Jewish essence of her own mother, my Grandma Rose. They were both connected in their love and care and respect for each other, just as my mother and I were also strongly connected to each other through our love and knowledge of our goodness. And that is the essence of Jewish life.

Joan Moran
Austin, Texas
October 2024

PROLOGUE

LIGHTING THE CANDLES

Rose Rosen Lanch stood smartly tall as she cut a fine figure in her plain, gray, cotton dress. It was her favorite dress, and she loved to wear it on Friday nights for Shabbat. The miniature pansies dotting the material gave her frock a holiday look. No matter how many times she washed it, the dress smelled of lilacs. The scent made Rose happy and brought a serene look to her beautiful olive skin, shining without a blemish or a line. She was a stately woman who carried her head high, as if she was reaching for the ceiling. Her back was razor straight, which gave her an air of confidence and control. That was who Rose was – a warrior standing in front of the mantle above a stone fireplace ready to strike a match with immaculate precision and light the candles for Friday night Shabbat prayers.

Blessed are You, God, Ruler of the universe, who sanctified us with the commandment of lighting Shabbat candles.
May God bless you, Esther, and protect you.
May God show you favor and be gracious to you.
May God show you kindness and grant you peace.

Rose felt her daughter's presence, and a chill rose up her spine. She heard Esther breathe and whimper ever so quietly. She glanced at the front door. Had she remembered to secure the lock? It was too late to check. Prayers had to be said.

Yesimech Elohim k'Sarah Rivka Rachel v'Leah May you be like Sarah, Rebecca, Rachel, and Leah.

When Rose was young sitting in temple, she was forever trying to understand the prayers. Yet other things captivated her – the warm glow of the candles, the solidity of her Jewish congregation, and the cantor's pure voice leading the songs in Hebrew. Her strong memories distracted her momentarily. Suddenly she was aware of Esther hiding behind the brown door that connected the small, cluttered living room to a narrow hallway – a hallway engulfed in semidarkness, except for a sliver of light shining from an outside gas lamp that pushed through a bedroom window.

Rose stared into Esther's fearful dark brown eyes. She smiled at her daughter as she held her hands against her heart and whispered, "I love you." She turned back to the altar to continue her prayers:

Shalom aleichem mal'achei hashareit mal'achei elyon mimelech malchei ham'lachim, ha-kadosh baruch hu…

Rose stopped praying when she heard the door crash against the hallway wall with such fierce velocity that it smashed a hole in the unpainted surface. As a cold wind blew through the apartment, Rose turned to Esther and put her index finger to her lips.

"Don't hurt Esther," whispered Rose, more to herself than to her raging husband. "She is innocent in this."

Jake's arm flew up and knocked the candles to the floor. He threw Rose's prayer book against the sofa.

"Papa, don't!" screamed Esther.

"I'll do what I want to your mother," he yelled.

Jake grabbed Rose by her shoulders, released one hand, and slapped her across the face with terrifying anger. Rose stood tall and refused to move.

Esther propelled herself in her father's direction and grabbed his arm. "Stop! Mama did nothing. She was saying her prayers."

"We're done with this, Rose. Do you hear me? No more!" Jake pushed past Esther, tramped down the hallway, and disappeared into darkness.

Esther straightened her back and walked steadily to the kitchen. She got a rag and held it under the cold water faucet. The rag dripped as she walked to the sofa and held it against her mother's cheek.

"The sting is gone."

Esther started to whimper.

"No, no, my darling, you mustn't cry. This moment does not deserve tears. We are fine. We are together. *May you be like Sarah, Rebecca, Rachel, and Leah.*"

"Mama, is he so mean to you? I don't understand."

"You will understand one day."

"I'm old enough to know, Mama. I'm four years old now. I should know."

"Later, darling, and then it will be better."

Grandma Rose & family

PART 1
CHAPTER 1

ROSE

Rose Rosenbaum was the second born child into a wealthy Jewish family in Odesa, Russia, during the late 1880s. She was bright and full of smiles and spread her joy among her family. The titular head of the Rosenbaum family was Abraham, a handsome, gregarious man whose ability to organize a successful confectionary and bakery business while providing for his wife, Vita, and a growing family was exemplary among his contemporaries in the city of Odesa. As Jews living among primarily Christians, life did not always feel comfortable. Unless wealthy and had social status, the Jews of Odesa did not live among Gentile residents. Despite Abraham's success in business and his wealth, he was wary of intermittent waves of antisemitism, sometimes rising to the level of a pogrom. It happened that at the time of the assassination of Tsar Alexander on March 13, 1881, Christian councils began to believe foreign agents who pushed the propaganda that Jews were complicit in the Tsar's death. Russian agitators blamed the Jews for other troubles, such as limited employment opportunities and lower wages. Increased Jewish population growth in Odesa during the 1800s contributed to suspicion that Jews possessed great wealth, power, and influence in Odesa. Even though Jews held high positions in manufacturing, the majority of wealth in Odesa belonged to non-Jews. Without political power in Odesa, the Jews had little means to use their wealth to gain higher positions.

In 1888, when Rose was seven her father set up his business in London. At the time, Rose's mother had given birth to four more children. Everyone waited patiently for two years while Abraham found a location in a fashionable London neighborhood. He discovered a city that was open, exciting, and cultured. In London, Abraham was accepted by like-minded English businessmen for his fine mind and quick wit. During the two years he was away from his family, he insisted that Vita, and the children were to be instructed in English. Abraham had his own tutor in London, a beautiful young woman who caught his fancy. He purchased a large home in London and prepared to move his family into a new life. His business was called Knightsbridge Confectioners and Bakery. Rose was the child who was the most excited to move and was the first to learn English. She practiced daily to be perfect.

The move was quick and uneventful. The stately and beautiful Vita settled Rose and her siblings into a large Victorian house and cloistered them in a world of tutorial education and religious teachings at the Jewish temple. The children learned Latin, mathematics, biology and music. Rose was thrilled with her new life. By the time she was in her teens, she was a classic beauty, the perfect Gibson Girl, an ideal woman of the times whose figure and musical talents were displayed in lavish music halls where dance and pantomime were popular spectacles. Rose was accepted into a theater group. She glowed under the stage lights. For the next fifteen years, the Rosenbaum family grew in size, several more children were born, and thrived despite Abraham's absence from home. He cared more for his own status among men and his attraction to women, both of which were palpable. Late nights were common. He ignored his children, and he certainly did not encourage interest in his business among his five sons. The only one of his four daughters, Rose was curious about the family business. It was a pity that her father could not see her talent for organization and management.

After the last child was born, Rose saw her mother spend more time in her bedroom alone and let the nannies take care of the needs of the younger children. Her mother's depression weighed on her mind. She suspected the marriage was falling apart. At least, he still lived at home. It would be worse if everyone knew of their troubled marriage. Rose worried that something bad was going to happen.

One day, without saying goodbye, Vita left the house and was gone for hours. When Rose asked her mother where she had gone, Rose replied, "I've talked to a solicitor about divorcing your father, darling. We no longer have a marriage."

Several times, Rose would hear her parents fighting in Vita's bedroom behind closed doors. She heard a slap, and then another. Vita screamed. Abraham stomped out of her room.

"You will not talk to any solicitor," he yelled. "There will be no divorce."

"Papa," she said to her father. "Why did you hit Mama?"

"Get away from me. It's none of your concern."

One of Abraham's trusted friends told him that his cousin, a solicitor, received a visit from Vita to seek a divorce.

"I hope it is not true, Abraham," said his friend. "It would cause a huge scandal."

Abraham was furious that his family was about to be involved in a scandal. He would not countenance it. The divorce was not going to go through. He was not going to be humiliated and become a subject of ridicule in the business community.

He manically followed Vita around London for weeks until he saw her enter the building where her solicitor's office was located. He shifted from one foot to another as he waited for her to come out of the building. When Vita walked onto the sidewalk, Abraham took out a revolver and pointed it at her. She looked at him with horror and disbelief. He waited several seconds before he shot her without a word. He studied the gun in his hand, then stared at Vita's lifeless body splayed out on the sidewalk. Without taking a breath, he pointed the gun to his head and pulled the trigger. Anyone who witnessed the murder-suicide on the street that day would never recover from the despicable, violent action. Abraham's name was never uttered again in polite society.

There was chaos in the family. Rose tried to hold the children together despite the shock and trauma caused by the deaths of her parents. No one knew what to do or how to grieve this unspeakable tragedy. Rose knew that her siblings were considered pariahs and would always be excluded from having a comfortable life in London. Every sibling was responsible for his or her own destiny. The older daughters felt desperate and hopeless that they would never marry. At almost eighteen, Rose found no one to give her council. She had to be practical. She must get a job and leave London. She could not live in a city carrying her family's name and shame. The story of how her parents died would forever tragically linger in the public view. Worse, Rose worried about her relationship to the temple congregation. As a single woman without parents, she may not be accepted. She might have to bear witness to the Jewish community by carrying her grief and sorrow and the unexplained circumstances of her family's murder-suicide.

Rose knew enough about the way London's business community comported itself that they would never forgive Abraham's offense. On the surface, Rose was old enough to understand that the pretentious Victorian society considered wealth the highest priority. Victorians were the proper models of propriety and restraint. Yet beneath the straight-laced, corset wearing, top hat attire, there were myriad hints of scandal throughout the business community. How could she not know when she socialized with the daughters and sons of the upper class and heard some of their secrets regarding illicit affairs? It seemed that her father had also succumbed to the idea that the certain forms of debauchery and skullduggery were legitimate pathways to achieve wealth.

The Rosenbaum funeral was a small affair. Rose sat in the front row of their Jewish synagogue with her grieving siblings, a few of her father's business friends, and a small number of prayerful congregants. Rose remained stoic. She only thought of how proud she was that Vita held firm to her religious beliefs and saw to it that her sons had bar mitzvahs and her daughters were confirmed. It was Vita who educated her daughters to attract well-established young men who would one day come calling for her daughters.

But no one came calling after the death of the Rosenbaum's, no one went to their home except Abraham's business friends who offered to buy Knightsbridge Confectioners and Bakery. Rose watched the slow demise of the Rosenbaum family. She doubted that she could keep the family functioning. Her older brother, Ollie, planned to sell the confectionery and bakery business and split the proceeds with his brothers. They needed money to live and start a business. However, the selling of the Knightsbridge property was executed by Abraham's lawyer. Rose was surprised that the sons did not receive any of the proceeds from the sale of Knightsbridge. They left the contents of the house. The irony was that the bulk of the estate was left to Vita. The next in line to receive monies generated by Abraham's legal trust was the lawyer, a man named Simon Silberman. Rose would never forget this ugly man with veined, gnarly hands who received and controlled the Rosenbaum fortune through his legal manipulations. Not only did Mr. Silberman receive Abraham's hard-earned wealth, but he also procured all the proceeds from the sale of the other Rosenbaum properties. No one knew Abraham owned other properties. The family felt betrayed. When the news of the disbursement was revealed to the Rosenbaum children, Rose told Ollie, the oldest male, not to employ another lawyer to contest the will.

"The family has been hurt enough," she said. "It will take years and money that we don't have to fight off Mr. Silberman's lawyers. It will be a fool's errand. Scrape up enough money through the sale of every piece of furniture, artwork, silver, crystal, and furnishings and get yourselves either a ship's passage to Canada or to the United States, or for a nest egg to start a small business in the suburbs of London. But get out of London. Otherwise, you will have no life worth living," Rose said.

The daughters were encouraged to marry for money, or they could start a new life elsewhere. Some of the Rosenbaum cousins had already emigrated to Toronto and New York, even as far away as San Francisco. Most relatives were doing well. Rose was completing a secretarial course at a business school for women at the time of her family tragedy. She wanted nothing from the estate. Her preference was to make it on her own. Rose wanted to work in the British embassy. In 1905, at the age of eighteen, she applied for a secretarial job at the embassy and was immediately accepted in the diplomatic secretarial pool. Within months, she was transferred to Toronto, Canada. If her father had seen her in another light with her quick head for business, Rose knew that she was the only family member who could have successfully managed Knightsbridge Confectioners and Bakery. She was the only sibling who came to her father's factory to watch how the assembly line worked, what jobs were needed, and how the accounts were managed. She left notes and memos on her father's desk with suggestions, only to be ignored. She watched him flirt with young women and knew that his behavior should not be allowed. The end of the Knightsbridge enterprise was not so much a surprise for Rose, but that it ended because of violence proved devastating.

CHAPTER 2

ROSE & JAKE

The excitement that the nineteen-year-old Rose felt in 1906, as she boarded a passenger ferry from Southampton to Toronto to work in the British Consul General's office was overwhelming. It was her first journey of independence. Every decision she made, every article of clothing she brought with her in her brown leather valise, how she walked with a straight spine in order to appear older and more mature, was created from her astute intelligence, social awareness, and her warm and natural beauty. Rose made a bold move before she left London. She changed her last name and left Rosenbaum behind. Fifteen days later, the voyage was over, and Rose Rosen walked down the plank and onto the port of Toronto. Rose was a courageous and brave young woman in a time when women were not perceived as having the fortitude to be adventurous and take chances. Her first courageous experience set the tone for the way she would live her life and defined her goals. She would always make life work for her.

On her first day of work, she was told she was not needed in the Toronto British Consul General's office. London made a mistake. Instead, she was supposed to go to the High Commission Office in Ottawa.

"I'm sorry, Miss Rosen, but we don't need another secretary for our pool," said Mr. Monahan. "We don't want to inconvenience you, so please work here for the month. We are sorry the position did not work out."

The Consul General's office agreed to pay for Rose's first month rent in a nearby boarding house.

Rose was not inclined to move to Ottawa. Toronto was a beautiful city – not as large as London, but it was not as dreary as some of her co-workers ascribed. She wanted to stay in her accidental job, and she had an idea about how to do it.

Rose knew she was more than capable. After a month of diligent work, Mr. Monahan approached her at her desk at closing time.

"This is the end of your month's stay, Miss Rosen, and you've done splendidly. You are a fast learner and we can use you in other areas. Rarely has a new hire accomplished what you have. Of course, you were highly recommended. We want you to stay. I've cleared it with the High Commission Office in Ottawa."

Within three months, she was writing and sending dispatches back to London and delivering security information packages to Toronto's diplomatic offices. She knew she could have been given more responsibility, but women had their place, and Rose knew by instinct that her position was secure for as long she wanted – as long as she played by the rules. Rose had been working for a year when the head secretary asked her to run an errand to the port authority of Toronto. She was to collect an important document that arrived on the last ferry of the day. Rose looked particularly fashionable that day. She enjoyed looking stylish. She wore a grey poplin skirt that skimmed her ankles, high leather black boots that hooked up underneath her skirt, which added a fine detail to her small feet, an ivory colored blouse cinched in by a decorative belt made of copper, a short, black bolero jacket, and a stylish teal wide-width Watteau hat popular with the young ladies of the day. There is a photograph taken of Rose on this day that lives in a special place in her granddaughter's home. When she was introduced to the operating manager of the office, a Mr. Sheldon, her smile lit up the room. And when Mr. Sheldon gave Rose the envelope for the British Consul General's Office, he smiled with a nod of approval for her comportment and beautiful visage.

"Thank you, miss ..."

"Rosen," said Rose.

"You should be photographed today," said Mr. Sheldon. "You look stunning." As Rose turned to go, a handsome man of five feet eight inches, with shiny black hair, dressed in dark slacks, a white shirt, and an unstructured jacket, stepped inside the door of the purchasing manager's office. He tipped his hat to Rose and smiled.

"Come on in, Jake," said Mr. Sheldon. "Miss Rosen, let me introduce you to Jake Lanch, our purser. How many times have you crossed the Atlantic, Jake?"

"Probably six or seven times now. It's a long journey, all right."

"Nice to meet you, Mr. Lanch."

"Likewise, Miss Rosen."

Rose loitered by the door for a few seconds to see what this Jake person was about to do for the shipping company. She waited a minute or two and left.

"Jake, after you take the boxes off the shipping container, I want you to sort the fabrics by color. That's what the customer asked for. The boss does not have enough men to do the job."

"I'll sort them out and distribute the clothes in the boxes with labels," said Jake. "Maybe I'll find a few more men who need some work. Times are tough."

"That's right," said Mr. Sheldon. "You said you did some design work in a fashion house before you came to Canada."

"That's right, sir, kind of like that lady who just left. She can put together what she wears with style. And she has an eye for color. She's tall. Clothes look good on her figure."

"You're right on that score, Jake. You have a good sense for fashion."

Rose hurried out of the building to the railway platform to catch the next trolley back to her office. She clutched the envelope tightly to her chest so she wouldn't drop it. Jake walked toward her with determination.

"Please excuse me, Miss Rosen," said Jake. "I saw you when you came into the office."

"Yes, I remember," said Rose.

"Who do you work for?" he asked.

"I can't tell you that, Mr. Lanch."

"It doesn't matter. More importantly, would you mind going out with me sometime?"

At that moment, the trolley pulled up. "I won't be able to meet you since I don't know you, and I don't go out with strangers."

Jake offered his hand to help her up the steps. "Think about it. I'm Jake Lanch, and I'm not a bad guy once you get to know me."

Days went by and Rose worked diligently. She learned some accounting practices and improved her shorthand skills. It was fun and freeing to be independent, to go out to lunch or dinner with friends, or to take in the cultural arts of the city. Then one afternoon, when she came back from her lunch break and saw an envelope on her desk, Rose knew who sent it, but wondered how he was able to get the letter delivered.

The letter read: *I still want to go out with you. I have an important job with the shipping company that will keep me from crossing the Atlantic. Can you meet me at O'Doul's after work one night? I will be there every night until you decide to meet me, Jake.*

On the fifth night, Rose walked into O'Doul's, an Irish drinking establishment, and saw Jake at the bar drinking a beer. He jumped off his seat and guided her to a quiet table.

"Too much noise in here," said Jake. "You know how the Irish love their pints."

"How did you find out where I worked?" asked Rose, settling into her chair.

"I am the purser, Miss Rosen, and I can look up deliveries of packages and letters. I looked up where your package was to be delivered."

"That was quite dishonest."

"Yes, and clever." Jake lit a cigarette, "Miss Rose Rosen."

They talked for hours. Jake was from Kraków, a city in Poland that had a history of being part of Prussia, Germany, and Russia. He was sure that when he was born, Kraków was governed by Russia, but he was also sure he was Polish for all that mattered to anyone else.

"I learned that Poland is a major Jewish cultural and religious center," said Rose. "How lucky for you and your family."

"How would you know that?" Jake asked.

"I'm from Odesa originally, then I lived in London."

"I wouldn't know about that either," Jake told her. "I was fifteen when I left Poland for Paris, and five years later I came to London."

"How exciting. What did you do in Paris at fifteen? You were so young."

"I knew from the time I was a kid that I could draw. What women wore caught my eye. There was no beauty in the shtetl. Women wore worker's clothes – dark, no shape. On holidays, women dressed up in traditional clothes, long dresses in vibrant colors, that kind of thing, and I would draw those fancy clothes, but it wasn't enough to make a living. The damn Russians were always trying to take our land so we couldn't become prosperous."

"You don't seem like a man who would waste time."

"I left one day and worked the rails for passage until I got to Paris, where I wanted to make my fortune."

"Did you, Mr. Lanch? Did you make your fortune?"

"That all depends on what you mean by a fortune. I mean fortune as the way to describe doing what you love to do. I went to all the fashion houses in Paris, but the most exclusive was the house of Lavin. One day, as I was standing in front of the baroque building on the Champs-Élysées, a wealthy lady dressed in rich clothing that I could never have imagined walked out of the fancy double doors and gave her packages to a man in uniform. She noticed me before he helped her into her carriage."

"Did she say something?" asked Rose.

"Not at first. She looked me up and down and asked me why I was dressed in rags, and I told her I had gotten off many long train rides and was looking for work in fashion illustration. She marched me in the front door and addressed Monsieur Jean Claude."

"Who was Jean Claude?" Rose asked.

"An assistant designer. She told Jean Claude that I was going to design a velvet jacket for her. She said I didn't look like much, but I had a desire to be a fashion illustrator. I got to work, took her measurements, picked out a purple velvet fabric, and within an hour, the wealthy woman, whose name I didn't know, bought the jacket on the spot and told the assistant designer to hire me as an illustrator. She also gave money to me for the jacket."

"You experienced a moment when luck and opportunity met. How fortunate for you."

"By twenty, I was done with illustrating their fashion collection because they would not move me up to a designer for couture. That's when I left and came to London and was hired on with a ferry company to get to Canada. And now you are caught up with my life, Rose Rosen."

"I'm completely impressed, Jake. And speechless."

Their courtship began. The couple spent the next six months together. Rose was excited when Jake was able to move on from shipping to selecting and ordering fabric for a large store in the garment district of downtown Toronto. Jake took an interest in attending union meetings in the garment district and was soon organizing for the workers, most of whom were immigrant Jews from Russia who leaned toward communism as an economic system.

"As a young boy in Kraków, I was ready to receive the Communist Manifesto. I never wanted anything to do with religion, let alone being identified as a Jew," said Jake.

Rose listened intently as Jake described how, as a young boy, he was introduced to Marxism and communism in Kraków, then under Russian control.

"I heard about the first Russian Revolution in 1905 under the leadership of Leon Trotsky," said Jake. "He rejected his Jewish roots. He's my hero."

Rose found nothing to admire in Jake's politics. They were incompatible with her upbringing. "You're Jewish, and yet you don't go to Shabbat services."

"Communists are atheists, Rose. There is no religion in politics. I thought I was clear."

"But you were born in Kraków, a Jewish center of religious culture."

"I never practiced the religion. I have to tell you this so you won't be angry later. I don't believe in God."

"I do believe in God, and I practice my religious beliefs, Jake, so we'd better come to some agreement about this situation."

CHAPTER 3

TEST OF ENDURANCE

Rose Rosen married Jake Lanch three months after he told her he was an atheist. It was 1907, and she was twenty. The moment they married, she knew it was a mistake. It was all too fast – she did not think it through completely. Jake was a fast talker, and fast talkers do not always tell the complete truth. It was impossible to read him correctly without the details. She did not know that before he left Paris, Jake changed his last name from Lanchesky to Lanch. He had no papers, no identity, so he could be anyone he wanted.

Rose wondered if she understood love. Did she mistake his energy and talent for love? She hoped she could change him. He possessed a native intelligence that compensated for his third-grade education, and she thought she could smooth out his rough edges. It only took a short time after they married for Rose to know better. The revelation came in increments. She learned that once Jake lifted the curtain on his violent temper, he was a monster and a bully.

She was always on her guard.

Within a few months, Jake took a job in the International Ladies' Garment Workers Union. He joined a group of communist labor leaders who formed an influential cell, which brought him recognition as a force for labor reform. He began to climb the leadership ladder and was promoted to a union position in Montreal in 1911. Their first daughter, Esther, was born in October of that year. She was an exquisite baby, even if she was born with a small goiter on her neck. Rose did not think of removing the lump of cells. After all, it was not life-threatening. She never dreamed that Esther would be stigmatized due to a goiter.

Jake's star continued to rise in his union. His reward was the presidency of the International Ladies' Garment Workers Union in Montreal. Increasingly aggressive in recruiting workers to the communist cause, he worked longer each night talking politics with the union workers. It was a hectic time for Jake. Rose felt nothing when he was away from home, other than relief that she could live without fear of Jake's abuse. She was free to light the Shabbat candles and say her prayers. Her spirits lifted. She brought her enticing smile to the surface again. Free to make decisions, Rose found a free Catholic preschool for Esther. Rose did not trust a public school. She thought the education was inferior. Then she went back to work at the British Consul General's office. Jake did not say a word.

When Jake found out about the Catholic preschool, it was a different issue. "What the hell do you think you're doing, Rose? It's a Catholic hellhole. Get her out of there." Once Esther started school, she was often crying when Rose picked her up.

"Mama, the kids make fun of the thing on my neck and tell me that it's because I'm Jewish. I don't want to go there anymore."

That was all Rose needed. She quit work and became Esther's tutor, just as she was tutored as a young girl. She taught Esther how to read and write, to add and subtract, to speak elementary French and sing French songs, as well as learn geography and Hebrew. The arrangement was perfect for Rose because she was pregnant again,

Not long after Rose quit her job, the union assigned Jake to Winnipeg, Manitoba, where he was directed to grow the Ladies' Garment Union into a recognized labor force. Rose did not want to go with Jake. She was six months pregnant, had her own doctor, and she did not want to uproot Esther. Jake said he'd send money back to her. He was never good at keeping his word. She tried to make ends meet after the second baby was born

– a daughter, Mildred Rose. Three months later, Rose went back to work full time at the Consul General's office, or there would be no food on the table. Rose felt sick at heart that she was not basking in Mildred's new life. During Mildred's first year, Rose bartered meals with an elderly lady who would babysit. Esther had to go back to Catholic school. Rose put a scarf around her neck to cover the goiter. The scarves served as a distraction. Her classmates loved the colorful designs.

For several years, Jake went back and forth from Montreal to Winnipeg and then to Ottawa to see to the organization of Canadian unions. He made a name for himself. But for all of his successes as a union organizer, Jake was not someone who got along with people. He held strong opinions, carried the communist banner and carried grudges.

Jake got in trouble again. He made a few enemies. He told Rose that they were moving to New York. He has a good job there.

"You mean America?" asked Esther. "We're going to America?"

"Rose, pack your things," Jake said. "We leave this weekend."

The Lanch family took the Adirondack train from Montreal to New York City in the winter of 1919. Esther clutched her doll to her chest on the train and asked Rose why they were moving to America. Jake was silent as he looked out the train window.

"Tell her, Jake," said Rose. "Talk to your daughter."

He gave Rose a withering look. "I gave her a doll. What more do you want?"

"That was years ago," said Rose.

"Can you teach me how to make clothes for my dolly, Papa?" asked Esther. "I want to make dolly clothes."

"Tell her why we had to move in three days – what kind of trouble you got into with the union, how you didn't know how to play by the rules."

"I got a job in New York," said her father.

"Not true. There was a riot at the union hall in Winnipeg. Someone set fire to the building. You were blamed because you stand with communists."

"You don't know anything. It's a better job I'm after. I can finally design."

"You were successful, even got your name on a plaque at the union building in Winnipeg," said Rose. "Jacob Lanch is a big macher. What more do you want?"

"Yes, I'm a big macher, Rose," he responded with disdain. "I'm so well-known that the president of the International Ladies Garment Workers' in America, this guy named Dubinsky, asked me to join forces with his American union. There was disorganization in the States and Dubinsky wanted my help, but I didn't want to be an extension of America. Dubinsky – that son of a bitch had his own ideas. I told the workers I didn't like the way they ran their union. But the real reason is that the new job in New York is a step up – more money. So shut up and be satisfied."

"What about citizenship for us?" asked Rose.

"We'll deal with it when we get to New York."

As the train pulled into Penn Station, Jake Lanch and his family departed the Adirondack and joined the throngs of travelers on the platform. As Rose tightened the scarf around Esther's neck to cover the goiter, she looked up and saw Jake's name on a sign. She felt sick. It confirmed the move to New York was real. His anger would never be tamed.

"Look, Papa! There's your name, up on a sign!" said Esther pointing.

Jake approached the young man holding the sign. He was dressed in pressed dark suit trousers, a wrinkled white shirt, and glasses too small for his face. They followed him outside the train station and into a car. Rose was trying to stifle her tears as they drove through the city to the crowded Lower East Side. People were packed into the streets and sidewalks. The driver stopped in front of a building in decline. Rose straightened her back, fighting her anger. The driver helped carry their bags upstairs to a third-floor walk-up that was dark and dismal and smelled odious. Rose hoped it was not a poison chemical. Crammed into the five-hundred square-foot apartment were two small bedrooms, one small bathroom with no bathtub, a living room with a moth-eaten sofa, and a glass coffee table with a crack in the middle. The kitchen included an icebox and two-gas stove tops. A wooden table with three well-worn chairs was placed next to the kitchen.

"The boss will see you tomorrow at nine," said the driver as he handed Jake a card with directions. "If you need to find a school, there is a grammar school in the neighborhood."

The driver left and Jake closed the door behind him. Rose comforted Esther who was hot, miserable, and confused. Mildred was crying.

"Don't unpack," Jake said. "I'll be back."

Rose opened the two cabinet doors and looked for a glass so that she could give her daughter a drink of water. She found two glasses and opened the water faucet. A dribble of brown water came out. She held Esther's hand and they both sat at the kitchen table waiting for something to happen. She gave Mildred milk out of a bottle.

Two hours later, Jake came back, gathered his family, and walked them to another apartment building two blocks away. The evacuation was done in silence, but Rose could feel Jake seething. On the walk to the apartment, Rose passed a school that had a cross on the door. She held herself rigid as tears welled up in her eyes because Rose knew that was going to be Esther's new school until they moved again – for it was clear they would always be moving somewhere. A synagogue appeared two doors down from the Catholic school. There was no way to join the congregation. At the least, Jake procured his family a better apartment complete with a set of glasses and dishes, newer furniture, a bathtub, and clear drinking water.

"How did you do it, Jake?" asked Rose. "How did you get us out of that hole?"

"I walked into the factory and told that son of a bitch I was quitting before I started. I told him he could not treat me that way, like a slave on a plantation. I told him to provide us a decent place to live and give you a job or I was leaving. I told him I'd organize the garment workers' union against his company and he would be living in a hell of his own making."

Estelle & John

PART 2
CHAPTER 4

ESTHER

Esther Lanch was a strong child in mind and body. She was Rose's daughter in most ways – aware, astute, bright, self-confident, and beautiful. Her mother taught her well. And yet, her definite likes and dislikes, and her preferences were not always compatible with her mother's desires. Sometimes, Esther gave in to her emotions. One morning as she walked to the neighborhood Catholic school on the Lower East Side, she was in tears because she hated where she lived and where she went to school. At almost ten years-old, she worried about her family and never felt safe, and she worried that the kids in school would see her goiter. Mostly, they did not because as Esther got older, she found a way to keep the scarf tied securely around her neck to hide it. The girls in school again loved the scarves and the problem went away.

Esther was about to get an education outside the classroom and on the streets of the Lower East Side. The Roaring Twenties had arrived, but that meant nothing to Esther in the beginning. She didn't know about speakeasies or wild drinking or police raids or mafia shootouts. She was too young to understand the ramifications of Prohibition under President Harding and his Republican cronies. She heard Jake tell Rose that they were a pack of thieves and liars. Her understanding of that would come later.

Esther got her best education from the newspapers and rag sheets sold on every street corner in the Lower East Side. On the way home from school, she would hang out at the news kiosks and read about everything happening in New York and in other big cities like Chicago and Philadelphia. Even her citizenship was a mystery. Her visa was stamped in New York City, so she thought that was how you become an American citizen – get a new visa when her family moved to another city. Sometimes, Esther listened to Rose talk to a woman named Golda, who took care of Mildred after school in the afternoon, about the evils of drinking and how Golda thought Prohibition was going to solve the immorality of America.

"But Rose, drinking is a symbol of evils of city life," said Golda as she itched under the headscarf she wore. "The government has to control modern society by eliminating alcohol so politicians can turn back the clock to an earlier and better time."

"Golda, my dear," said Rose, "the Volstead Act doesn't make drinking illegal, it only makes the manufacturing and selling of alcohol illegal."

"People still can't drink," said Golda as she again pulled at her headscarf.

"The truth is that everyone has been stockpiling liquor since Prohibition began. Rumor has it that even the Yale Club, with all those rich politicians, stacks alcohol to the ceiling in the basement. The ladies at my work make bathtub gin when they give parties on the weekends."

"How does the alcohol get into the speakeasies?" asked Golda.

"The men who run those places buy it from gangsters and hide the alcohol behind closed doors. Their clubs are only open to people who know the secret password. Everyone knows how the system works, including the police who raid the clubs every now and again, so it looks like they're doing their job. Did I mention the murder rate?"

"How do you know all this, Rose? It sounds like you made it up."

"I listen to the radio and read the news." Rose took Mildred's hand and walked with Esther out of Golda's apartment. "I'll see you tomorrow."

Esther was getting her first education about Prohibition and how it works in real time.

Esther was a curious learner from a young age. When she was twelve years-old, her civics teacher, a pretty nun in her mid-20s, selected three topics for an assignment, one of which was "How the Women Got the Vote." It was 1923 and the women's vote was relatively recent. Esther knew about women marching for equality and heard from her mother that the ladies garment workers were protesting low wages, long hours, and poor working conditions. She asked the librarian at school for books on the women's voting movement. "I'm glad to see young women like you interested in this subject, young lady," said the librarian. "Do you know that the women's vote has altered men's attitudes toward women? It changed the way women thought about themselves – how they dressed, pursued education after high school, and how they could make a choice to enter politics and fight for their rights."

"I think it's thrilling," said Esther. "I want to read all about it."

When Jake brought his dress designs home, she studied his latest styles for a new kind of woman, known as a flapper. Esther skipped the politics section in the newspapers and read about the flappers – young, energetic women with short bobbed hair who preferred sleeveless dresses to show off their slim arms, wore knee-length skirts to show off their calves, and bound their chests to flatten their busts. Flappers drank alcohol and smoked and talked freely in sexual terms. Esther watched ladies walking the city streets and noticed that most women who followed the fashion of the day were young, forward-looking, and appeared completely independent.

However, Esther had no one to talk to about such things. Once again, Jake was not in Esther's life. And when he came home, he talked about union politics, not design. Her mother said he could not help himself. It was his passion to mix his profession with politics. At night, he attended union meetings and won supporters for his communist cause. New York was a bastion of Eastern European Jews, mostly from Russia and they were ready to hear the message of equality – join unions and be paid a fair share for a day's work. But Esther was not interested in what her father did. She wanted him to notice her and help her design clothes.

Rose was pleased that her husband was busy with the union almost every night, especially on Friday nights. She took advantage of the time to prepare for Shabbat, by lighting the candles and reciting the prayers. It was her time with Esther and Mildred to bring them to an awareness of Jewish tradition. Esther complied so as not to upset her mother. But she did not have her heart in it. All the stories sounded like fairy tales. Esther did not understand belief.

"One Friday night, Jake came home early. Rose had brought the candlesticks out of hiding. When she heard the door open, she stuffed them back into the hiding place. "Rose! Rose, you won't believe what happened today. I met a husband and wife, Ida and William Rosenthal, French Jews who owned an undergarment company named Maidenform. We talked about designing functional undergarments that would be comfortable and support a woman's bustline. Ida asked me to sketch out a design. But not just any design – one that showed off the curves of a woman's body."

"You should become a millionaire with this idea," said Rose. "Women will love it."

"This is swell, Papa," Esther said. "You'll be famous one day."

"I'm going to call it the Maidenform Bra."

But Jake's happiness lasted only a short time. The Rosenthal's paid Jake what amounted to his salary for the design and then went back to France.

The cycle began again. Rose told Esther that Jake's anger got him into trouble again for his union work. He suspected he was about to be fired. The last straw was his union organizing. He was bringing too many communists into the union and asking for more pay increases. Almost three years after he started his job in New York, Jake came home and announced he found a company that needed a full-time designer to work in the nascent garment district in downtown Los Angeles. It paid more money than his union job. "When the school term ends, we're moving to the other side of America – to California – to a city called Los Angeles."

"Promise me you won't put me in Catholic school anymore," pleaded Esther.

"Don't you worry about that," said Jake. "No more of that crap." In June, Jake took all of his and Rose's earnings and boarded his family on a train to another job in another state on the other side of America.

Esther and her family debarked a Southern Pacific train from New York and stepped onto the platform at Los Angeles Central Station. She had been riding the train for almost a week and she felt happy. The ride was filled with beautiful landscapes and interesting sights.

The move was no panacea. It was far from what Esther expected. She wanted to take herself to bed and never wake up. Jake immediately settled his family outside the city of Bell Gardens, an unincorporated area northwest of Los Angeles, one of the first cities to define suburban sprawl in the 1920s. Esther looked out over the acres of weeds – dry, ugly, hot, without a trace of green. Jake told Rose that it was cheap living. His employer owned the house.

"This is a slum," said Rose as got out of the car and she looked at the compact house.

"No, the slum is downtown Los Angeles where the sweatshops are located."

"You were hired by a slumlord, and you've got no unions to protect you. Los Angeles is not going to let you bring in your communist workers to run the show."

"The sweatshops here aren't as bad as New York," said Jake.

"They're all bad, falling-down fire hazards and overworked women who die underneath their sewing machines. This is another one of your batty ideas. When you get in a fight with your employer, you run to another stupid, damn job."

Jake slapped her across the face. "You wouldn't have a roof over your head if it weren't for me. And besides this time you don't have to get a job."

Esther and Mildred ran after their mother and hugged her. Rose held her hand to her red face and refused to cry. Her heart turned to steel.

"You can't grow a vegetable or get to a store within an hour. What kind of life is this?"

"You're safe here so don't worry about it. I'll be sleeping at the fabric company most nights. I can earn extra money by watching the building."

Esther and her mother stole a glance at each other and breathed a sigh of relief. Each was relieved for different reasons – Rose knew she would be able to keep to the rituals and teaching of the Jewish faith, and Esther knew that her family would be happy without having to dodge the emotional ups and downs of her abusive father. Jake would not be a daily presence.

Soon hope vanished. The two years in Bell Gardens were a continuation of Esther's unhappiness. She protested going to the school, worried that every day, as she walked with her sister almost a mile and a half through the weeds, she would encounter three or four mean girls who made fun of her goiter and tried to pull the scarf off around her neck, revealing the odious outgrowth. Esther would fight them off like a warrior to get her scarf back. Then she and Mildred would run to school.

The taunts and teasing continued into eighth grade. Mildred was miserable and tired from getting up early and walking to and from school. She itched all over from rashes caused by heat.

Esther suffered from headaches. There was never enough food. She wanted to skip school, even though she knew she did not have the nerve. After all, she was a good girl. She did everything right. Pride and responsibility stopped her from rebelling or doing something rash.

"Why do you even go to school?" asked Mildred. "You hate it, and so do I."

"It's the kids, not the teachers. All my teachers praise my work and that feels good."

Life got more interesting when their neighbor Mr. Osloff, an attorney who lived about a half a mile away, paid Rose an introductory visit one Saturday afternoon. While having iced tea on the porch, he bemoaned his lack of office help. Esther was standing at the door listening.

"People, especially women, don't want to work so far from Bell Gardens."

"I'm sorry to hear that," said Rose.

"Mama," said Esther, "why don't you work for Mr. Osloff? You can do the typing and office work. And he doesn't live too far away. Mildred and I can help out and learn to cook."

"Aren't you smart, Esther," said Mr. Osloff. "How about it, Rose? And you can keep my accounts in order. It's a win-win all around."

Even though Rose agreed to offer her services to Mr. Osloff, Esther felt resentment – in fact, she was angry – not at Rose, but at her father who put them all in the situation. Esther suspected that whenever her mother worked, she made more money than her father. So Rose went back to work. Her mood grew lighter, and she wore a smile instead of a frown. Mr. Osloff would drive Rose home every night with an armload of food.

Late one night, Esther couldn't sleep and wandered into the kitchen. The light was on, and Rose was diligently composing a letter.

"Why are you up so late, Mama?" asked Esther.

"Sit down, Esther. I have to tell you something. I'm writing to your Aunt Anya, who lives in San Francisco, and telling her about the difficulty I have had living and working in New York. I'm still suffering. The sweatshop was dirty and the air was polluted. It seems the perfect moment to plan an escape."

"You mean an escape from Papa?" Esther asked.

"I mean a divorce," said Rose. "I'll have to borrow some money from Anya. I can also use my mad money from the cookie jar."

"And I'll add my babysitting money to the jar. And when I grow up, I'll always have a mad money jar, too."

"That's a good plan, my smart girl."

"I was wondering about Papa – what happened to him? He was so talented as a designer. He could have been famous."

"He still is talented," said Rose. "But two things fight against your father succeeding. He can't get along with the people he works with, and he can't take criticism. The other thing has to do with how people look at immigrants. When a Jewish immigrant succeeds, the Christians believe they don't deserve it. They don't understand that we value education and encourage young people to excel in whatever they do. When they disparage us, it's called antisemitism. It's been with us ever since the Jews walked the earth over four thousand years ago."

"What does that mean?" asked Esther.

"It means that the Jews have been persecuted since the beginning of time, my darling. As long as there are Jews walking the earth, there will be people who hate us. It's a simple truth that the Jewish faith rouses suspicion and hatred."

"What does that have to do with Papa?" Esther asked.

"Because Jake has been fighting against discrimination all his life. Communism and atheism were his weapons, and neither brought him peace or success. It would be better if he stayed quiet, blended into the background, and put aside his injuries. "

"Why do people hate the Jews, Mama? Why aren't we just like others?"

"Our customs and beliefs are not Christian. You've spent enough time in Catholic schools and know that Christians believe their savior already came to earth to save mankind."

"His name was Jesus," said Esther.

"The Jews are still waiting for our savior, dear."

"Mama, I don't believe in any savior. I don't need to be saved."

"Maybe in time you'll change your mind when you get older, my darling."

Mr. Osloff gave free legal advice to Rose about a potential divorce. He took a shine to her. Rose still had her beauty and charm. It was Mr. Osloff's idea to base the divorce on abandonment. It was also his idea for her to secure a job in San Francisco so she could go directly to work. He gave Rose a list of job opportunities that fit her skills. Within a month, she procured a job with Schlage Lock and Key, which had offices in downtown San Francisco.

Rose wrote to Anya that she did not need a loan because she already procured a job. She did need a temporary place to live with her two daughters. They plotted their escape together.

Anya wrote back:

Get the train schedule and find a departure day when Jake isn't home. Pack light and bring food for the journey. You will live with me in the Fillmore section of downtown San Francisco. Bring a copy of the divorce papers with you.

Rose wrote back:

I'll leave everything else to Mr. Osloff. Jake will figure the rest out.

CHAPTER 5

THE CITY BY THE BAY

Rose, Esther, and Mildred got off the train at San Francisco's main train station at the Third and Townsend Depot in June 1924. It was a glorious feeling for all of them. They were free.

"Mama," said Mildred, "does this mean we won't have to walk in the weeds again?"

"The weeds are a thing of the past, my love," Rose said, her English accent lilting through the air. "We'll now have the ocean and music and good schools, and hope."

"And you have your new job, and we'll get to meet our Aunt Anya," said Esther.

"Yes, and my sister has done very well for herself. She finished her education, decided not to marry some old Englishman whom she would have to take care of for the rest of her life and started on her adventure. She didn't have much money, but she had fortitude. You could learn from your Aunt Anya, Esther. This is a mitzvah for us all."

They carried their bags to a trolley outside the train station, boarded, and headed for the Fillmore area in the district known as the Western Addition.

"It's the Jewish section," Rose told her daughters with pride as they found seats on the trolley. "It's where Anya lives."

As delighted as Rose was to live in the Jewish district, Esther had no emotional attachment to being Jewish. It was not so much that at an early age she was sent to Catholic school in Montreal and New York, although she felt isolated and embarrassed as she struggled with prayers in Latin or in French. The stories from the New Testament seemed to be made up, like fairy tales. Walking the streets of the Lower East Side, among a population that was mostly Jewish, especially in the garment district, was another form of strangeness. There was the total immersion of the Jewish working and living environment – like in Brooklyn or the Bronx or Queens and the Lower East Side. where immigrant Jews settled in those cloistered boroughs with a suffocating sameness. Somewhere outside of the Jewish world, there was the Christian world where Jews were not accepted. She could not understand why everyone could not live together. Esther was confused why religion even mattered? It seemed that religion got in the way of moving forward because tradition and language were limiting to one's thinking. She thought it would be easier not to be who she was. If children asked her where she came from, she would say she comes from wherever all the rest of the children come from.

As Esther looked out the windows on the trolley on the way to the Fillmore, she wondered what it would be like to be exposed to the big city of San Francisco. Did Jews live outside the Fillmore? Could she move around silently and observe and then create a way not to self-identify as a Jewish girl, but as a person without religious attachments? It felt scary to imagine living outside the walls of a Jewish section. In time, she'll move away and not be confined and defined by the Fillmore and the Jewish way of life. With all that was happening so quickly in her life – Rose's new job, finding schools for herself and Mildred – she thought maybe her Jewish confirmation would be an afterthought.

"Darling, Esther, what are you thinking?" asked her mother. "You are very quiet."

"I'm excited to see Aunt Anya. And there is so much going on in the streets that I don't know where to look. I have so many questions."

"They will all be answered in time. We have to get settled now."

"Does Aunt Anya go to the temple, Mama?" asked Esther. "Is she religious?"

"In her way, I'm sure she is religious," said Rose.

"Everyone is different with religion, right Mama?" asked Esther. "But you pray and do all the practices."

"Yes, my darling. I hold my religion tightly. I hope you and Millie do the same. Just breathe this air and think of the possibilities in this community."

Esther held out hope that Rose's plans for her would get lost between the long hours of her mother's work at Schlage Lock and Key and her entering high school.

As Rose, Esther, and Mildred walked through the Fillmore, the first thing Esther noticed was that it did not look like the Lower East Side in any way. People and clothing carts were not filling the streets. Fabric companies and garment racks were not smashed up against each other, overwhelming every inch of space and blasting fierce competitive commerce on the streets. The shops in the Fillmore were above ground, on the second and third floors hidden by a multitude of storefronts. There were Jewish markets and kosher restaurants stretching for a mile. Along the walk to Anya's, Esther saw two Jewish temples within blocks of each other. In front of each temple, there were Jewish men coming in and out of the large carved wooden doors. Some were smoking or taking in the cool summer air. Others were entering the temple to pray.

"Mama, why do these men stand outside and pray instead of inside?" asked Mildred.

"You have to pay to attend services at the temple, my darling," said Rose. "And today, there are probably more men than usual since it's Shabbat."

"I know what that is, Mama," said Mildred. "It's Saturday."

"It starts Friday at sundown," said Rose.

"Did you join a temple?" asked Mildred.

"You know your father was against religion and praying."

"And even if you did, Papa would find out," said Esther. "Then more fighting and screaming."

"Even though temples are places of worship, they require other services that have to be paid for like the rabbi and cantor, secretaries, and upkeep costs for the building. There are no dues. Who pays if not the congregation?"

"But Mama, don't you think it's unfair to exclude Jews from the temple because they can't pay dues?" asked Esther. "Why should money have anything to do with praying?"

Rose was distracted by the Jewish men congregating outside the Geary Street temple. Esther turned away, preferring to study the wide expanse of the streets that accommodated the trolley cars, similar to those she remembered when living in Montreal. The landscape was relatively clean – not like the stench of the Lower East Side with overflowing garbage. Esther noticed newsstands on every street corner carrying papers in English, Hebrew, German, and Yiddish. She spotted Jewish bakeries within arm's distance of each other selling fresh bagels. The Lower East Side was becoming a faded memory.

"Thank God there are no bars in this area," Rose mumbled.

"It's Prohibition, Mama," said Esther. "There are no bars anywhere that you can see. They're all behind closed doors."

"How do you know about this at such a young age, Esther?" asked her mother.

"I learned about that in Lower Manhattan. I heard people talking in the streets."

"It's ridiculous, this thing about Prohibition, no drinking and such," said Rose. "Nothing good will come of it."

They came upon Aunt Anya's apartment building – the finest one on the block, painted brown with cream trim. It reminded Esther of the brownstones she had seen in Brooklyn on the one occasion when they took a trip out of Lower Manhattan. Before they could climb the seven steps to ring the bell at the entrance, Aunt Anya rushed out the door. "I've been waiting for you for hours, and looking out my front window with joy and excitement!" They hugged and kissed and cried, and before they knew it, they entered paradise. Everyone was overcome with emotion.

"Anya, my darling, your apartment is spacious and glorious," gushed Rose. "Two bedrooms and a toilet. My, my, and all your rooms filled with beautiful furnishings – soft gray sofa, carved end tables, and plush chairs. You certainly have done right by yourself."

"It's gorgeous because of the absence of a man," Anya said. "Men bring clutter and bad manners and terrible odors inside the house."

"You're not married?" asked Esther.

"Why would I want to be married, dear one? I live better single than married, and I have a better job than most women due to my independence and lack of children. We have women's groups in the Fillmore that will teach you another vision of yourself."

Rose was not listening. She was looking out the front window admiring the well-dressed women displaying the new 1920s fashion trends: shorter, low-waisted dresses and bobbed hairstyles, cloche hats, the casual, haphazard fashion of a mixture of brightly colored clothes, scarves and stockings with bold Art Deco geometric designs of the era.

"The first thing I want to do is to buy a new scarf for Esther. See how colorful and beautiful they look on the ladies walking outside."

Anya studied Esther. "Why did you name her Esther? That name doesn't have a pleasing sound. It's too biblical."

"Esther's story in the Bible is compelling," said Rose. "I'm sure you know the Book of Esther, Anya. We learned our Old Testament stories in London and repeated them for years growing up. She risked her life to save the Jewish people."

"What does that have to do with your Esther?" asked Anya.

"You don't understand. She was the most beautiful woman in the Achaemenid Empire, and she was chosen to marry the Persian king. When Haman, his most trusted advisor, persuaded the king to authorize the extermination of the Jews, it was Esther who stopped the pogrom. She is the inspiration for Purim."

"It doesn't matter now, Rose. We are not living in those times, and there is no pogrom in America."

"I think you're right, Auntie," said Esther who was listening to their conversation.

"Don't fill her head with that stuff, Anya. She's on her way to being confirmed. You have to remember that Esther is not worldly like you are."

Esther turned away. Anya pulled her Rose aside.

"What's wrong with wanting to be a modern woman? And, by the way, a woman can be modern and Jewish. Jews don't have to follow every single dictate of Judaism. The modern thought about Judaism today is more freedom to express the way a person thinks about religion. Even some Conservative temples are moving to become something called *Reformed*."

"You live in the Jewish section of town, and so why is that?" asked Rose.

"I'm comfortable where I live, and I know how to straddle both worlds. I'm modern with the best accounting job at the Call Bulletin. I have Jewish and Gentile friends. I was at Langendorf Bakery before my accounting job. You know that I've always been a rebel, I admit, but I can speak freely when I want. We live in America, Rose. And while I'm on that subject, I think you should change Esther's name. It's old-fashioned. Too biblical. How about Estelle? It sounds dramatic, like a movie star's name."

"I like the name Estelle. Mama, can I please change my name before I go to high school?

"I'm opposed to it," said Rose. "Esther is her identity, but you'll likely do what you want. Just make sure you get the name change on your visa. It's your only identification."

"Why doesn't Esther have her citizenship papers?" asked Anya as she turned to Rose. "Rose, you need to get Esther's citizenship papers before she graduates."

Rose picked up the suitcases and left the room. "Why did you want me to change my name, Auntie? Is Esther so bad?"

"It's old-fashioned, my darling. You are stunning and smart and vibrant, and Esther sounds old and boring. You need a fresh start – a modern beginning to this next adventure."

"Mama didn't put up a fight. I think she's mad."

"Rose is more traditional than I am. We were raised in the same religion, but I wasn't devoted and didn't follow all the rules. Being Jewish has come and gone with me through the years. I don't embrace the whole tradition. I love it in bits and pieces. I'm simply suggesting that being modern might give you a leg up in the world."

"I have a goiter on my neck, Auntie," Esther blurted out as she pulled the yellow and brown scarf to the side of her neck to show Aunt Anya.

"That has nothing to do with who you are. I suggest you wear longer scarves in the flapper style. That would make a more dramatic statement, more about the times you live in. The scarves will be your trademark. You are more than your goiter, my beautiful niece."

By the end of June, Rose and the girls moved into a small but cozy apartment in the Fillmore, several blocks away from her sister. "The place has good bones, and, in time, I'll fix it up and make it almost as lovely as Aunt Anya's apartment. It's just a little dark, that's all. It could use more windows."

"Mama, since this is a new place and we're starting our new lives, I want to be called Estelle. It's important to me because I'm going to high school and I want a fresh start."

"I still don't approve, but you seem to be determined to take another name. In that case, you need a middle initial. So keep the "E" from Esther and become Estelle E."

"I love it Mama." Estelle hugged her mother.

"That reminds me, we have to fix your name on the Visa, otherwise San Francisco won't recognize you. And you might need it in school."

Rose got her daughters settled, then spent the summer working twelve hours a day at Schlage Lock and Key. Estelle was once again the babysitter for Mildred. The good thing about Mildred was her curiosity. She was smart and quick-witted. The bad thing about her was that she tested limits and was tenaciously contrary. It got her into trouble. Estelle had little patience with her because her nature was the opposite – Estelle was a pleaser, the good girl. Mildred pleased herself. During the first summer spent without their mother's supervision, the sisters were cautiously hopeful and moderately gregarious about being on their own. After they made the apartment neat and clean, the sisters left every day around noon to explore the Fillmore district. As a fun bonus, the apartment next door had a record player, and whoever lived there played popular songs all day and jazz long into the night. Rose rarely heard it – she was too tired after working a long day, and she fell asleep after she had something to eat. But the sisters danced while doing the dishes or cleaning up. They were determined to find a dance club when they got older so they could learn the Charleston and the Black Bottom and the Varsity Drag, the most popular dances of the 1920s.

"Hurry, hurry," said Mildred. "We have so much to see today. I want to see the flappers. I'm going to draw them."

"And I'm going to copy their fashion so I can be in style."

"This will be the best day yet."

After lunch they ran out the front door and raced down the stairs to the street. To their surprise, they discovered that summers in San Francisco were not always the sunniest of seasons. Most days outside the building, they encountered dense fog.

"Why isn't there any sun in this city?" Mildred asked.

"It's hiding in plain sight behind the clouds," Estelle answered.

Estelle was pleased that even in the Fillmore's sedate Jewish world, there were signs that the progressive age was in full swing. She noticed the subtle tone and style of the district. It was not only the fashion and hairstyles and long, flowing scarves that caught Estelle's attention. She noticed fashion and style in New York's Lower East Side's garment district, but the Fillmore didn't possess the constant energy and hustle of the crowds. It was a small district, compared to the other districts that made up San Francisco, and might present limited opportunities. She dreamed about living in a bigger world that was more exciting and less restrictive. Estelle went to the first newsstand she saw on the street. "What are you looking for?" Mildred asked. "I want to see what this place is all about. Look around, Millie. See all the merchants and bankers and businesses on the streets. And it looks so clean. It's called the Western Addition."

"I thought it was called the Fillmore," said Mildred.

"The Fillmore is part of the Western Addition. This district is larger than we think it is."

The man running the newspaper stand, an elderly gentleman with a kind face, adjusted his yarmulke on his head and pulled a book from a stack in the back of the kiosk.

"Are you girls tourists?" he asked.

"No, we just moved here, and we want to know about where we live," said Estelle.

The man handed her a book. "Here, keep it. It'll come in handy."

"Thanks. I sure appreciate this."

"This tourist book will get you around San Francisco. Good luck."

The sisters walked around the streets until they found a park bench. "Hey, listen to this, Millie. It says the Jews helped develop the Fillmore. They put money into the district and made it grow along with most of San Francisco."

"I can't wait to go to the ocean and see the harbors and go to the beach."

"Let's think of ourselves as adventurers and explore every nook and cranny and find all the city's secrets before we have to go back to school.

On one afternoon walk along Webster Street, Estelle and Mildred passed a synagogue with an elaborate carved wooden door drenched in gold leaf and a sign on the side of the building: Keneseth Israel.

"What is that, Estie?" asked Mildred.

An elderly Jewish man, dressed in an old-fashioned black suit and carrying a prayer book, stopped on the top stair in front of the temple doors.

"It's a Jewish synagogue," whispered Estelle.

"Do they have these synagogues outside the Fillmore?" asked Mildred.

"Probably not. There are hardly Jewish people outside of the Western Addition."

"What does that mean?" asked Mildred.

"The Christian people live outside the Fillmore, Millie. A whole other world lives and breathes and eats outside our area."

"What's our area?" asked Mildred.

"Silly girl. This is the Jewish area. We're inside the Western Addition district, but because Fillmore Street takes up most of the district, people call it the Fillmore. Mama says we are living among our own people. And it's safe here. But I'm not going to live here forever."

The man adjusted his prayer shawl with a long fringe hanging almost to the ground and pressed his round, fury black Russian hat down on his head. The wind was blowing, and his long coat was whipping around. His clothing looked like it originated from another century. He wore large, bulky, black wool pants that dropped to his ankles. But the oddity the sisters were intrigued by most was the small double box held to his forehead with black leather straps. He seemed to be fighting with the straps as the wind came up and scattered them around his body. When he tried to control them, he looked like a dancer in motion.

Millie took a few steps toward the man. "What's that on your forehead and why do you wear a funny hat?" she asked.

"It's called a tefillin," said the man. "We wear these two boxes for morning and evening prayer. I forgot to take it off inside the temple. I'm getting forgetful."

"Are you hot?" asked Mildred. "It's summer."

"We wear our clothes all year long – in summer or in winter – out of respect to God, our creator. And our clothes are one of the ways the Orthodox Jews identify themselves. Our dress comes from centuries ago in Poland."

"We saw Orthodox in Lower Manhattan, Millie. But they live mostly in Brooklyn."

"There are different ways to worship," said the man. "We have more rules, different clothing. Our prayers are in Hebrew, and we go to temple every day, perform rituals, and keep kosher. In the Conservative temple, men wear simple hats, yarmulkes, prayer shawls and also keep kosher, but they are not as strict as Orthodox Jews. They do not wear our clothing, and they can speak either English or Hebrew in temple. And there is the Reformed temple where Jews speak English and do not maintain dietary rules. I'm not sure these people are truly Jewish."

"What's kosher?" asked Mildred.

"Aren't you Jewish girls? You live here among your own kind and you know nothing."

"Why are you always among yourselves?" asked Estelle. "Because you are different?"

"It is all for the highest glory for God," said the man. "You should learn from your parents about your religion, otherwise, it will disappear."

The Jewish man walked unsteadily down the rest of the stairs and turned down the block. The sisters did not speak until they walked four blocks. They came upon another, more modern synagogue. The sign outside the temple read Beth Israel.

Mildred walked up the stairs to the front doors to peek inside and, just then, a man came through the doors dressed in a dark, tight-fitting modern suit with a yarmulke on his head, which he quickly took off upon leaving the synagogue. He nodded at Mildred and she giggled.

"Are you Reformed, sir?" asked Mildred.

"I am a Conservative Jew," said the man. "This is Beth Israel, which used to be completely Orthodox, but it is now Conservative. Come and visit us sometime, and bring your parents, too."

"Can you imagine our father inside a temple?" asked Estelle.

The sisters laughed and skipped down Geary Street, looking into every deli and clothing store, especially the Fillmore Fashion Store filled with dry goods and ready-to-wear clothing. Several Langendorf bread trucks stopped to deliver fresh bread to the markets. They waved to the drivers and shopkeeper and moved on down the block to the National Theater.

"Look," said Estelle. "Al Jolson's playing here!"

"He's on our radio, Es. But how can he be in the Fillmore and on the radio?"

Along the way, they passed the Eagle Market. "This is the biggest market I've ever seen," said Mildred. "What are all these foods?"

"Smell the dill pickles in barrels, Millie. And garlic tomatoes are in barrels, too."

They passed by the Jefferson Market. "Why are chicken feathers around here? What's going on? The chickens are screaming."

"Customers buy live chickens here. It's a kosher market. Then they take the live chicken to the back of the market to be butchered by – wait a minute, I have to look in the book – a shochet, a kosher slaughterer. Then they wrap it in newspaper and pass it back to the customers."

"That sounds awful," said Millie, holding her nose. "Who wants to eat that?"

"If we want to eat out, the tour book says there's Diller's Strictly Kosher Restaurant on Golden Gate between Webster and Fillmore. That's the most popular. But I hate kosher food. And how can anyone give up eating milk and meat together?"

Estelle and Mildred walked around a section of the Fillmore almost every day. One day, Mildred didn't want to walk so Estelle went to Aunt Anya's apartment.

"What's on your mind, Estelle?" she asked as she indicated for Estelle to sit on the sofa.

"You're not working today?"

"Oh, darling, I only work when they need an extra typist or I can help in various departments like accounting. This accounting office pays well. What's on your mind?"

"Millie and I have been walking for days and watching how the Jewish people stick together. I wondered why they always stick together with each other in each family, and always doing their activities together. Is that normal?"

"I don't know if it's normal," said Anya, "For me, it is a limiting way to live, not open to new ideas, only surrounded by Jewish dogma, repeating rituals and chants day after day because they were born into that religion and know nothing else. But religion is complex because it means different things to different people. I'm Jewish, but I don't follow all the dogma of the Old Testament, nor do I go to temple often. I live my life on my own terms."

"Do you believe in God?" Estelle asked.

"Believing in God comes from faith," said Anya. "You believe because you want to believe. Faith comes from your heart. Jews believe we are bound together by faith that has been both our heritage and the cause of our persecution. We remain together because of our respect for Jewish life."

"I don't believe you, Auntie. None of it seems real. Maybe it's a fairy tale, but not a bad fairy tale. There is no God that fixes things. I don't believe in praying. Prayers don't tell me what to think. We fix things. Religious Jews think there is one way to live, to eat, to dress, to pray, to believe only in the Torah. Women cover their heads with scarves or wigs and wear long modest dresses and huddle together in the background. I don't want to be like them."

"Not you, Estelle. You will be educated, not forced into a marriage with a man you don't love, or you don't know, or worse, meant to bear a child after exchanging marriage vows. That is not freedom. That is not life. Now let's get some milk and cookies."

The summer went by fast and soon it was the end of August. Along the way, the sisters found a radio in an alley and got it to work after they plugged it into a socket in their apartment. It was a highlight of summer. The sisters danced and sang and learned about jazz and who were the popular singers and orchestras – Louis Armstrong, Josephine Baker, Jelly Roll Martin, Ethel Waters, Ma Rainey, Bix Beiderbecke – and hobbled together a vocabulary that suited their age, especially Estelle, who was more than ready to tackle being a teenager.

"Where am I going to school, Estie?" asked Mildred as they took their afternoon walk along the perimeters of the Fillmore. "You know where your school is, but what about mine?"

"It won't be a Jewish school. We would have to be a member of the Jewish temple, and we don't have the money. Maybe it will be a Catholic school like I went to in Montreal."

"I want to go to a public school like you."

"We'll go to the library and search, but not now. We have to start dinner for Mama."

Estelle and Mildred were getting dinner together when Rose came home early from work.

"I've got to change my clothes," she said. "It's hot today."

Estelle put stuffed bell peppers on a plate and Mildred finished the salad. Water glasses were filled and napkins were added to the table.

Rose came in and sat at the table.

"How was your day, Mama?" asked Estelle.

"There is always too much work. I can't wait until Sunday for my day off. Tomorrow I want you to go to Commerce High School and register for classes. It's almost Labor Day."

"What about me, Mama?" asked Mildred.

"I haven't decided yet what to do with you," said Rose. "I don't trust the public schools."

"On our walk today, we saw a Catholic school called Sacred Heart Cathedral," said Mildred. "It's an old school, but I don't know how much it costs."

"Thank you, darling. I'll see about that. I can't afford to join a temple, and I certainly won't go to the Orthodox synagogues. And you have to be married to be a member, I'm sure."

"What about Reformed?" asked Mildred.

"How do you know about Reformed? Where did you get that?"

"We walked by a Jewish man and he told us he was Reformed," Mildred said.

"I see you both have learned quite a bit this summer."

"I haven't learned much about sewing," said Estelle. I want to make my own clothes."

"Get a job after school and you can do anything you want, my darling."

"You'll find my school, Mama," said Mildred. "I'm not worried."

CHAPTER 6

COMMERCE HIGH SCHOOL

It was the end of summer, the Saturday before Labor Day, and there was a heat wave in the San Francisco Bay Area. Rose got the day off, so she did some shopping in the morning and returned around noon. Bundles of groceries were still in her arms when she spotted a letter on the credenza close to the front door. Estelle was fanning herself, reading a good mystery while the radio played Bessie Smith singing "Baby Won't You Please Come Home" in low tones.

"Hi, Mama," she said. "How was it out there?"

Rose did not answer her. Instead, she dropped her bags of groceries on the floor and opened the letter. As she began to read, her face flushed and her hands shook.

My dear Rose, I hope you and your daughters are settled in comfortably and have had a good summer in San Francisco. I know you will thrive in that beautiful community and come to prosper soon. You are a hard worker and extremely loyal to whoever you work for. Now, for the real purpose of my letter. It is to inform you that I ran into your husband, Jacob Lanch. When

I say that I ran into him, that is not actually correct. He came to my house, the place where I work, and demanded answers to his questions about why he was served with divorce papers. What right did I have to do that? I had no permission to do that. Evidently, he did not know you worked for me, or with me, and he went, shall I say, berserk. When I threatened to call the police, he backed off, but said he would not sign any divorce documents. He said he would be married to you for the rest of his life and you could never marry another man. This was your punishment for going behind his back. He said he would never marry again. I caution you to be careful of contact with Jake. I would not put it past him to come to San Francisco to bully you into taking him back. I have an idea that I will write in another document, which not only accuses Jacob of abandonment, but also accuses him of abuse. If you have any objection to this plan, please let me know, and I will not draw up the papers. I want the best for you. I will always be forever grateful to you for helping me out at a difficult time in my life. If your circumstances had been different, I would have chosen another course for us. I developed a fondness for you that could not be matched.

Yours truly,
Mr. Osloff

Rose dropped the letter on the credenza as tears rolled down over her smooth, unlined, face. Estelle watched, scared for her mother. Rose entered her room and didn't come out for the rest of the night. Estelle walked to the credenza, read the letter, then returned it where Rose had left it. She cried. Estelle didn't know why she cried, only that one day she would be like her mother – strong and committed to living an honest and true life. Mr. Osloff's words were kind and sweet. He wrote to her about her beauty and loyalty. Estelle knew that if anything would bring her father to San Francisco, it was Rose's wish to divorce him. Mr. Osloff also feared Jake's response would harm Rose. Estelle knew the games he played with Rose. She knew he might slap her. But Estelle knew one thing about her mother – Rose would never give in, never take him back. She possessed a strong sense of pride in who she was and what she had to overcome in life. Rose would not lose herself in Jake's obsessive drive to hurt others. There was no love left.

The next morning Rose came into the living room dressed to the nines wearing a new dress – a blue and white floral pattern, belted with a white lace neckline with three-quarter sleeves. She wore a new pair of white shoes with a two-inch heel.

"Mama! You look like a movie star," Estelle said with excitement. Mildred jumped out of her seat and hugged Rose.

"We're going out today, girls, to see things we've never seen before. This is a new day, and a new month, and you'll be locked up in school until Thanksgiving, So let's have some fun."

"Yes, yes!" Mildred blurted out. "I want to go to Fleishhacker Pool."

"It's not open yet, my darlings, but we'll go one day. Neither is the zoo. But there are hundreds of places to go in the city."

"Sutro Baths, then," said Estelle. "They have seven saltwater pools and a glass roof, and there's lots to do there. We can explore the museum and eat at the restaurant. I think it's time to celebrate our new life. I'm almost fourteen and going into high school and Millie is going to be eleven. And we'll make new friends and learn new things."

"And this is a perfect birthday celebration," said Rose. "We'll have a choice of the saltwater pools and you'll have plenty of time to try them out."

"What are you going to do, Mama, while we swim?" asked Estelle.

"I'm going to swim, too, and then we'll go to the museum and then eat lunch, then walk along the cliffs and look out over the Pacific Ocean, and all will be well."

Estelle thought it was the best day they ever had together – frolicking without a care, without a thought as to whether Jake would invade their world. When they returned home after the long day, Rose sat the girls down in the living room.

"Tuesday's your first day of school, but Monday is Labor Day and a holiday. I get the day off, and we're going on another field trip to the Emporium department store to shop for something new for school."

"Mama, you don't have to spend lots of money on us," said Estelle.

"Well, don't fret, my darling. I got a raise. All the hard work and long hours paid off."

"I'd love some fabric to sew my clothes. It will be important for me in high school."

"Let's see what we can find on our travels tomorrow. We're clever and resourceful women, and we will find what we need."

As they road by trolley to the Emporium, Rose told Mildred that she was not going to Sacred Heart school because there was tuition just like the Jewish schools, plus they required a uniform. "I asked one of the ladies in the secretarial pool at work if there was a public grammar school in the Fillmore. Lo and behold there is one on Scott Street in the Western Addition. It's called Benjamin Franklin Middle School."

"Oh, Mama, you're the best." Mildred hugged her mother for a long time.

The Emporium had a section of fabrics that covered half of an entire floor. Estelle did not know how much yardage to buy, but she had watched her father design and sew garments in his various jobs, and she felt confident that she could come up with the right yardage for the cotton fabric she selected – an eggplant color for a skirt and a soft yellow and orange plaid for a long blouse that fell to the hips – it was the new flapper style with the skirt dropped over the knees. She studied patterns and picked out needles, thread, and fasteners. There remained the problem of not owning a sewing machine. Estelle combed the area to see if there was a sewing room in the back where the store did alterations. While her mother was paying for her fabric, Estelle took a tour of the back rooms and dressing area. There it was – her sewing room with five or six sewing machines separated from each other by worktables. Estelle stood in awe. She wanted to sit down immediately in front of a machine and learn how to operate it. She saw the head seamstress hovering over an employee who made a mistake. Estelle waited patiently for her to finish her consultation.

"May I help you, young lady?" she asked Estelle.

"Yes, ma'am. I'm Estelle Lanch. I have sewed by hand for many years. I learned from my father who was a designer and could sew anything. I was wondering if I could watch and learn how to use one of the sewing machines when they weren't in use."

"My name is Mrs. Greenburg, young lady," she said. "And while I applaud your interest, I can't let just anyone sit at machines that belong to the Emporium."

"I thought about that, and I would be happy to do alterations after school."

"How old are you, Estelle?"

"Fourteen." It was a small white lie. She would not be fourteen until October.

"My father was famous in New York. He created and designed the Maidenform Bra."

"This is interesting information. I suppose we can try this out. No reason why not. When you're ready, come by after school and let's see how fast you can learn to sew on the machines. By the way, I like the way you wear your scarf. Very stylish."

Estelle pulled the scarf away from her neck to show Mrs. Greenburg her goiter.

"So that's why you wear a scarf. It turned into a good fashion statement. It gives me some ideas on how to incorporate scarves into designs."

If Estelle could get through the first six months of high school hiding her goiter by cleverly dressing herself in the latest fashion, she could find the acceptance she sought outside her world. That, and a new pair of stylish one-and-a-half-inch heels with a T-strap would complete her dreams. They would also make her legs look longer.

Tuesday after Labor Day could not come soon enough for Estelle and Mildred. They were both up and dressed before the sun rose. As they entered into an already hot and muggy end-of-summer day, they felt nervous as they headed to the trolley.

"It's so nice we can take the same trolley, Millie," said Estelle, as they hiked up their skirts and greeted the conductor. "This will be a great adventure."

"You look good, Estie," said Mildred. "I like your yellow scarf because it sets off your dark hair. Even though we are wearing our old clothes, we still look fresh. Right?"

"Yes, but why didn't you wear the new skirt and blouse Mama brought for you?"

"I'all wear it for a special day."

"Please don't tell Mama that I'm going to the Emporium after school," said Estelle. "I'll be home in time to help with dinner. Please do your homework while I am learning to sew."

"I won't tell. But what if I get asked to go to the soda shop with a friend? Can I go?"

"Of course, but make sure it's on a day when you don't have too much homework. And watch the time. We don't want to make Mama angry."

The first few days at school were difficult for both girls. Mildred had an easier time making friends. She was in sixth grade, and her classmates were more friendly than snobby. Estelle tried to remain calm as she walked through the front doors of her new high school. She was overcome by so many different types of people. No one looked at her, and she was happy about that, but she was nonetheless intimidated. She knew there was no reason for her to think she was odd or strange, except her own insecurity. She felt no one looked like her, dressed like her, or wore scarves. Freshman classes at Commerce High were spread throughout the school. Hallways were long and crowded and walking through them was uncomfortable. Estelle was glad she did not have shoes with heels. Students bumped into each other, dropped books and binders, and started and stopped conversations that caused traffic jams.

There were many more nationalities than Estelle expected. The students were not only from the Western Addition, but they also came from beyond its borders – from the lower socioeconomic Mission and Tenderloin districts with their predominantly Irish and some Italian immigrants who chose not to settle in Little Italy or the North Beach District. The Japanese lived in Japantown and crossed borders north of the Fillmore to attend Commerce High School. Estelle settled into her homeroom and held her breath as she assessed the other students. Her eyes wandered to the brown bags on their desks. A sinking feeling overtook her. She inhaled with a loud yawn because she realized that she had forgotten her lunch. At that moment, she thought she would die of starvation. The next thought that popped into Estelle's head was more important. It was a thought so big that it changed her life forever. After looking around the classroom at her peers, she noticed that most of the girls were slim. Estelle decided then and there that she was going on a diet for the rest of her life. She would never think of herself as fat again. She would stop cursing her waistline and begin to think of herself as thin. Of course, these body-image thoughts were only in her mind. She was developing a lovely body. But there was no way Estelle was going to stop fretting about her weight. She vowed to weigh herself every morning, and she would diet if she gained an ounce.

"I'm not going to be fat anymore," Estelle told Rose when she handed her daughter a brown bag lunch the next morning.

"Oh, my darling, you are not fat. That's in your head. You have a beautiful figure."

"Then, what's this?" Estelle pulled on her waist to show off her extra skin with disgust.

"Leftover baby fat is all you have. In six months, that will all go away as you walk and take your P.E. classes and eat sensibly. You have that nice long waist. Perfect physique."

"I'm going to make my lunch from now on, Mama. You don't have to do that for me."

Estelle was furiously sewing every afternoon at the Emporium with dedication. She finished her first piece of clothing, a dark jersey sleeveless flapper dress cut on a bias. Mrs. Greenburg was so impressed that she offered Rose a job after school for three hours every day. She was to hem skirts and dresses. Mrs. Greenburg would teach her tailoring if she was talented enough. Estelle decided she was going to learn to design her school wardrobe and earn money for herself and Rose. She was giddy with joy. Life was beginning to take shape. It was time to tell her mother what was happening with her life. By December of her freshman year, Estelle settled into the school environment and slowly grew out of her shyness. It all began the day she wore her newly made outfit to school. Estelle spotted some leftover fabric in the sewing room – a subtle print in blues and browns that matched the colors of her brown skirt and a long, blue blouse that hugged her hips. She was proud of her new ensemble. She added a slight smudge of eye shadow she found in a dressing room at the Emporium. It changed her look slightly because it accentuated her eyes.

"Your outfit is smashing, Estelle," said one of the girls as they came out of civics class. "I see you sewing up a storm in home economics. I'm Lucille Flynn by the way."

"Thanks, Lucille. I've got an after-school job at the Emporium sewing hems and doing alterations. When it's slow, I work on my own clothes."

"Maybe you can help me in home economics because I am lost," Lucille said. "I can't even hold a needle. It keeps falling out of my hands."

"Of course, I'll help. This will be fun."

"How come you always wear a scarf? I mean, it's your trademark, at least, that's what the girls say."

"Are they making fun of me?" asked Estelle.

"No, they were complimentary. I told them we were friends, and they were kind of jealous. You can meet them after vacation."

An Irish boy from the Mission pushed his way between the girls. "Hey what did you think about this new law Mr. Edwards told us today about kicking a bunch of Jews and Chinese out of our country? Finally, getting rid of the riff raff."

"Get away from me, Billy," said Lucille. "We're not friends."

"You mean the Johnson-Reed Act?" asked Estelle. "It's called a quota system. The U.S. isn't kicking people out. It's about how many new people they're going to let in."

"Yeah, well, they're not letting in as many," said Billy. "That's what my pa said."

"Is that a good thing or a bad thing?" Estelle asked Billy.

"That's good," said Billy. "They aren't Christian, and they didn't go to school like we did. Besides, the Jews speak Yiddish. And they're not good at business and they cause trouble."

"That's not true," said Estelle. "They fit in fine. I read in *The Chronicle* that they've been in America since the Spanish Inquisition. Wherever do you get your information from, Billy? The Jewish people helped to make San Francisco what it is today. Remember Levi Strauss?"

Estelle held her breath, thinking of her father and how he achieved something most immigrants did not. He was exceptional at what he did, and then he threw it away out of pride or anger or his belief in communism.

"Ask your pa. He knows the history of San Francisco, and maybe he'll tell you the truth."

Lucille and Estelle quickly became best friends. Lucille was grateful for Estelle's help as she learned to sew and Estelle was happy to see how much progress she was making.

"Are you going to be a seamstress after you graduate?" asked Lucille.

"No, I'm happy to design my own clothes. I watched my father design and sew clothes, but he didn't teach me much. He wasn't around."

"Do you have to work every afternoon during vacation? We could get a Coke at the soda shop, or maybe one afternoon I can come with you to the Emporium and watch what you do."

"That's a great idea. Then maybe on some Sunday I can go to the Mission. I've never been there. I'm bored with the Fillmore."

"It's a dump, Es," said Lucille. "Why do you want to see the Mission District?

"It's just different from what I see all the time. I don't mind if the Mission is a dump. If you have time, you can look around the Fillmore, but there's nothing much to do. Just shops and restaurants and some clothing stores. Sundays should be our exploring day."

"I'm stuck at home on Sundays taking care of my sisters and brothers after church, just as I do every day and it's not fair. When I finally get away, I want to go to North Beach because my older brother said it's a fun place."

"I heard the same thing. Let's make a plan. Maybe we can take a trolley during Christmas vacation. We're smart girls. We can figure it out."

On the last day of school before Christmas vacation, Estelle and Lucille passed the sparsely decorated Christmas tree in the lobby. No one noticed the tree as the students pushed through the front doors of Commerce High School.

"What are you doing for Christmas?' asked Lucille as they walked to the streetcar.

"We celebrate Hanukkah, and don't ask me to tell you what it means because I don't know exactly. My mother tries to tell us the story every year, and then Millie and I forget."

"I'm sorry. That's sad."

"Why sad? I live in the Fillmore because my mother is Jewish. I'm not."

"I don't know why you say that," said Lucille.

"It's the truth. It's my mother's religion, not mine and not my father's. My father is a communist and doesn't believe in God or religion, and he and my mother don't get along about that. What are you going to do over the holidays?"

"Babysit. Just like every day. Both my parents work. Really, Es, I never understood why the Irish have so many children. They use the older kids to take care of the young ones. There is never enough to eat, never enough beds or clothes or anything. They come home exhausted, expecting that one of us will make dinner, and they leave early in the morning expecting us to make breakfast. Who knows if the young ones even get lunch? We're all stacked together living with no air to breathe and no place to study or play. What's the point of having kids if parents are never around?"

"My mother says all you need is two kids. Just double yourselves."

"I like that idea. But a better idea is how we can figure out how not to have any kids."

They hugged, and Estelle got on the streetcar. The ride always gave her time to think. Most of her thoughts were about Mildred. Estelle thought she had it bad having to look after Millie, who could be a handful – spirited, challenging, often getting into trouble skipping school with friends. Estelle tried to curb Mildred's strong-headed and impulsive behavior. But she refused to monitor her schoolwork. Estelle felt that their mother should take care of school issues. Millie's saving grace was that she was a wiz at math, and she was a natural at the piano. Even in the sixth grade, without any lessons, Mildred taught herself the popular songs of the day in music class. It was difficult to stay mad at Millie for long. First things first. Estelle was intent on making a new outfit for herself, and she would make a shawl for Rose and a new skirt for Mildred for Hanukkah. She hopped off the streetcar and walked several blocks down Market Street to the Emporium. Stacks of clothes needing hemming and alterations were folded on her sewing machine.

"I'm so glad you're early today," said Mrs. Greenburg. "It's the holidays, and we need all hands on deck. Let's start with the easiest and work up to the most difficult. Hems first."

The holidays passed quickly. Even though Estelle did not get her presents finished until the last day of Hanukkah, Rose and Mildred were happy with their gifts. As usual, Rose gave Estelle money to buy fabric for her clothes and gave Mildred small jewelry trinkets.

Estelle managed to visit Lucille on New Year's Day, but found that everyone had gone to church. It was Sunday. She sat in front of Lucille's house and watched a few boys on rickety bikes riding up and down Noe Street. After an hour, she saw a group of people walking toward her. Estelle stood up and waved. Lucille came running up to her and gave her a hug.

"This is my family, Es," she said.

They all nodded hello and went inside.

"Not too long, now," Lucille's mother said. "You've got chores."

"I'm sorry. This was the first time I could get away," said Estelle. "I had to work all during the vacation. But look what I brought you."

Estelle took out a silk scarf from her purse splattered with the colors of the rainbow. Lucille put it around her neck, thrilled to have a present for herself.

"I didn't get anything for Christmas, and this is so beautiful."

Estelle held her hand and they began to walk. "Don't worry about things like this."

"We'll get to North Beach some Sunday in the future," said Lucille, "even if I have to ditch my family. I'm so tired of being a mother. I'm never having kids."

"We don't have to do anything our parents did. We can be who we want and do what we want," said Estelle as she adjusted Lucille's new scarf.

"I want to be a seamstress like you, Es. You sew like you are playing the piano. It's your talent. Plus you have beautiful dark eyes. So dramatic."

"I love sewing, but for now, it's my hobby. Next year I want to learn to type and take dictation so one day I can work in an office. I'll design and sew on the side and I'll own my own business."

"Those are good dreams, Es."

They stopped walking when Estelle saw a school. "What's this school?"

"St. Paul's Grammar School. I didn't go there. We don't have enough money to go to Catholic school."

"Religion is a waste of time. And you even have to pay for it."

CHAPTER 7

JAKE

By the time Estelle was a junior in high school, she was at the top of her class in most academic subjects. Her favorite classes were home economics and business, which included typing and dictation. Estelle hung out with Lucille and a group of her Irish friends from the neighborhood, All the girls wanted to copy Estelle's style of dress, and even though they could not afford the flapper look, Estelle was generous and clever in helping them add items to help give hints to the modern style – the signature scarf or a dropped waist. The girls went together to a thrift store when they needed an item or two, such as low heels. Estelle usually found something to embellish their wardrobes.

Since she was still sewing at the Emporium, she offered to alter or hem any of their clothes. When they were all dressed in their finest, they would take a trolley to North Beach and walk among the exciting streets. There were speakeasies and restaurants, and everyone was speaking Italian and singing Italian songs. The area was lively and fun and different from their world in the Mission or the Fillmore. Estelle was having the time of her life. She was blending in and accepted as one of the girls – part of the gang. It's what Estelle dreamed about.

"We're coming back here when we are grown up, Lucy," said Estelle. "Then we can find a speakeasy and we can drink gin and dance the Charleston."

During the summer between their Freshman and Sophomore year, Lucille was finally able to visit the Fillmore. "I'm free, Es. It's a miracle I was left by myself today. Something about a field trip and they would be late getting home. There is a God."

"No, Lucy. There is luck."

It was a late Saturday morning in mid-June, and it was overcast. Not many people were on the streets. Most of the Jewish community found solace in attending Saturday morning temple. After services, they would buy groceries for their family dinners.

"There's so much food on the streets," said Lucille. "And kosher signs everywhere. What does that mean – kosher?"

"Most religious Jews don't mix milk and meat when they eat. But I'm not sure why. Milk and meat are not allowed to touch, so you have to put them in separate dishes."

"The food is different from how we eat, I imagine," she said as she pointed to a sign that read "Live Kosher Chickens"

"A Jewish butcher slaughters the chickens in the back of the store. It's different from how regular butchers slaughter. Something about how the blood drains out of the animal. It's part of the Jewish dietary rituals."

"Does your mother cook this way?" Lucille asked.

"She hardly cooks because she's tired all the time. She grew up religious, but her circumstances changed with work. My mother didn't lose all her rituals. She has a few left."

A block away Aunt Anya was waving and walking towards the girls. She was dressed to the nines, wearing a flirty yellow dress with a crochet neckline, a dropped flapper waist, a straw cloche hat, and a light green wraparound shawl – her curls flowing down to just below her ears.

"Auntie, you cut your hair! It looks wonderful," Estelle said. "You have a bob cut."

"Don't you both look terrific! Who is your friend?"

"This is Lucille, my best friend in high school."

"Hello, Lucille," said Anya. "I love your red hair. And it looks like Estelle dressed you."

"She's a great seamstress. We all think she is the bee's knees."

Anya takes her niece by the shoulders and looks into her eyes. "I knew you would be a stunner, my darling. And talented. Let's walk a little. Where are you girls off to?

"I'm showing Lucille the Fillmore. She's never been in this district before."

"She's missed something special. Lucille, the Fillmore is the best district in the city."

"I love all the smells and looking at the different storefronts. And everyone's talking at once."

"You are right about talking, Lucille."

Anya took her attention to Estelle. "Your mother and I had lunch last weekend and she is very, very tired. What are we going to do about that?"

"I told her to ask for a raise."

"I told her to get a boyfriend." Anya laughs. "Both are good options."

Anya hugged Estelle and kissed her on the cheek. "Goodbye for now, little ones. We'll check in later about your mother. See you soon."

The girls watched as Anya sashayed down the street.

"She's wonderful, Es. You are so lucky."

"My mom's sister is special. When I was little, she changed my name. I was born Esther and she didn't think it suited me. She also told me to wear longer scarves to hide my goiter." She untied her scarf, and Lucile stared in disbelief for a moment before Estelle quickly retied her scarf and brought herself back to her normal state.

"Oh, Es, I'm so sorry. I never knew. How could I know?

"When I started kindergarten, my mom covered my goiter with a scarf because the kids teased me, but Auntie Anya showed me how to make the scarf into a fashion statement. So it's no big thing. Come on, let's get a Dr. Brown's cream soda. They're delicious in the Fillmore."

Sometime before Thanksgiving in Estelle's sophomore year, she came home to an empty house. Mildred was nowhere to be found. Her mother was not home from work. Both were late. A table lamp was on in Rose's bedroom, and Estelle turned it off. No use wasting electricity. Estelle could not help but worry. She left the apartment with her coat and purse and ran outside, hoping to intercept them coming down the street any minute. She leaned against the wall, clutching her purse and started to cry. It was getting dark and the temperature was dropping fast. She considered looking for them, but realized that they might come home and find her missing. She decided to run back upstairs.

When she turned on the light, Estelle noticed a letter. The handwriting was familiar – Mr. Osloff's handwriting.

My dear Rose,

I hope this letter finds you well. It has been too long since I have written with news. Life has proceeded with the sameness of work, while I carry your memory in my heart.

Your husband, Jacob Lanch, has finally signed the divorce agreement on the condition that he brings you a copy of that agreement to your home in San Francisco. It was a quick exchange and not to my liking. In the agreement, you accused him (referenced in the document) of abandonment and abuse. I told him that he had to accept your conditions if he was to sign the divorce agreement. He would accept abandonment but not the abuse. I reminded him that I saw his wife, Rose, walk into my office to work and her face was red and she had bruises on her swollen jaw. There could be no doubt that your husband is guilty of outright abuse. I never said anything. I didn't want you to feel shame.

To get him out of your life, I accepted his offer to deliver in person a copy of the divorce decree officially signed by the court of Los Angeles. When I asked him why he wanted to deliver the decree in person, he told me he had a job in San Francisco, but that he wouldn't bother you. And he wanted to see his daughters.

This is a trade-off, my dear Rose. A matter of negotiation. If he can't see you, you will not obtain a legal divorce, which I think is healthier for you than holding the line against him. I know you, Rose, and I know you will benefit more from this compromise than not. Time to let go; time to move forward to a new life freely and willingly.

Yours forever truly,
Mr. Osloff

As Estelle put the letter back on the end table, she heard the door open and the shuffling of coats being removed and hung on the entry hooks. Rose saw Estelle on the sofa.

"Where were you Mama? I was scared."

"Millie and I went to my office to type a response to Mr. Osloff's letter. I told him he did right by me even though he made a Faustian bargain with Jake. I assume you saw his letter on the table. The letter was half hanging out of the envelope."

"I didn't mean to snoop, Mama. You deserve better. Mr. Osloff loves you."

"It doesn't matter," Rose said stoically.

"It does matter. You are a beautiful woman and smart and clever."

"I don't need a pep talk," said Rose. "I know what I need – the strength to face your father and get the divorce papers in my hand without incident. Then he can be on his way. There is nothing between us but a piece of paper. I'll get it anyway I can."

"What about Millie and me? What are we supposed to do with him?"

"Whatever you wish to do with him. See him. Don't see him. Have your fill of him or let him go out of your life"

"Aren't you afraid of him?" asked Estelle.

"I have nothing to lose, my darling. He will not lay a hand on me."

Estelle and Mildred could not wait for Thanksgiving vacation. They needed a break and were happy to have the holiday to look forward to. Anya and Rose went shopping on Wednesday afternoon for turkey, squash, cranberries, potatoes, carrots, and a pumpkin pie. It would be a simple meal but filling and tasty.

The girls were busy at home setting the table for the following midday meal and creating a centerpiece from flowers that they picked in the park. The usual darkness of the apartment was blessed by a stream of sunlight shining through the small living room window facing O'Farrell Street.

Mildred came into the room and turned on the radio. Jazz music floated through the apartment. Mildred took her sister's hands and they began to dance to "Heat Wave" sung by Ethel Waters. Rose stood at the doorway and watched her daughters playfully dance to the modern jazz tune. Estelle grabbed Rose's hand and included her in their joyful circle. For a minute, the Lanch household forgot all cares.

The next morning, Rose got up early to stuff the turkey.

"I'll peel and cut the carrots," said Mildred as she threw down a magazine and marched into the kitchen. She pulled a peeling knife out of the drawer and picked up a bunch of carrots.

"Do that later, darling," said Rose. "Get yourselves dressed, girls. Anya will be here late morning. We'll have plenty of time to put out the hors d'oeuvres."

Within the hour, there was a knock on the door. Rose entered the living room first, followed by Estelle and Mildred. They were all dressed in their best clothes, hair curled, shoes polished. There was a moment of silence as they all looked toward the door.

"It's too early for Anya," whispered Rose.

Estelle walked to the door and opened it. Jake stood straight with a bouquet of flowers.

"Hi, Esther," Jake said.

"I'm Estelle. My name is Estelle now."

"When did that happen?" he asked. "Your mother wouldn't change your name."

"What do you want, Jake? And no, you cannot enter my apartment. If you are here to give me the divorce papers. I'll take them now."

"Hold on, hold on. Can't I say hello to my daughters? Where's Mildred?"

Mildred came out from behind her mother.

"There's my girl."

"We're not your girls," said Estelle. "We're not anything to you. Please give Mama the papers and leave."

"They're not on me," said Jake.

"Then why are you here, Jake?" asked Rose. "You're not coming in. You're not invited."

Estelle noticed Anya standing behind Jake's back.

"Jake," Anya said. "Nice to meet you after all these years. I'm sorry I didn't come to your wedding in Toronto."

Jake turned around and sneered at her "Isn't this the happy family? I guess you're here to eat dinner with everyone."

Anya pushed past Jake on her way into the apartment as Rose said. "Get out, Jake, and don't come back unless you have the divorce agreement with you."

"That would be a wise move," said Anya, "considering you have already signed it and it needs to be filed legally." She closed the door on Jake and turned to hug her sister.

"Mama, why didn't he bring the agreement?" asked Estelle.

"He'll bring it over to me when he's good and ready. God have mercy on his black soul."

Before school let out for Christmas vacation, Estelle sat at the counter of the St. Francis Fountain with her friend Margaret Richmond. It was a classic soda fountain with three gooseneck soda spouts of carbonated water with syrups to make colas, milk shakes, malts, and egg creams.

Photos from the early days of the soda fountain flanked the ornate gold mirror frame.

"What are you having, Margaret?" asked Estelle. "I have to watch my figure so I'll have soda water with a little bit of syrup."

"I'm probably going to stuff myself over the holidays so I'll go easy, too," said Margaret.

"Hanukkah is early this year. Did you notice?"

"I don't pay attention to the Jewish holidays. My mother does, and that's when I know."

"Don't you go to shul on Friday nights?" asked Margaret.

"We've never belonged to a temple. I don't know much about the religion."

"You are very worldly, Estelle. You live in the Fillmore, but you aren't connected to it."

The soda jerk, a tall, sixteen-year-old, pimply teenager sauntered over to take their order.

"What do you want?" he asked.

"Soda water with some flavor. Maybe you could add a little squirt of Coca-Cola."

"Make it two, please," added Margaret.

"I'll try," said the soda jerk as he walked off, shaking his head.

"Why do you like it here?" asked Margaret. "I mean, this place is the Mission. It's kind of low rent. The Fillmore is much nicer."

"I come here with Lucille when she doesn't have to go home to babysit after school."

"It's all Irish. And Catholic."

"That's the point, Margaret. Don't you get tired of always being around the Jewish district? Don't you want to meet other people and learn about how other people live?"

The soda jerk set down their drinks, abruptly turned, and walked away.

"That's what I mean," said Margaret. "The soda jerk didn't try to be polite. Not like the Jews who schmooze and kibitz. They're always so friendly. The Irish are kind of rough around the edges."

"The Irish can be standoffish, but Lucy is a good friend and fun to be with."

A bell rang above the door, surprising the teenage boy who entered. Out of concern for his yarmulke, he put his hand on his head.

"Hi, Moishe," said Margaret as she turned to see who entered. "Come and sit with us."

Moishe stood for a moment and looked at the soda jerk. "Hi, Frank."

Frank didn't acknowledge him.

"See what I told you," said Margaret. "You can't find a friendly face. Sit down, Moishe. You know Estelle." What are you doing here? You never come to the Mission."

"I was looking for Estelle and thought she might be here," he said.

"I know people in the Mission," said Estelle.

"Your friend is Lucille, right?" he asked.

"She's my best friend. You do good research, Moishe."

Frank walked to the end of the bar and stood in front of Moishe.

"May I have a Coke, please," said Moishe.

"This isn't your part of town," said Frank. "Why are you all here? "

"Don't you have a job to do, Frank?" Estelle said. "I see you at school, so I know who you are, and I know you and your gang think you're the be-all and end-all, but you're here to wait on us and get our drinks, not to give us the third degree."

"Why did you say that?" whispered Margaret as Frank walked away. "It was rude."

"He was rude," said Estelle. "We come from the Fillmore, and he wasn't keen to serve us. What do you think, Moishe?"

"I get it, Estelle," said Moishe. "But you don't have to point it out."

"We all have to notice, otherwise, you won't see prejudice when it's in front of you."

"I see it, but I live in the Fillmore with other Jews," said Moishe. "I think that's what all Jews do, live together, just as Catholics and the rest do. Why did you have to go there with Frank?"

"I was testing to see how uncomfortable I could make him with two Jews and an atheist sitting at his counter. I wanted to see what would happen."

"It's your choice how you want to live your life, Estelle. I wanted to talk to you because the journalism department needs another opinion writer for the newspaper, and I thought of you."

"Are you serious, Moishe? I'm not a writer."

"Yes, you are. Your English papers always get As, and you're a good writer."

"You can do a fashion column, Es," said Margaret. "Or tips on sewing."

"That's not what I have in mind," Moishe said. "More like current affairs."

"You mean like politics? Come on, Moishe, I'm barely politically literate. You should do current affairs, and if you need help, I'll edit."

"How about human interest stories?" he asked. "Would you consider that?"

"A fashion column is more up my alley."

Frank came up to Moishe, set down the Coke, and walked away without a word.

"Let's go, everyone," said Margaret, "Drink up, Moishe."

Moishe took two big gulps, left money on the counter and followed Estelle and Margaret out of the St. Francis Fountain.

"Hey, Estelle, I'll let you write about fashion but you have to promise me that I can give you a couple of human interest stories along the way."

"You got it. But I can't start now. The holidays are coming up and I'm still working at the Emporium. See you guys later."

Estelle was not happy working at the Emporium. Lately, Mrs. Greenburg was using her designs, telling customers they were her own, especially styles with scarves. When Estelle first began to work for Mrs. Greenburg, the head seamstress gave her the credit for her designs.

However, for the past six months, the recognition had stopped. Estelle thought it was dishonest.

But leaving Mrs. Greenburg was out of the question until she had another job. Her idea was to find part-time work as a typist. And that would require more than good luck.

CHAPTER 8

HOLIDAYS

Before Estelle made any rash decisions like quitting her job as a seamstress at the Emporium, her idea was to talk to her typing teacher, Mrs. O'Conner, about opportunities for becoming a typist. She was a straight A student and typed 90 words a minute. Surely, she could find a part time job. Maybe Mrs. O'Conner could suggest a way to find a job.

The Tuesday before school let out for Hanukkah, Estelle waited for all the students to leave the classroom and walked up to Mrs. O'Conner.

"Excuse me, Mrs. O'Conner. I'd like to find a part-time typist job. I am hoping you might have some suggestions."

"Oh, dear," said Mrs. O'Conner. "You're much too young to work in an office. It's hardly worth the effort to go out there and look."

Estelle thanked her typing teacher and left the classroom. She held her tears until after she left the school that day. The holidays were approaching and Mrs. Greenburg was waiting to pile work on her during the break. She had no time to focus on writing for the school newspaper. And how could she do justice to papers she had to write that were due in English and in U.S. history. Her sophomore year was demanding.

She also wanted to show good faith by writing at least one or two articles for the school newspaper on fashion. Working at the paper could get more interesting in her junior and senior year. She wanted to show good faith. One step at a time. Quitting her job at the Emporium in the middle of the holiday season was not an option. Planning to look for work next summer was a better idea. Maybe Mrs. O'Conner was right. She was too young. Estelle was always in a hurry.

Estelle ran home from school. She was out of breath and hot despite the cold San Francisco winter. She threw off her coat and scarf and plopped on the sofa.

"I came home as soon as I could," said Estelle.

"Good. Hanukkah is in two days, and Auntie Anya is coming over with a few of her friends. I want you both to know that I have invited a friend as well. He is a Schlage customer. Jewish, of course."

Estelle and Mildred exchanged a knowing look.

"Stop it, you, two. He has nowhere to go."

"Mama, you've got to get those papers from Papa, right?" asked Estelle. "Do you know where he works or where he lives?"

"Where is this coming from?" asked Rose. "You saw him when he came to see us on Thanksgiving. I know nothing more."

"I'm going to the library to look up information on a paper I'm writing about the Gold Rush next semester. I'll be back in an hour or two."

"Can I go?" asked Mildred. Before Estelle could answer, Mildred put her coat on and followed her sister.

The library was quiet in the late afternoon when Estelle and Mildred arrived. It was a large but plain room, mostly painted in drab browns without much decoration except the unusual high ceilings and carved wooden desks that did not fit with the austerity of the space. A librarian was at the front desk with stacks of books all around her. Mildred stopped and gazed up at the intimidating size of the library.

The librarian pushed her glasses up on her nose when Estelle walked up to her. "Hello, Miss, I'm looking for job postings."

"They are on the bulletin board near the restrooms, young lady," said the librarian.

Estelle walked to the job board. She took out a notebook from her purse and wrote down the names quickly. Mildred started to wander off into the library proper, but Estelle grabbed her hand and sat her down at a table while she opened the drawers to several cabinets searching for information. She pulled the drawers out as far as she could and made notes.

"What are you doing, Es?" Millie whispered.

"Trying to find out where Papa might be working. I'm looking for union meetings."

Estelle found four locations of union shops in the Bay Area. From her research, she learned that communism with a big C had a weak presence in the 1920s in San Francisco and around the Bay Area. The worldwide communist philosophy didn't carry weight with the labor and manufacturing sectors on the West Coast. Unions were more important when Jake lived in Canada and New York. That's where he hit his stride – organizing workers was what he did best. What was her father doing in San Francisco walking into virgin territory?

Estelle was going to fix everything up, find her father, and give Rose a new start in life. Maybe the man Rose asked to Hanukkah dinner was someone she was interested in and would like to spend more time with. She made notes, put the cards back in order.

"Time to go, Millie," said Estelle. "We have to help Mama prepare for Hanukkah."

Anya was the first to arrive for Hanukkah dinner. She was dressed to the nines with perfect makeup and hair and her outrageous laugh. She brought a kugel to complete the dinner of brisket, potatoes and carrots. Several of her girlfriends came in behind her bringing cakes and cinnamon desserts. Rose was preparing to light the first candle on the menorah and all joined in for prayers.

Estelle knew no prayers. She stood still with respect and cast her eyes down. Mildred poked her sister mischievously and tried to make her smile. Every Hanukkah made her think of her youth in Montreal when her mother lit the two candles for the Shabbat prayers and Jake crashed into the apartment. She could still feel his rage. Her own trauma was always a fresh wound.

The man named Louie did not make it to Hanukkah. Rose felt sad but did not let it ruin the evening. There was dancing, music and good food and everyone was grateful for each other's company.

The following day, Estelle arose early in an anxious state. She was going in search of her father. It was important to look perfectly dressed when she saw her father. She put on a gray wool skirt, which she designed herself and a maroon sweater that creased her hips. She tied a gray long silk scarf around her neck and let it fall to the side. She put on a black wool coat that she found in a used clothing store. The saleswoman thought it looked so stunning on her that she let Estelle have it for free. The finishing touch was her favorite cloche hat. She picked up her blue notebook from the entry table and left.

Estelle took streetcars to all four union halls. Two of the halls were in the Inner Mission District south of the Market and east of the Western Addition. The other two were downtown on Geary and Van Ness. Estelle was struck by the similarity of them – a small building housing a cramped dirty room and smelling of smoke and coffee. Most of them had small groups of workers hanging around under dim lights, while a few union bosses tried to provide help to those who asked for information.

In the last union hall she visited on Geary, there was a secretary sitting behind an old wooden desk shrouded in cigarette smoke. She waited until the secretary finished her typing.

"Excuse me," said Estelle. "I'm looking for my father, and I know he is a union man; in fact, he was president of the Ladies International Garment Union in Ottawa, Canada. His name is Jacob Lanch. Do you know him?"

The secretary did not look up.

Estelle continued. "Do you have a roster of names? In the other union halls, they didn't have anyone to talk to."

"Isn't that something," said the secretary as she looked up. "Why, dear you are a child."

"Excuse me, ma'am. I'm asking if you have a roster of your union members."

"I shouldn't do this, but since it's your father you're looking for." The secretary pulled out an old ledger book and gave it to Estelle. She went through every page and there he was – Jacob Lanch with an address. It was getting late. Estelle would find her father tomorrow.

Estelle was bone tired and needed coffee and maybe a piece of kugel. There were leftovers at home but they were probably eaten for lunch. As she made her way to Diller's Kosher Restaurant, she looked around for help-wanted signs. She checked the notes she took at the library but did not find many options for a typist. It was the holidays and probably no one was hiring. During vacation, when she had free time away from the Emporium job, she vowed to walk the entire Western Addition, up and down Geary Street, then past the Fillmore Auditorium, Market Street, and the financial district to find any signs of job offerings.

She entered Diller's and decided to treat herself and sit in a red booth and order off the menu like a real adult.

She entered the busy restaurant and met the host, a young man in his early twenties with a big smile, white teeth, and darting eyes. A black tie peaked out of the top of his apron, and he wore a yarmulke.

"May I help you?" he asked. "I'm sorry we don't have any booths available but you can sit at the counter if you like. "I'm Daniel, by the way. I haven't seen you here before."

"Estelle is my name. This is my first time at Diller's."

Estelle walked over to the counter and took a seat between two Orthodox rabbis. The rabbis exchanged glances at each other, then went back to slurping their matzo ball soup. She studied the menu but was distracted as the rabbis continued to exchange glances.

"Excuse me, rabbis, but I'd be happy if you want to sit next to each other."

They shook their heads in the negative and resumed slurping. She closed her menu, got up from her seat, and headed for the door.

"Something the matter?" asked Daniel.

"The two rabbis I was sitting between were strange, and I can't eat when I feel people are staring."

"Let me wrap up a couple of brisket sandwiches for you to go," he said, "and it's on me."

Estelle watched the rabbis as they ate in silence, never looking at each other again. The space between them remained vacant. She checked her watch and knew she was going to be late for dinner. Daniel returned with the brisket sandwiches in a brown paper bag.

"I threw in some dill pickles," he said. "Kosher, of course."

"My mother will be pleased. Thanks so much."

"Will you come back?" asked Daniel. "I mean, you are always welcome, and next time you won't have to sit between two rabbis. For a fact, they are kind of weird. They are brothers who never leave each other's side."

"Why do they leave an empty space between them?" asked Estelle.

"It's a cloistered Jewish community, like monks. It's part of living a hallowed life."

"They shouldn't get too close because they might touch each other?"

Daniel held the door open for Estelle. "Something like that."

She stopped and looked directly at Daniel in a businesslike manner.

"If you ever hear from customers or business people in the Fillmore needing a typist, you know, after-school work, can you let me know? I'll drop by from time to time to check in. And thanks again for the food."

"You're welcome. I'll look around for you."

When Estelle came home, Rose and Mildred were sitting down to eat dinner.

"Nice of you to join us," Rose remarked. "You're late."

Estelle set the bag on the table and slowly pulled out two brisket sandwiches with dill pickles. They stared at the sandwiches with lust in their eyes.

"Did you steal these, Es?" asked Mildred.

"Don't be silly. I went to Diller's because I wanted to be a grownup lady and order off the menu. Just a snack, mind you, and a cup of coffee. Silly, I know, but I went to the counter and sat between two Hasidic Jews who were the strangest people I had ever seen. They acted like I shouldn't be sitting at the counter. I couldn't stand how odd they were acting, so I left."

"You shouldn't have done that, Estelle," said Rose. "That's just not done in the Orthodox community."

"I shouldn't have done that because they smelled and slurped their matzo ball soup? Take a sandwich, Mama. I couldn't eat a whole one, so Millie and I can share the other."

"Tell us more, Es." Mildred bit into the brisket and her eyes glazed over. "Mama, you've got to taste this."

"When I was leaving, the host, Daniel, asked why I was going without ordering, and I told him. He went to the kitchen and brought me the brisket sandwiches. I think Daniel felt bad that the Orthodox men put me off eating at Diller's. He thought he owed me a favor for the awkward situation."

"You shouldn't be eating out. It's an extravagance. Keep your job, darling, and save your money if you plan to quit in six months. I still say you would be putting yourself in an awkward situation with Mrs. Greenburg if you quit at the beginning of summer."

"I told you why it was a good idea, Mama. Mrs. Greenburg is taking my designs and claiming they are her work. That's cheating. Besides, I'm going to be working like a dog all vacation hemming and doing alterations without the prospect of a raise."

"You're going to get fired if you take another day off. Are you going to work tomorrow?"

"Mama, I'll take it from here. I have a few ideas."

"And just what are those ideas? What are you up to, Estelle?"

Rose faced her daughter. "I hope you are not doing what I think you are doing, Estelle Lanch. It's none of your business."

"I don't mean any disrespect, Mama, but I know his address. And I'm going to get your divorce papers so you can start living a life."

Rose gathered her darning and left the room. What Estelle found curious was what Rose did not say to her; she did not forbid her from getting the divorce agreement. Estelle studied the address of Jake's place of work. She would wear her best dress and coat and her cloche hat. A little makeup would make her look older. If she appeared adult and mature and presented herself calmly before him, she would be able to make her argument to get her mother free from him forever.

Estelle got off the streetcar. Her breath was short, and she found it difficult to walk a few more blocks up Geary to Larkin. Even though it was a cold December morning, she was feeling sweat running down her back. It was ten o'clock when she arrived at the door to her father's shop. The sign read Furrier. She loosened her coat and made sure her scarf was securely in place. When she opened the door, a bell rang overhead. The shop was ensconced in half-light with dust particles floating in the air. It was cluttered, and reeked of cigarettes. A colorful array of black and red furs – mink and fox – hung on hooks around the edges of the small store.

Jake walked out of the back room wiping his hands on his dirty apron. He showed no surprise.

"Hello, Jake," she said.

"How long did it take you to find me?"

"About two days. You're not hard to find. There are only about a hundred union communists. It's not a big ledger book."

"You're smart, Esther. Sorry. You're Estelle since you or your mother decided to change your name. Suit yourself. Let this go, Estelle. You've got no business butting into my affairs."

"I'm here to get the divorce papers."

"If your mother wants them so much, why isn't she here?" asked Jake.

"Because she won't lower herself to come into your shop and ask. She won't humiliate herself. I want you to finally do right by her."

Jake walked through the archway into the back room. Estelle stole a glance into the messy workshop. It looked as if Jake was working on two pieces of fur, sewing them together to make one long piece that was made to hang around the neck. He returned carrying an envelope dotted with grease in one hand, and in the other the long fur piece.

"You still have that goiter?" asked Jake.

"How would I get rid of it?" she said. "What do you know about furs? You didn't do this kind of work before, did you?"

"When I was in New York, I worked with some fur pieces. In Los Angeles there wasn't much interest in furs except for movie stars in Hollywood. Costume designers would come to me downtown in the garment district and ask me to work on fur designs. It paid the bills."

"Where'd you get the money to buy these furs?" asked Estelle.

"It's my shop, Esther. Where do you think I got the money?"

Jake put the fur around his daughter's neck. "It suits you. I take it you made your dress and altered the coat. You did good work. Who taught you?"

"Not you. You were hardly a good father. And I'm Estelle now. Not Esther."

"Harsh words. I should have been around to see your talent. You can design clothes and sew them. But designers are a dime a dozen. You should think about learning how to make hats. When we were in New York, I worked on a few hat designs for a Frenchwomen who sold hats at Macy's. A shopgirl, she was. She was still at the beginning of her career as a milliner, but we kept in touch, and she wants some of my designs for Macy's here in the city."

"What's her name, this Frenchwoman?" asked Estelle.

"Lilly Daché. She'll be successful one day. I can teach you how to make hats if you want. Maybe you could learn a few more things from me before you decide I'm worthless."

"What happened with the bra design in New York?"

"The goniffs stole my bra. They are thieves. Just because Maidenform named it as the pushup bra, they thought they owned it. They thought it was theirs and they got the patent. You know that's why we left that pigsty of a city. The Jews ran the garment district, made the rules, got their unions to back Dubinsky. The lot can go to hell."

"You're Jewish. Why do you say that about Jews?"

"I'm a communist before I'm a Jew." Jake said as he handed the divorce agreement to Estelle. "What difference does it make anyway? I always land on my feet."

Estelle opened the greasy envelope and took out the document. It was signed.

"You thought it wasn't signed? I couldn't get out of Bell Gardens until that lawyer your mother worked for got his pound of flesh. He must have loved that woman."

Estelle turned to leave, but one of the fur pieces caught her eye.

"That's mink in case you're wondering," Jake said. "Take me up on my offer to teach you how to make hats."

"I might. Hats are the rage today, especially the cloche."

Estelle left Jake not knowing whether she would see him again. Somewhere inside of her, Estelle hated her father. His abuse was abhorrent. Another part of her knew he was a talented genius tortured by his gifts, never feeling respected, always fighting and raging at the wind. She could not understand someone like that. Jake made life difficult for himself and for others. It was hard to love such a father. Then at the last minute, he offered to give her something. Teaching her how to make hats, something she would love.

Estelle did not go straight home. She had to think, to understand the dysfunction of her father. She did not want any of that to taint her. Estelle walked briskly on the cold but beautiful day towards the streetcar. She felt happy but did not know why. After she got off the streetcar in the Fillmore, she sprinted to Diller's. As she entered, she felt dripping sweat on the sides of her face. There were only a few men milling around. Most Jewish families were probably eating leftovers from Hanukkah dinner the night before. She sat down in a booth for four, pulled out a few crumpled papers, and examined the three job offerings she found in the library. None of them looked appealing for her job skills. She was taken away from her thoughts by Daniel sitting down across from her.

"I'm sorry I didn't greet you. I was on the phone with the boss. This is a surprise. Or maybe not. I thought I might see you again."

"I was out on an errand today, and I'm tired and need a cup of coffee. I'm going over the jobs that I found on the work board at the library.

"Sure thing," he said as he reached into his apron pocket and gave her a few work notices. "I'm sorry they're so crumpled. And I must warn you that during the holidays, hardly anyone needs workers."

Daniel left the booth and brought back a cup of coffee. "Any luck?"

"I can draw a map of the buildings and offices and then visit them later. I'm making a plan. You don't happen to have any kugel left over from Hanukkah. We don't need much."

Daniel smiled and went back to the kitchen to get the kugel while Estelle got her money out of her purse. A few minutes later, he came out with a pan wrapped in tinfoil. She handed Daniel her money, but he would not take it. "Please, this doesn't cost much, and you don't have a job now."

Estelle stuffed the money into Daniel's apron but he would not take it. "I still have a job at the Emporium, and I wanted to quit over the holidays, but I have to get better skills. I don't qualify. I mean, I'm not good enough. My shorthand needs to be better."

"Funny you should say that. But before I tell you this, and you say no, I want you to think about the potential for the job. Do you remember the Orthodox rabbis who sat next to you at the counter? Well, their temple needs a typist during vacation."

Estelle sipped her coffee and pretended to think about it.

"Daniel, there is something you don't know about me and probably won't like about me, but I'm not religious. I don't go to shul, I wasn't confirmed, and I will never say Kaddish. Those rabbis were weird. Thank you for thinking of me, but I would rather starve than work for them – especially in a temple."

"How about a Reformed temple like Beth Israel?"

"That's Conservative."

"Kind of. They need a typist, too."

"I want a job outside the Fillmore. And that's where I'm going to look. Thanks, Daniel. I appreciate your help."

"Where are you going to look?"

"Market Street, in the Financial District. I'm going to work right after I graduate, and that's where I want to start my career."

"You're sure?"

"I'm sure. Thank you, Daniel, for your help. By the way, what's your last name?"

"Goldfarb."

"The rabbi?"

"My father," he said. "I only know about contacts in the Fillmore. Sorry I can't help."

As Estelle slid out of the booth. Daniel stood up. She gave him a hug.

"Thank you. I have to get home. I have something for my mother."

She could not get out of the restaurant fast enough. She was confused by what she was feeling for Daniel. He was kind, sweet and helpful. The opposite of the cruelness of her father. Some day she wanted to tell Daniel about her father. From Jew to communist. And why she was not a believer.

"Come back soon, Estelle, and tell me about your adventures."

Estelle entered the apartment with the kugel under one arm and a folder under the other arm. She entered Rose's bedroom and placed the folder on the nightstand. When she came out, she noticed Mildred sitting in the living room, crocheting a sweater. Estelle went into the kitchen, set the kugel down on the counter, and poured herself a cup of cold coffee. The smell made her close her eyes.

"It's undrinkable," said Mildred.

Estelle drank it anyway.

"Where were you?" asked Mildred.

"I went to see Jake and got the divorce papers for Mama."

Mildred threw down her crochet sweater and stood up. "How did you ever find him?"

"Detective work at the union headquarters. It wasn't hard. Mama's free now."

Mildred hugged her. "Mama won't know what to do, she'll be so happy. We should have a party for her when she comes home from work."

"He won't be coming around much, if at all. Mama's life won't change. She's been a single mother forever, but she won't have to worry anymore. She's free. I need to go to work at the Emporium this afternoon. Tell Mama I'll be home late."

"I thought you were going to quit."

"So did I, but it isn't the time. I'll quit next June. I hope this next semester goes fast."

CHAPTER 9

DILLER'S KOSHER RESTAURANT

The second semester of Estelle's sophomore year went by in the blink of an eye. The last day of class in mid-June was filled with anxiety. She was going to the Emporium to tell Mrs. Greenburg that she was quitting. "I'm determined to prove Mrs. O'Conner wrong," she told Lucille.

"You're so brave," said Lucille. "I couldn't do that. Looking for a job at the beginning of summer will be difficult."

"I know. But I've got to try."

Mrs. Greenburg was not happy with Estelle leaving. She gave her last paycheck and told her that if she ever wanted to come back, she would think about it. "Thank you, Mrs. Greenburg. I learned so much."

Estelle's face carried no expression.

Diller's was packed with people eating lunch. She went to the counter and ordered a cup of coffee and sipped it as she read *The Examiner's* want ads.

Most of the secretarial jobs were full-time and required at least three years of previous work. Daniel approached her from behind and peered over her shoulder.

"I guess you've already walked up and down Market Street. Stay here. I'll be back in a minute."

He walked into a small office, pulled out a ledger, and returned to Estelle. Let's go sit in a booth. I've got something to show you."

They sat at a booth in the back and Daniel opened a ledger.

"We're in a mess here at Diller's. Papers piled everywhere, orders for food, letters in need of answering. It's a job, but it's more than typing. The ledger indicates we have funds to hire someone to organize Diller's, but week after week, Mr. Solomon ignores the problems. What if you were to work here, in the back office? This would be after school between lunch and dinner. You'll learn more than typing. You'll learn how to work in an office. Think about it. I'll speak to Mr. Solomon and see what he thinks."

"Thanks, Daniel. I'll come back later. I really appreciate you thinking of me."

Estelle spent the next two hours walking the streets of the Fillmore. Once again, there were no jobs available. Granted it was the beginning of summer, and all the part-time jobs were snatched up weeks ago. She was late to apply. She gave up and decided to visit Lucille. Four of Lucille's siblings were outside playing on the street. Lucille was sitting on the stoop reading a book. When she saw Estelle trudging up the hill, she put the book down and ran to meet her friend. They hugged with delight.

"I'm so happy to see you," Lucille said as she pointed to her charges. "And you can imagine why. Look at those dirty kids."

"It's a handful." Estelle laughed. "I don't know how you survive?"

"I'm going to run away after I graduate from Commerce. Want to come with me?"

"Jeez, count me in. Nothing I'd like better, but I have to take care of my mom and sister for a few years. She works hard, and I need to help out. Mildred is a handful."

"I see her after school with boys, and she is only in the eighth grade."

"That's not the worst, Lucy. High school boys from Commerce hang around sometimes. When I told her to stop that behavior, she laughed and told me to mind my own business. You never know what's going to happen with her, so I need a good job, and it can't be too far away."

"You have two more years, Es," said Lucille.

"I think I might have a part-time job at Diller's if I want. Daniel is going to talk to the owner about my working there this summer."

"Is he sweet on you?" asked Lucille.

"I don't know."

"Are you sweet on him?"

"Probably. Maybe. He's a good friend. And we can talk. He's smart. But no matter how I feel about Daniel, I'm not sticking around in the Fillmore after I graduate. I'm getting out, even if I have to move Mama and Mildred with me. The Fillmore's too small – like living on an island."

One of Lucille's siblings started screaming when her brother took away her toy. She disengaged them from each other and grabbed the toy. She sat down on the stairs and cried.

Estelle comforted her. "Things will get better, Lucy. I'll help you anyway I can," said Estelle. "I was thinking on the way over here that since I'm not working at the Emporium anymore, why don't you ask her for my job?"

"My parents wouldn't let me. Besides, I'm not half as good as you are."

"They might if you tell them that you will be paid for two or three hours of work every day, and you'll bring in extra money home for them. You can even keep a little for yourself. Tell them you're working toward being on your own someday. Your sister is only sixteen months younger than you, so she can watch the younger ones after school."

"I don't have the skills yet to do what you did. You're a professional. I'd be better after a year from now. I promise I'll try next summer. Es. Really, I will. I need your courage. The hardest part will be getting their attention. They're always so busy. And when they get home, they want dinner. It seems impossible."

"Nothing is impossible," Estelle said. "I'll help you all I can this year. Our home Economics teacher asked me to help out in class. I'll get you in shape. Now that's settled, let's take these kids down the block to get them an ice cream at the corner store. My treat."

It was foreordained. Estelle got the job at Diller's. Within a week, she sorted out the office, balanced the books, corresponded with the suppliers, and typed up a list of responsibilities for the kitchen and staff. She was experiencing real office management. Daniel was right. She could also make more money working less hours if she was efficient. Estelle didn't see much of Daniel during the summer. He took time off in the afternoon to take a class at the junior college. He tried to get back to the restaurant in time to see her, but she had often left. During the day he helped the owner, Mr. Solomon, with ordering food or shopping for specialty items. When they did connect at work, they had a friendly connection. And he was always ready to help her with algebra problems or science projects.

"You're smart, Daniel," Estelle said one day. "Why didn't you go to college?"

"I plan on it. I'm actually taking a class this summer. That's where I go in the afternoons. Mr. Solomon is going to sponsor me in a few years. In the meantime, I'm saving my money. You definitely should go to college. You could be anything you wanted to be."

"I've got two more years of high school, and someday I will. Now I have to take care of my family. I'll get a good job after I graduate, then we can move into a better apartment."

"I hope you don't move too far away," said Daniel.

"Before Estelle knew it, summer ended and school was about to begin. She asked Daniel if she could work part time at the restaurant. She promised him eight hours a week. He was happy with that, but they both knew they would see little of each other since he was going to take another class in the afternoon during the time she would be working.

During her junior year, Estelle began to write more articles for the school paper even though she had a full roster of classes, assisting the home economics teacher, working eight hours a week, and getting dinner ready for Rose and Mildred. Most of the time, she was able to take out food from Diller's. She was excelling at typing and a business class, but disappointed in the learning curve on shorthand. Estelle did not have the extra time to practice on her own.

On May 20, 1927, something spectacular happened. Charles Lindbergh took off in his monoplane, *The Spirit of St. Louis,* from an airport on Long Island,

New York, and flew the first nonstop solo flight across the Atlantic, landing in Paris thirty-three and a half hours later. It seemed the world was not the same after that flight, and neither was Charles Lindbergh. San Francisco opened its arms to Lucky Lindy. Even in the Fillmore, his reception from the crowd was worshipful. Estelle witnessed the parade in awe and embraced the pageantry. She was drawn into the crowds and screamed and waved an American flag along with everyone in the neighborhood. The aviator was the number one sensation in America.

The school paper wanted Estelle to write an article about the Lindbergh flight even though it was not her area of expertise. She was interested in Lindbergh, the man of the moment, the man who changed aviation forever. After flying 3,610 miles in 33.5 hours, Lindbergh landed at Le Bourget field in Paris, becoming the first pilot to accomplish the solo nonstop transatlantic crossing. Lindbergh was an instant hero, America's hero, and he changed the trajectory of commercial aviation. She felt she wanted to know him better. Besides, who could resist an embracing story of courage, tenacity, and faith? Except she only had three weeks to write the article before school was out for the summer. This assignment complicated Estelle's hunt for a job that would take her out of the Fillmore and into the big city.

Thankfully, the article on Lindberg was an easy assignment. The story flowed out of her the day after the parade. Estelle delivered it on time, perfectly typed with no misspellings. The article was the hit of the school, and even though she was congratulated by teachers and students alike, Estelle knew she had more important things to do.

Two weeks before school got out, Estelle was once more combing through the want ads. Times were good in 1927. San Francisco was prospering and she thought there would be plenty of part-time jobs all over the city. Estelle kept her vow. She was not going to work in the Fillmore. This would be the summer of Estelle's emancipation from the Jewish world she had grown up in. Some days, the thought of leaving all that she knew weighed on her and consumed her with dread. Yet, when she thought of summer and learning new skills, she was excited and hope returned. When she told Daniel some of her dreams, he cautioned about moving too fast.

"I want something new for my life – something not attached to the past. The Jews are always living in the past because the past is their present, but I want a future, a new society with different ideas, different foods and clothes and work opportunities. If I don't see it happening where I live now, here in the Fillmore, I can't imagine staying in the Fillmore."

"I have to agree with you, Estelle, but you are a pioneer, and most of us are holding places for the next generation."

Estelle took every opportunity to find a job outside the Western Addition before school let out for summer vacation. She roamed the Financial District, downtown, and around Civic Center. From her journalism classes, Estelle learned of the four or five daily newspapers around town. The best of them were *The Examiner* and *The Chronicle*, but she knew they would not hire rookies, especially a soon-to-be senior from Commerce High School. But Estelle knew she could tell a good story, so she huddled around the job boards and gauged whether she could pass the front desk with her modern clothes, cloche hat, and sophisticated airs.

Weeks went by without success. Estelle applied for several typing jobs, and even though she scored at the highest levels on the typing tests she took, she never got the jobs. If it was not her typing that prevented her from getting the job, she thought it must be something else. She studied the applications and pondered over why they asked the applicant his or her religion. She always left that question blank. Next time, she would write Protestant. Rose was getting annoyed with her oldest daughter. It was taking her too long to find a job. To make matters worse, Mildred was slipping through her hands. Estelle was not available to be a buffer between home and school for Mildred, who was coming home later and later. Sometimes on the weekends, no one knew who she was with or where she spent her time.

"Why can't you keep an eye on your sister on the weekends?" asked Rose.

"Because I'm trying to find a job," she told Rose. "I only have so many hours in the day, Mom. But I'll have a talk with her."

Estelle decided to take a leap forward and rewrite her article on Charles Lindbergh in case she was able to get into one of the newspapers in town. She went to the library and took a deeper look at Charles Lindbergh. Who was this man whose bravery changed the world? How could an airmail pilot get the guts to enter a competition to fly a monoplane from New York to Paris? It was impossible to think the pilot would not land the plane. But it was suicide, nonetheless. And it was reckless to fly solo nonstop across the Atlantic. Lucky Lindy's greatest challenge was staying awake. Estelle read that Lindbergh had to hold his eyelids open with his fingers. Reporters wrote that he hallucinated ghosts passing through the cockpit. Estelle was staying up later and later trying to rework her Lindbergh article to submit to one of the newspapers. Her mother was reading on the sofa and watched her daughter struggle.

"What's going on with your article, darling?" asked Rose.

"What makes a hero, Mama?"

"One person's hero is another's coward," Rose said. "A hero's life has the potential to change society. A coward's life is kicked to the ash heap of the forgotten."

"Where did you learn that? It's wonderful. So Lindbergh was a hero. His flight, his daring brought change to society well after the moment he landed. Smashing idea."

Estelle began rewriting her article on Lindbergh and focused the piece on the importance of Lindbergh's colossal feat to young high school students. She had to demonstrate how his solo nonstop flight changed the future of aviation forever and opened up possibilities for the next generation to imagine more challenges without fearing the outcome. Although her article was not a typing audition, its merits were based on the creative argument for heroism – no guts, no glory.

In late June, Estelle entered the office of *The San Francisco Examiner* on California Street at ten o'clock in the morning. Like a professional, she held her head up and her back straight. She was dressed, as Rose would say, to beat the band, with a matching dress and coat in a nutty brown color, complete with a scarf, an old remodeled hat, and a fold-over leather case that held her Lindbergh story. The large reception area was decorated with sofas and chairs and a low table which held the latest editions of *The Examiner*. A lady receptionist of about forty – neat and trim, sporting a bob of black hair and wearing a long necklace of pearls – sat behind a sturdy desk. A stack of files rested on the left and a telephone was on her right.

"Excuse me, mam, I am Estelle Lanch, and I'm looking for someone to talk to who is in charge of local stories," said Estelle.

"I'm afraid we don't take stories from the outside of the paper," said the receptionist. "We hire reporters and editors for those activities."

"My article is about how Charles Lindbergh has influenced the next generation, my generation. I write for the Commerce High School newspaper, the Crimson, and I thought the reaction to Lindbergh's feat by my contemporaries has a place in the future of America."

"That's mighty bold of you, but as I said, I don't know who you should talk to because everybody is working and busy."

"Maybe someone in local or neighborhood news?"

The receptionist picked up the phone. "Operator, please connect me to local news." There was a slight pause. "Yes, hello, Miss Peterson. I have a young lady here who wishes to speak to someone from local news. She has written an article about Charles Lindbergh for her school newspaper and the reaction of the students to this event. Would you be interested in speaking with Miss Lanch?"

The conversation ended quickly. The receptionist put the phone in the cradle. "Miss Peterson is too busy to talk to you. Come back another day."

"I see. By any chance, do you ever hire typists?"

"Not usually. I presume you need a summer job. You can try other newspapers. We sure have enough of them in this town. Don't go to *The Chronicle.* They have no openings. My girlfriend is in the typing pool there."

"Thanks for your help," said Estelle. "And your pearls are smashing."

"Come back here if you want. No harm in checking."

Estelle went to *The San Francisco Call & Post* and to *The Chronicle,* knowing she was going to be rejected. Rose encouraged her daughter to try a smaller newspaper. Estelle went to *The Daily News* on Powell Street and was greeted by a young man at the reception desk on the side of a crowded newsroom floor that was full of loud voices and clacking typewriters. Somewhere in his twenties, the receptionist was handsome and boyish at the same time. The peach fuzz on his face made him appear even younger. "How may I help you?" he said to Estelle with a devastating smile.

Estelle used her charm, her intellect, and all the professionalism she could muster to sell her project, Lindbergh through the eyes of the next generation.

"I'm not the guy who has the last say," he said. "And by the way, I'm Steven. And another by the way, we're now *The San Francisco News* as of this year."

"Good to know. I'm Estelle Lanch," she said. "Nice to meet you. Who do I talk to?"

Steven picked up the phone and spoke to someone about her story idea, "already written and edited," he said as he winked at her. He nodded and hung up the phone. "Mr. Durant said to go on back. He's in the middle of the third row, wearing a hat with a cigarette sticking out of his ear. Good luck."

"Thanks, Steven. And I was wondering if you have any need for an extra typist for the summer and maybe after."

"I'll see what's needed. When you come back, I hope to have an answer." He smiled again and watched her walk back to Mr. Durant. As she walked into his cubicle, Estelle took her article out of the case. Without looking at her, Mr. Durant took it from her hand abruptly and read it. She could not believe anyone could read that fast.

"It needs a new headline – 'What Commerce High School Students Think About Charles Lindbergh,' blah, blah, how his solo flight affects their lives. It's a mouthful. Headlines are short and to the point. 'The Next Generation and Charles Lindbergh.' His name stands for everything he's done. It's provocative. It's about the future. It's about America's new hero."

Estelle fast-walked to Steven's desk after her interview with Mr. Durant.

"Steven, good news. I'm going to be published for the first time," said Estelle.

"I expected as much, Estelle. And by the way, I fixed it so that you'll enter the typing pool tomorrow."

"And I expected as much from you, Steven. Thank you. See you tomorrow."

"First thing is to sign up at the hiring desk. Welcome to *The San Francisco News*."

CHAPTER 10

1927

Summer felt like it was on speed dial for Estelle. She was only seventeen years old, and her new job was unrelenting. Eight hours a day in *The San Francisco News* typing pool was drudgery. One story blended into another. Estelle wanted to use her editing skills to rework an article every now and then, but it was not her job and nobody asked. Once or twice Mr. Durant asked her to fix this or that grammar issue, but usually, even if the slant of the article was obtuse, it was nevertheless published.

Once in a while, Estelle visited Daniel at Diller's. They told each other stories about their daily activities. When she thought about the end of summer, she was worried she would have less and less time with Daniel. Between starting her senior year with a full roster of classes, journalism assignments, and homework, she worried that her friendship with Daniel would suffer. In a way, she wanted to get closer to Daniel, but it would be at her own peril. Suppose she fell in love. Suppose she was trapped by love. It was confusing and that relationship did not have a conclusion that would work for her. Her determination to get out of the Fillmore always came first.

Sometimes Steven asked her for coffee after work. He was fun and interesting because he lived in the Mission District on Noe Street. That meant he was Catholic, like Lucille, with a bunch of sisters and brothers. He asked her several times if she wanted to go to North Beach, but there was no way she could get home in time to make dinner. Steven was a "good time Charlie." He would not be a serious boyfriend. And she did not want a serious boyfriend anyway.

On a break one Friday afternoon, one of the ladies in the typing pool asked Estelle where she bought her clothes. When Estelle told her she made her own clothes, the lady almost fainted.

"They're so stylish and the fabric is heaven," she said.

The comment made Estelle think of her father and his offer to show her how to design hats – the Lilly Daché model. She began thinking she should check in with him.

Estelle made an excuse to Mr. Durant to leave work a half hour early on that Friday and took a streetcar to Geary Street to see Jake. It was the end of summer in San Francisco, balmy and warm. The fog was tired of creeping into the city every day and decided to let the sunshine roam through downtown.

As she approached her father's shop, Estelle noticed a new sign on the door: "Jake's Furriers." The cigarette and musky smell inside the shop made breathing almost impossible.

"Who is it?" Jake yelled from inside the work room then walked through the arch and into the front of the store.

"Look what the cat dragged in," he said without malice.

"Is that a joke, Papa? Or are you glad to see me?"

"I was expecting you before school starts, but I thought you'd be here earlier."

"I have a full-time job at *The San Francisco News* in the typing pool."

"You should have come to work with me," he said.

"You don't pay, and I'm not slave labor. Besides, I made enough money to buy a second-hand Singer sewing machine."

"Why are you here?" asked Jake.

"I've got an hour or so free. If you have some time, maybe you could show me the basics of making a cloche hat."

"I don't have time. I'm busy."

"Yes, you're busy. You offered once. Did the offer expire?"

"I have to fill some orders. Come back tomorrow."

Estelle decided to walk home. She needed to think. Would she return to see Jake the next day? He was impossibly resistant, and it was perhaps not worth the effort to try to forge the faintest of familial bonds.

Estelle decided to get Lucille's advice. Her friend was able to get her old job at the Emporium for the summer. It was a full time summer job, maybe a part-time job for the school year. Estelle was so pleased that Lucille's sewing skills had advanced almost to a professional level. It was near closing time for Lucille and Estelle hoped they would have some time to talk. It was rare that they saw each other.

Walking into the store was comforting. It still possessed that familiar smell of sweet perfume mixed with lavender powder. On her way to the back of the store, she examined the fabrics and notions on display. It brought back good memories.

Estelle peeked around the corner of the sewing room to catch Lucille's eye. Her friend saw her, smiled, and waved her inside the room.

"Hi," said Lucille. "I was hoping you'd come by one of these days."

"I left early because I wanted to visit my father. He promised me he'd teach me how to design and make hats. But he told me to come back tomorrow."

"I thought I heard a familiar voice," said Mrs. Greenburg as she entered the room from the back. "Nice to see you again, Estelle. Lucille said you were in a typing pool at a newspaper. Wasting your time, I think."

"It's good money, Mrs. Greenburg. It's not what I want to be when I grow up."

"What did I hear about designing hats?" she asked.

"My father designs hats for Lilly Daché once in a while. He sends his designs back to New York for her approval. But right now he's a furrier."

"You should let him teach you to be a milliner, Estelle," said Mrs. Greenburg. "That's a promising skill. By the way, thank you for recommending Lucille. She is doing a fine job."

Lucille and Estelle walked arm in arm down Market Street. They were happy to be free, off for the weekend, and looking forward to getting a Coke at a soda fountain or maybe taking a walk around Golden Gate Park.

"How are you getting along at the newspaper?" asked Lucille. "Summer is almost over. Are you going to be at the paper much longer?"

"Working two hours a day is probably not going to happen."

"You'll never be able to go back to Diller's after working downtown. It's more exciting. Mrs. Greenburg will let me work after school like you did.

I'm happy about that. And I owe it all to you. I can't believe my parents let me work. All I had to do was say I'll bring home money."

"Don't ever be afraid to ask, Lucy. A yes is better than a no, but you won't know the answer until you ask. And I knew you were good."

"What are you going to do about your father? Are you going to have him teach you how to make hats?"

"You know I'm nervous about that and I do and I don't want to learn. If it was anyone else, I'd jump at the chance."

"He's your father, Es. Give him a try and if it doesn't work out, you can leave. Remember, don't ever be afraid to say yes."

On Saturday, before Estelle went to Jake's shop, she told Rose where she was going and what she was thinking about doing with Jake.

"I don't want you around him," Rose said. "He's not a good person."

"I'm not going to catch his evil, Mom," said Estelle. "I want to learn something from him. You can't deny his talent, and it might be useful to me in the future."

"Watch yourself, darling," said Rose. "Come home directly. By the way, I noticed you're calling me Mom instead of Mama now. I guess you're growing up, my darling."

Jake unlocked the front door to his shop when he heard the knock at the door. She followed him through the arch and into the back room. Cigarette butts were overflowing in ashtrays, dust floated in the air. For the next two hours, Jake explained how to shape a hat design by using the dummy heads on a long wooden table cluttered with unfinished hats and fur designs, measuring tapes, and fashion magazines. He showed her a hat in one of the magazines – it was a pretty cloche, a light pink with gray trim, tipped slightly to the right on the head. It left room for short curls to inch out under the hat and fill out the underneath sections of the semi-round shape. Then he fashioned the same shaped hat on a dummy head and turned it around so the back was the front, and the front was the back. It was a simple calculation that suddenly made the hat look original. Then he pulled the fabric out on the side of the hat to give it a little height, which exaggerated the slant of the brim.

"It's very clever, Papa. I like it. Can I put it on?"

He gave her the hat. Even without the under-stitching and the need for a thicker piece of fabric to hold the height up securely, the look was Roaring Twenties.

"Okay, I want you to do this on three samples from one of the fashion magazines. Pick three hats and make them your own. Take any thick fabric you want. And mind your colors."

For the next two hours, Estelle worked on the hat designs like a professional milliner. She was focused and excited. Her father paid no attention to her and worked on his fur designs. She was immersed in getting the feel of designing something she never thought possible. Catching a glance at her father from time to time, Estelle thought what he was doing – designing fur pieces – seemed another impossible effort.

"Papa, can you tell me what kind of furs you're working on?" she asked.

"Finish your work first, and then we'll talk furs."

An hour later, Estelle finished her third hat. She was beaming. Jake looked at each one and made a few adjustments, pulled, pushed, reset, and refined. Estelle studied the adjustments and began to see the hats through his eyes – the eyes of an artist who wasn't a nice man but was probably a genius. Jake had a madness about him when he retreated into himself to create his work and Estelle found it appealing.

"I work with all types of furs, depending on what comes my way – mink, sable, fox, possum, raccoon and seal. I've got cheaper furs like rabbit and chinchilla. I design coats or jackets, furs to drape around the neck and shoulders, and, of course, fur hats are an important look for the rich."

Jake checked his watch. "It's too close to five. I'll see you another day. Are you still typing at the newspaper?"

"I'm going to put in my notice to leave in a week. I'm sure they won't use me part time once school starts. Then I'll look for something else. Maybe I should go back to retail."

"Let's see what I can work out for you. It depends on how much business grows. I have an idea to let you run around the city with my hats and a few furs and sell them to department stores. We'll work out a percentage. When you officially quit, they'll be a plan for you."

On her way home, Estelle tried to think her way through her father's offer to let her sell his designs. There would be no salary, only a percentage, so she couldn't count on a consistent salary for her senior year. More importantly, it was not compatible with building a resume for a full-time stenographer's job she wanted after she graduated high school.

Rose watched her daughter enter the apartment and silently hang up her coat on the rack by the front door, put down her purse and walk into the living room. It was well past five.

"Sit down, Estelle," Rose said.

"I'm sorry I'm late, Mom. I told you I was going to see Jake."

"You've got lint on your dress. And you smell of smoke. Why are you doing this to me?"

"I'm not doing this to you. He's got something to teach me. I learned how to make hats."

"He's using you. That's what Jake does. He uses people. And whatever it is you're thinking about doing for him, Jake won't pay you a dime."

"Then, that's it?" asked Estelle.

"Selling a few hats won't give you enough to compensate for your services or prepare you for what happens after graduation. Don't be taken in by him. You were the one who was hell-bent on getting me the divorce papers. You saw that was the future for us – a future without Jake for all of us. Yes, I was mad at first, but in time I realized it was the right thing to do, and I am grateful to you. I have a few clients at Schlage who can help you get a good job that pays well. For now, keep your job at the paper for the next two weeks. In the meantime, think about what kind of job will impress your next employer – that's the way it's done. Don't sabotage your career by listening to your father."

Estelle went to her room and cried. When she finished crying, she pushed her disappointment down inside her and held up her head. The door to her room opened and Mildred walked in. She saw her sister's red face.

"Looks like Mama's in a rage. What happened?"

"Nothing. Where were you? Never mind. I can smell cigarettes on you."

"Out with friends," Mildred said. "I forgot to bring home food for dinner."

"I'm not going to lecture you, Millie. I won't be around much this school year with a job and schoolwork, so more times than not, you will need to prepare dinner. Maybe you'll get a part-time job, too. Don't put it all on me. You should be working to bring home money and not fool around with men. And stay away from sex. You best be careful."

Estelle got up from the bed and threw on a sweater. "I'm going to Diller's to get sandwiches. Meantime, set the table and talk to Mom about jobs. Maybe you could be a waitress at Diller's for a couple of hours after school. I can help arrange that."

Estelle put in her two-week notice at *The San Francisco News*. The following Saturday, she went to Jake's shop and told him she would not take his job offer. She felt good about her decision. This was a "no" she could live with.

The first day of Estelle's senior year started out precariously. Her classes were not all stimulating, and to make it worse, Lucille was not in many of them. She missed her company, missed Daniel, and Steven was long gone. He flirted with her but nothing developed – they were two ships passing in the night. She still had no job and her prospects looked slim. Even Rose had not yet come up with a referral from her co-workers at Schlage. Estelle was growing impatient and disappointed with her progress in getting a job.

On a sunny autumn day, Estelle went to see her journalism teacher, Mrs. Potter. She was a woman in her late fifties wearing a black funeral dress with her gray hair pulled back in a bun and schoolmarm rimless glasses perched on her nose. She was writing in a binder and then looked at Estelle without recognition.

"Hello, Mrs. Potter. I'm Estelle Lanch, reporter for the school newspaper."

"Yes, of course. Forgive me. Yes, of course, I know you. What's on your mind?"

"I was wondering about my assignment to write about Langendorf Royal Bread."

"Is there something wrong?" asked Mrs. Potter.

"No, nothing is wrong."

"You live in the Fillmore so you must know something about Langendorf. All Jewish people know Langendorf. They deliver all the bread in the Western District and around San Francisco. I thought you'd be the perfect person to take the assignment."

Estelle stared at Mrs. Potter unable to fathom how she knew where she lived. "We have lots of Jewish students at Commerce who would be interested in the Langendorf story," Mrs. Potter continued. "I thought I made your assignment clear. You're to uncover how a long-running business sustains the quality of its product and manages to keep its business organization running smoothly while growing into the most successful bakery in San Francisco. You have a week to do it."

Estelle walked out of Mrs. Potter's office confused and somewhat angry by the encounter with her journalism supervisor. Mrs. Potter assumed that because she was Jewish, she would have an interest in the Langendorf bakery. Yet, Estelle had no interest in a Jewish bakery in the Fillmore. In fact, a non-Jewish student in the newspaper could handle the assignment just as well. Estelle didn't like that she was called out and identified, separated from the mainstream. On the other hand, it could be that Mrs. Potter truly thought she was the right person for the assignment because she was a good interviewer and one of the best writers on the staff.

She left the school building and walked with determination and speed from the edges of the Mission District, into the Western Addition, to a large plant on 1600 McAllister, the home of Langendorf Royal Breads – or as the Jewish population referred to it as Langendorf's Jewish Bakery. The major rush of deliveries happened early in the morning, so there were few delivery trucks outside the main plant at three-thirty in the afternoon. Estelle knew the story of the iconic Langendorf delivery trucks. Children loved watching the two-horse teams rented from a nearby stable deliver bread to Diller's or to Jefferson Market. Trucks also dropped off challah on Jewish holidays to the three synagogues in the Western Addition. In fact, Langendorf's delivery route included the Mission District, Mission Dolores, and North Beach as well as smaller neighborhoods in the Western Addition.

Estelle walked into the lobby of the plant and peered through a large glass window. The huge floor displayed dozens of machines that made the bread and dozens more ovens to bake the bread. The landscape was austere and gray without clutter or décor. She looked down one hallway, then turned to look down another and saw an open door. As she walked, Estelle heard her heels clack. The noise she was making from her shoes sounded like gunshots. She knocked.

"Come in." The man's voice was gravelly. "Door's open."

Estelle walked into a small office with a desk that was barely sufficient to hold all the papers, receipts, orders, and ledgers, and stared at an elderly man sitting behind the desk. The man was about sixty, wrinkled, with a twinkle in his brown eyes and a scarf wrapped around his neck. He had a few gray whiffs of hair on his head.

"I'm Estelle Lanch," said Estelle. "And I'm here to write an article about the history of the Langendorf Bakery for the Commerce High School newspaper. May I make an appointment with you or someone I can interview to get the history of the bakery?"

"Everyone leaves at three in the afternoon. We start baking at three in the morning."

"Then why are you still here?" she asked.

"That's a good question," he said. "By the way, I'm Bernard Langendorf, and if you want to get the true story of this bakery, you got to talk to me."

"I'm glad to meet you, Mr. Langendorf. You have an accent, but I can't place it."

"I'm from Vienna. Would you like to start your story from where I came from?"

"Possibly. Do you mind if I take notes?" asked Estelle.

"I would mind it less if you could type," said Bernard. "I need a secretary around here."

"I'm a pretty good typist, Mr. Langendorf."

"Good, you can start tomorrow. You see this desk? It's going to be all yours to sort out."

"I'm in school all day."

"Then come in at three thirty every day and work some magic. By the way, if you're going to live in San Francisco or anywhere in America, you need to be a citizen. Are you a citizen?"

"Not yet. My plan is to apply when I turn eighteen."

"Do it now – before you work for me."

"How did you know I wasn't from America?" asked Estelle.

"Everyone in America is from some other place. We're all immigrants. Now, sit down and I'm going to tell you a story."

The following is the article Estelle wrote for the Commerce High School newspaper:

Bernard Langendorf's story was one of hard work and a little luck. He came to America at sixteen from Vienna before the turn of the Twentieth Century. Like most young men, he never finished school; instead he apprenticed at a Viennese bakery. Bernard saw the signs that another pogrom was about to erupt in Vienna. He found work on a boat leaving the port of Wien and worked on every ship that sailed west on the Atlantic. In Liverpool, he boarded a cargo ship on its way to America.

Bernard came through Ellis Island like most Jewish immigrants. One of his mates aboard a ship sailing into New York harbor told him about a city with much opportunity, but not as crowded as New York. The city was Chicago. He set up a small bakery in that city but soon discovered that his neighborhood was too small and not to his liking. It was more a Jewish ghetto than a mixed neighborhood with Italians and Germans. And he was not making much money. He heard from a few of his customers that San Francisco was the most exciting city in California. After all, gold was discovered in northern California not that long ago and everyone was floating on dreams.

Bernard moved his bakery to San Francisco in 1895 and established Langendorf's Vienna Bakery on Folsom Street, south of Market Street and settled in the vibrant Jewish community. His rye bread was famous – reportedly made from an old Viennese recipe that included nuts and sweet cranberries. After the 1906 Earthquake and fire destroyed his business, Bernard re-opened his bakery at 878 McAllister Street, near Laguna. In 1915, with $400,000 raised from ten prominent San Franciscans, he built a new and expanded plant at 1160 McAllister. By the early Twenties, Bernard acquired a small fleet of delivery wagons, some pulled by horses and a few ran on gas.

When I asked Mr. Langendorf the secret of his success, he replied: *"At the end of day, I carry my cash in a paper bag and take it to the bank."*

CHAPTER 11

GRADUATION

Suddenly and without fanfare, Estelle's life took on a new dimension. Langendorf Royal Bread was the center of the San Francisco universe, at least a star in the business community south of Market Street. She was more excited that luck was on her side when Mr. Langendorf offered her a job for the school year. Or maybe the job found her. When she told Rose of her good fortune, her mother smiled like a Cheshire cat.

"You know your Auntie Anya worked there years ago. It's *bashert*."

"I'm sure it was meant to be, Mom. But before I can work there, I have to have my citizenship. I'm almost eighteen. I can take Millie with me, and we can start her process, too."

"Oh, dear, I kept forgetting to remind you. I applied when I went to work for Schlage, and I put off doing so for you girls. Forgive me, my darling."

"Mom, I love you and you had so much to do when we got here. I'll take care of it."

As it turned out, Estelle's article about the history of Langendorf Royal Bread was one of the most popular articles of the year. Mrs. Potter acknowledged her outstanding work in journalism at the high school awards ceremony before graduation in June. When Estelle walked up on the stage to accept the award, it was followed by cheers.

"I knew you were the right person to write this article," Mrs. Potter whispered.

Estelle did not smile at the recognition, nor did she demonstrate any particular joy, but she did have a revelation as she was walking back to her seat. She thought it was possible to be proud of one's heritage, faith, and identity and be a successful businessman like Bernard Langendorf. Bernard was not as rich as other Jewish merchants and real estate tycoons in San Francisco, such as Fleishaker, Haas, Dinkelspiel, Stern, Koshland, Steinhart, or Zellerbach, who were all German Jews, some of whom held public office. They all were held in high regard for their sophisticated business and commercial skills. None of these men had to hide their Jewish identity because their personal success did not reflect on their religious or cultural identification. Still, as a woman who wanted to achieve recognition in the world of business, she felt safer if she did not identify as Jewish.

Although Estelle tolerated Bernard's messy, disorganized desk, she moved quickly through the mundane office work and created space for other responsibilities that her employer gladly gave over to her since she got her citizenship papers. Because Bernard sent her on small errands around the city, she was able to expand her picture of San Francisco. Daniel was right. Diller's back room gave Estelle her first experience at learning how to manage an office. She was also grateful for his friendship and more because Daniel was the only boy she was close to during her high school years. He was never far from her mind. Since she had no experience with boyfriends, she thought she might have a crush on him.

One night, Estelle came home to find her mother playing cards with a man she never met. Rose introduced Louie Blum to her. Of medium height with black thinning hair and a warm smile, Louie was a prune farmer from Cupertino. He kept an apartment in the Western Addition for business reasons.

"Estelle, this is Louie who never made it to Hanukkah way back when. You remember I told you I met Louie when he came to Schlage needing a complete set of locks and keys for his storage unit on O'Farrell Street."

"Your mother is great at cards," said Louie.

"I'm glad you noticed," said Estelle, "because if you don't know that fact, my mother will beat you every time."

Graduation from Commerce High School in June of 1928 felt momentous. Estelle and Lucille stood next to each other in the auditorium, even though everyone graduating was supposed to be in alphabetical order.

"I wish we were going out with our friends instead of our families," said Estelle.

"I couldn't get away, but we'll go out tomorrow night to North Beach to hear jazz on Columbus Avenue. Maybe we can go to a speakeasy, if we can get a password."

"Or we could go to the Black Cat on Larkin," said Estelle. "Hey, I forgot to ask you if you got the full time job at the Emporium.?"

"I haven't heard from Mrs. Greenburg yet . What about you?"

"For now, but I'll be looking for another job. My mother's friend knows someone at Pet Milk."

"You mean like the condensed milk?" asked Lucille.

"We're up next, Lucy. Let's go onstage and get on with our lives. If I want to work on Market Street or in City Hall, I've got my work cut out for me."

Estelle got serious about finding another job the day after graduation. Times were good in San Francisco despite or because of Prohibition. She read *The Examiner* frequently at Langendorf – Bernard left newspapers strewn across his desk and floor. Journalists expounded about the noble experiment exemplified by the 18th Amendment. It was passed by Congress to direct efforts to reduce crime and solve social problems had the opposite effect. She wasn't shocked that crime and gang-related activities increased in American cities during the 1920s. On any night of the week in downtown America, bootleg gangsters were splaying bullets from machine guns to protect their territories and deliveries to speakeasies. Dead bodies were reported in every city in America. Ordinary citizens made their own hooch in bathtubs for recreational use in homes. or if they knew someone who could give them a password into gin joints, they dressed to the nines and took the party elsewhere.

Mr. Langendorf had his own opinions on the subject, and Estelle was eager to hear them.

"San Francisco is no different from any other big city trying to subvert the pleasures of drinking except we're known as a wild city," he said. "We are rebellious and free thinking. Bet you didn't know we have more bars per capita than any other city in America. That's because of the Irish. The Mission District has more bars than any section of the city. But the cops are mostly Irish, and they don't get in the way of their own kind."

Estelle was not worldly and thought Mr. Langendorf was probably right. The few times she ventured to the borders of the Western Addition, she saw shady characters hanging outside dark and mysterious doors with no identification. The men were shifting from one leg to the other, looking around to see who was watching. The speakeasies opened after dark, but men who needed their hooch would gladly wait hours before opening just to be the first inside.

Rose also had her own opinions on the subject.

"I'm not interested in speakeasies and gin-soaked nights," she told Estelle. "What interests me most is what's happening after women got the vote. How things changed, how in some quarters our opinions mattered, and our vote mattered. Jake and I didn't agree on much, but we were of one mind that all workers deserved better than a dirty and unhealthy work environment with little compensation."

"I never heard you talk like this, Mom. You sound like Papa."

"Maybe I do. We had that in common. That's why I tell you to aspire to white-collar jobs, like stenographers or sales girls in big, fancy department stores. Women earn more money and spend their days in nice offices or behind a beautiful perfume counter wearing lovely clothes. These working women graduated from high school and learned secretarial skills or developed sociable personalities that give them an air of having gone to finishing school."

Estelle knew her mother was right. Rose's hindsight as to how to overcome negative work situations was clear. Jake taught her that. In time, Rose got the best of him and became her own woman.

"You're smart, my darling, so don't waste a minute watching the world go by, waiting for a lucky break. Take advantage of what's in front of you at all times. Prepare to be the kind of woman who will be able to participate in this growing economy. Invest like Louie – and take advantage of the modern world."

"Too bad we didn't get to go out after graduation and explore North Beach," said Lucille as they were shopping for new dresses along Market Street. "We missed our opportunity. Maybe this weekend we'll get out. I'm bored. Let's go to the St. Francis Hotel and see Fatty Arbuckle's room, you know, where he killed his girlfriend. We'll be working full time soon, and we need to have some fun before we serve our penance in purgatory."

"You can't believe that, Lucy. When you're dead, you're dead. There is no purgatory along the way. Ashes to ashes, dust to dust."

"I was referring to how we'll be working eight or ten hours a day," said Lucille.

"That's not purgatory. That's hell. Come on, let's catch a trolley up to Union Square. I'm dying to see the jazzy lobby at the St. Francis Hotel. Everyone talks about it. All the hoi polloi go there and to Nob Hill."

"It's supposed to be smashing," said Lucille.

Estelle and Lucille hung onto the ropes above the seats on their way to Union Square at Powell and Post. It was a short hop, but they loved the scenery. Any place out of the Fillmore and the Mission districts was a good day. They got off at Geary and walked up Post, admiring the big department stores and small, cozy restaurants.

Even though it was mid-June, it was not a sunny day. Fog always rolled into San Francisco in June and wore out its welcome. Before they went into the St. Francis Hotel, they sat on a bench in the middle of the square and watched the pigeons gobble up breadcrumbs from people who had nothing else to do that day. They were mostly older men wearing tattered suits.

"Do you think these men are not out of work?" asked Lucille.

"It's sad, if so, considering the city has so much to offer."

"What's so great is that the city has the most theaters in America, even New York. Did you ever peak into the Fox Theater on Market Street? It's so jazzy. I can't wait to go to the pictures. Have you been?"

"Not yet, but I'm dying to go. Last year, Al Jolson talked and sang in *The Jazz Singer* in New York. Can you imagine? I wonder if Fatty will make a talkie. "

"I want to see where Fatty killed that woman," said Lucille. "If she wasn't his girlfriend, maybe they were hanging around. Maybe they were partying in the hotel and got a room. I know the room number – 1219 and it was Fatty's actual room."

"How do you know that?" asked Estelle. "What else do you know?"

"I just know that stupid stuff. Maybe I heard it on the radio. But Fatty came into the room, probably drunk and disgusting."

"He was three hundred pounds. If he fell on her, he would have crushed her to death."

"I love the mystery, Es. I don't care if the stories are true or not. I like guessing because everyone's been talking about it for years."

"No gun, no knife. What do you think happened?"

"If I was writing the story," said Lucy, "Fatty accidentally killed her with his massive body. He was huge and he didn't know his own strength. Fatty had to be drunk."

"I heard a story about Fatty on the radio," said Estelle. "It was something like 'Remembering Fatty.' The gossip was that lots of alcohol was delivered from Gobey's Grill the morning of the murder. It was really easy to get because Prohibition was only twenty months old. You could still get loads of gin and scotch."

"I'd love to see what the rooms look like," said Lucille.

Estelle took the lead as they anxiously entered the fabulously opulent European lobby, complete with gilded gold ceilings and the finest mahogany furnishings. It was massive. Estelle and Lucille looked up at the ornate gold vaulted ceiling.

"Once in a lifetime, Es," said Lucille.

"I hope not. Someday, I'm coming back. Let's ride the lift to Room 1219. We might get lucky if we can find a maid who has a key."

There was no maid and there was no key to Fatty Arbuckle's room. But they did get a peek into the room next door when a couple came out of their room. Estelle and Lucille almost bumped into them as the couple were leaving. They apologized over and over as the door to their room stayed open for several seconds. Suddenly, the man remembered something he'd left in his room and went back in to get what he needed. It was then that they got an even bigger view of the room next door to the scene of Fatty Arbuckle's crime.

Like thieves in the night, Estelle and Lucille ran down the hall and took the stairs to the lobby. Estelle opened the door slightly to see what was going on.

"Nobody in the lobby looks suspicious, Lucy," said Estelle.

"We're clear then," said Lucille. "Gosh, I can't catch my breath."

"Okay, one more streak to the front doors, and we'll make it out."

Four doormen stood at the top of the stairs, smoking and shifting from one foot to the other.

"Walk slowly next to me as if nothing has happened," said Estelle.

Estelle and Lucille clutched their purses and adjusted their hats and walked casually out the front door. Once they hit the bottom of the stairs, they hugged each other.

"Come on, Lucy. Let's get on the trolley and ride up to Nob Hill."

Every once in a while, the trolley stopped to chug up a steep grade. At the top of Nob Hill, they jumped off at California Street and squinted through the fog to see the beginnings of what was to become Grace Cathedral. Construction was in its infancy.

"The fog makes it freezing up here in the heavens," said Lucille as she and Estelle walked down California to Mason Street where the fancy Fairmont Hotel perched.

"All these swanky places remind me that I've got to get a job fast. I'm going to take the city government test and hope I get hired in one of the typing pools."

"Speaking of jobs, I'm not happy anymore at The Emporium. Time to move on."

"Not surprising. She piles the work on and doesn't increase your salary. Until you find a suitable job, stay where you are. You saw those gorgeous stores in Union Square. It would be smashing to work in an upscale workplace. We'll get this done in time."

CHAPTER 12

WORK, PLAY, LOVE

Estelle knew she had her work cut out for her after she graduated. She intentionally organized her life around getting a job in the typing pool at City Hall. It took two weeks to fill out the forms, and then she was required to retake a typing test that called for a different vocabulary – one that was directed to the kind of government work she would be doing.

When she filled out the personal forms, including proof of her citizenship, she had to include her address and phone number, high school attended, graduation date, prior work, and religion. Estelle knew not to check Jewish as her religion. She did a mental adjustment and thought about all the Christian religions she knew about and decided on Protestant. How could she go wrong with a religion whose ritual was noted for nothing in particular – no confession, kneeling, making the sign of the cross, or lighting the Friday night Shabbat candles? But there was one problem. Her address was in the Fillmore – and the address would give her away. She changed her address to Lucille's house in the Mission District and hoped her best friend wouldn't mind.

Mr. Langendorf was visibly upset when Estelle told him she would be leaving. He begged her to stay. She was resolute, telling him that she wanted a job in a bigger setting, maybe government work that could lead to other things. He was suspicious of her goals.

"You might be right, Mr. Langendorf, but I have to make my own mistakes. I'll be fine and so will you. You're the best boss ever."

"Stay through August, please, Estelle. You can help and train your replacement."

Estelle was finally notified that her typing score was so high that she was placed in the office of the city council. She was beyond excited. This was everything she wanted to happen. Estelle's preparation began with her wardrobe. Hours later, she decided to wear her finest work dress the first day on the job. Assuming she would have a brief lunch break, she carried her small sandwich and a piece of fruit in a brown bag. She wanted everything to be perfect.

Entering City Hall gave her a chill. Nervous, happy and set to learn, Estelle approached the receptionist.

"Hello, I'm Estelle Lanch, and I'm inquiring where the City Council is located."

The older lady with tight curly hair forced a smile and checked a log. "You are going to be assigned to Room 212 upstairs. They'll situate you."

Estelle thanked the receptionist and took the stairs two at a time to the second floor. At the top of the stairs, she was out of breath. Perspiration was settled above her upper lip. After taking several deep breaths, she opened her purse, powdered her nose, and rearranged her scarf.

The City Council's offices were already buzzing with activity before nine in the morning. There was an array of stenographers, secretaries, typists, and telephone operators in rows of cubicles. One of the councilmen was smoking a cigarette and dictating a letter to a stenographer who sat in a cubicle. Estelle's excitement turned into nervousness. She was energized but cautious as to how to direct her attention. Out of nowhere, an attractive mid-thirties stenographer came up to Estelle and guided her to a cubicle. The typewriter took up the entire surface of the desk. On one side, there was a holder that held sheets of paper.

"This is what we call a coop, and this is your assigned desk. I'm Evelyn Doughtery."

"I'm Estelle Lanch."

"I know. You were expected at eight thirty. I'm sure they told you nine, but no matter. Familiarize yourself with the typewriter, and there is a notebook about stenography in case you missed that class. I know they hired you as a typist, but you'll be expected to take dictation from a councilman if you want to stick around, and you are to translate his letters as fast as humanly possible from your shorthand. Use English words if you get lost. These guys talk fast. You won't last long unless you know shorthand, so do your homework to get you up to speed."

"I signed up as a typist," said Estelle.

"You signed up for wherever the big boys put you. If you can't learn the ropes, you will be let go. This is the best secretarial pool in the city, and if you want to be the best, you go the extra mile. This is the way things go around here. For every girl hired, there are ten more waiting."

"What are those machines on some of the desks?" asked Estelle.

"They're called Ediphones. It's a recording machine. If a boss wants to, he can speak into the Ediphone. Then you listen to it with an earpiece and transcribe it immediately, or keep it for later when the boss needs it. Meanwhile, Miss Estelle, you have homework after work. I'll have to cover for you until you get more than proficient in shorthand. And don't take too long. I can only cover for at most a week. After that, let's get a drink after work."

Estelle smelled Evelyn's perfume as she walked away as if she owned the office. In truth, Evelyn did own the office with her perfect short bob and neat summer skirt and blouse in the latest smoky blue and gray colors. She could learn a thing or two from Evelyn. Then she'll have that drink with her by next week. Estelle picked up the stenographer's booklet and scanned through it. She was familiar with the responsibilities of being a secretary, filing, creating files, writing letters, typing formats and the like, but the shorthand surprised her. She wanted to curse her typing teacher for scrimping on the fundamentals of shorthand without regular practice. She resolved to learn it in a week, including the weekend. Then she would tackle the Ediphone.

Estelle and Lucille met after work for a quick update.

"I'm miserable back at work," said Lucille.

"And I'm not happy about my lack of preparation as a stenographer, thanks to my typing teacher. That was a wasted class since I was already a proficient typist. I can't get out to see you for a week, and the weekend, too, Lucy. I have to review the symbols and marks of shorthand but be ten times faster. I'm way too slow because we never timed practices so we could improve. The only way I can see you is if you want to dictate letters to me or make up stories that I can record my shorthand times.

"I can manage that," she said, "but at your place, please."

"That would be smashing. I promise after I get this shorthand under control, I'll go around with you to other department stores for an alterations job. Let's start at City of Paris in Union Square. And then I. Magnin across the street. Reach for the stars. Why not? Then we can try Roos Brothers and H. Liebes. Look how many department stores are downtown, and since you've been working for years at the Emporium, you'll have a good reference."

"You're a peach, Es. Get to work on learning shorthand. In a month, you'll be the top girl in the office. They'll all hate you."

The following Monday, Estelle walked into her coop at eight fifteen ahead of the early birds. She set up her cubicle – steno book and shorthand notes on the left. Her note stand, as always, was to her right. As soon as she sat down, Evelyn appeared.

"Everything looks in place. Back straight as an arrow, and remember to sit slightly forward in anticipation of Mr. Crowe's dictation. It's scheduled at eight thirty sharp. Nice that you arrived in time to sharpen your pencils and prepare a clean page in your steno notebook."

When Councilman Crowe came out of his office, everyone in the coop looked up to see what was going to happen. He signaled to Estelle to come into his office. She picked up her steno pad and two sharpened pencils, and kept her breathing measured.

Councilman Crowe was from the Western Addition, which made Estelle a bit more comfortable. He smiled and greeted her politely. His gray suit fit him nicely, even though he was a heavy-set man with thinning hair and sagging jowls.

"Evelyn told me you were ready to take dictation," said Councilman Crowe. "I hope your learning curve is fast and efficient. I called you into my office to put you at ease. And I'm going to speak a little slower than usual so you won't make unnecessary errors."

"Thank you, Councilman. I appreciate the kindness."

"By the way, what district do you live in?" he asked.

"Mission District."

"I represent the Mission," Councilman Crowe said smiling. "Let's get to work."

The Councilman dictated his letter to the Building Trades on Guerrero Street. He did not, as promised, slow down his pace, and he was not helpful to Estelle. Instead he sped up his speech pattern. Estelle was unfazed because she made Lucille dictate to her as fast as she could. Allowing for a few errors, a symbol here and a sign there, she was able to handle the entirety of the letter. When she faltered, she made up shorthand signs that helped her capture the letter's intent without asking the Councilman to repeat or clarify. From then on, Estelle was asked by Councilman Crowe to come into his office for all dictation.

Estelle walked back to her desk with Evelyn at her side.

"How did it go? He did not speak slowly, did he?"

"He said he would, but he probably spoke faster to see if I could keep up," said Estelle.

"How about that drink? You haven't been to a speakeasy yet, have you?"

"No, but I'm ready."

"It's Monday, so let's go after work on Friday night with some of the gang. We have our regular speakeasy."

"Can I ask a friend? She's never been to a speakeasy either."

Friday could not come soon enough. After work on Monday, Estelle met Lucille in front of the Emporium, and she told her about their next adventure on Friday at a speakeasy.

"How am I going to do that, Es?"

"Tell her you have a birthday party for one of your co-workers. You have to go."

"I can't." Lucille started to cry.

"What is it, Lucy? The speakeasy?

"No, Mrs. Greenburg won't write a recommendation for me. I got a job at City of Paris as a seamstress, and she was mad and fired me."

Estelle took Lucille by the hand and marched her into the Emporium. They walked back to the alteration area.

"Hello, Estelle," Mrs. Greenburg said as she glanced at Lucille, "What can I do for you?"

"Lucille devoted several years to the Emporium, working hard, all through the summers and after school, and you won't write her a recommendation to take a job at City of Paris?"

"I don't owe her anything."

"Yes, you do, and you owe me something, too. Remember all those patterns I designed when I worked for you and you took credit for them with your customers? If you don't remember, I do, and I'm awful at keeping secrets. Management upstairs might want to know about your treatment of an employee who was devoted and whose work was exceptional. I recommended her, if you remember. Now it is your turn to recommend her."

Estelle and Lucille walked out of the Emporium with heads held high.

"Where are we going?" asked Lucille.

Estelle took her arm and led her across Market Street. "We are going to City of Paris, and you're getting a better job."

The transition from the Emporium to City of Paris took all of an hour. Lucille demonstrated her sewing capabilities at the time of her interview several days previously, and alterations asked for two recommendations. Lucille's new employer conducted another shorter interview with Estelle for her second recommendation.

"With respect, Mrs. Able, I've been working with Lucille for many years. We met in high school, and we've worked together on sewing projects for many years. I first worked in alterations at the Emporium and recommended Lucille when I left. She is also an excellent designer. In fact, she designed what I'm wearing. You'll see how valuable Lucille can be."

On the way out of the best department store in Union Square, Lucille hugged her friend. "You're the best, Es. I can't thank you enough."

"Now let's go celebrate. I have to get you a telephone number at City Hall so you can call me, and we can make plans for Friday night. I'll pick you up at City of Paris and we'll go to the speakeasy together. Stuff your flapper dress in a bag, and we'll change in the ladies room."

Estelle had no idea there was a speakeasy in the Fillmore and was curious that there was no ground floor or back door entrance on a lower level to keep the operation private. Bourbon & Branch was a second-floor secluded speakeasy facing O'Farrell Street. The hotel displayed a simple façade without outstanding markers to identify it as a classy or mid-level hotel. When Estelle and Lucille reached the second floor, clouds of cigarette smoke led them to a plain back door that blended with the dark walls and brown carpet. Estelle knocked three times. A peephole opened in the upper center of the door. She gave the password: "Chickens roost". They were let inside by a man in an elegant tuxedo.

Once inside, there were other secret doors, surrounded by exposed brick walls. The big surprise was the elegant lighting from top to bottom in the formal lobby. The girls headed for the ladies' room and changed into their dresses.

"We look like movie stars," said Lucille. "The lights make us look like celebrities."

"We look smashing, Lucy. This is the best moment for us."

The bar was crowded with young men lining up their drinks without coming up for air. From the bar, Evelyn waved wildly at Estelle. She and Lucille moved through a dense group of well-dressed businessmen and women to reach Evelyn who pushed herself out from the group to embrace Estelle and meet Lucille.

"What do you want to drink? There's everything at this bar, not just gin. There's whiskey and bourbon. I'll get one of these guys to pay for the first drink."

"We don't know, Evelyn," said Estelle. "We are new at this."

"Let's start with a shot of whiskey. That ought to last you for a few hours."

"She's nice, Es," Lucille said as Evelyn ordered their drinks.

"She's one of a kind in my book."

After an hour, a young man from the office came up to Estelle and introduced himself.

"I've seen you in the Fillmore. You live here, right?"

Evelyn set down a shot of whiskey for Estelle and for Lucille. They looked at each other with trepidation and consumed the alcohol with one gulp.

"Wow," said Lucille as she screwed up her face. "That's why men drink whiskey. You could kill yourself drinking this."

"I think you have to wait awhile so it sets in to feel any pleasure."

"So where do you live?" asked the young man.

"I live in the Mission right now," answered Estelle.

"I could swear I saw you at Diller's many times."

"Is that a question?" asked Estelle.

"I can make it a question by asking you if you know Daniel."

"Why is that important?" she asked.

"Maybe you hang out with him. Maybe you go to the same temple. His father is a rabbi."

"If this conversation has a point, why don't you let me in on it?" said Estelle.

"You never answered my question," he said.

"What difference does that make if I know Daniel or not?"

"Nothing. Nothing. I'm just saying – "

"You're just saying that if I know Daniel, I must be Jewish, I must like kosher food, and I must go to temple. What does any of this mean?"

The young man turned back to the bar. Estelle tapped Evelyn on the shoulder and gave her a warm squeeze. "See you on Monday."

Estelle took Lucille's arm, and they pushed through the door and left.

"What was that about, Es?" asked Lucille.

"I'm sorry, Lucy. I got spooked with all the liquor, and we're under age. "

"The guy at the bar saw you with Daniel," said Lucille. "Why did he bring that up?"

"He probably wanted to find out if I was Jewish. He works on my floor. I doubt if we'll be speaking to each other again. He's a creep."

"I'm glad we left," said Lucille as she took Estelle's arm.

By the beginning of 1928, America was growing tired of Prohibition. The thrill of going into speakeasies was waning. The secrecy behind the curtain, behind the mirrors, behind the barbershops, behind the hotel lobbies began to wane. However, the economy kept pumping out money. It looked like nothing could stop the forward trajectory of American commerce.

On New Year's Eve, Estelle decided to walk to Diller's, more in search of Daniel than to bring a surprise dinner home to her mother and Millie. She missed him – his warmth, his intelligence, and his kindness. When she walked inside, she saw him immediately. He was more handsome than she remembered. He had grown an inch or two, filled out, and no longer looked like a teenager. The overhead bell rang, but Daniel didn't turn around. It was as if he knew she had entered the deli. She stared at his back without blinking. He turned and smiled. She was unable to breathe, and it took her by surprise.

Daniel gave her a hug and a kiss on the cheek. She blushed.

"Happy new year," said Daniel. "You look smashing."

"So do you."

"Looking for something to take home for tonight's dinner?"

"Any suggestions?" she asked.

"I'll be happy to give you a brisket to take home with all the sides," said Daniel. "And then how about going out with me after your dinner?"

Estelle sat at a booth and took off her hat. A waitress brought her a cup of coffee. She tried to regain her composure when Daniel sat down across from her.

"I'm finally nineteen," she said. "Can you believe it?"

"And I'm finally back to school and taking more classes. It's junior college, but it's a good beginning. So, will you go out with me tonight?"

She squeezed his hand. "Let's go to the Fillmore and see *Lights of New York*. It's a talkie and all the rage. My mom is going out with her boyfriend tonight – he's Jewish of course – and Millie is wherever Millie goes."

A waitress brought the brisket dinner to the table wrapped securely in thick brown paper.

"Have a good dinner and meet me back here at eight," he said. "Don't change."

Estelle and Daniel held hands in the movie and sometimes he kissed her on the cheek or kissed her hand. She thought she might be in love for the first time. After the movie they walked and talked, and sometimes they were silent.

"We're almost at Golden Gate Park," said Daniel. "We can take the streetcar back later."

They sat on a bench at the edge of the park in the cold night air. Daniel put his arm around Estelle, and she rested her head on his shoulder.

"I went to a speakeasy a few months ago with my office workers. I'm a stenographer in the city council's office."

"Congratulations. You always wanted a job like that. Good for you." "I love it there, but a young man said he saw me at Diller's. He asked if I knew you."

"What did you say?"

"I said yes. And he asked me if you were Jewish."

"Because it's the Fillmore, and we have a good business reputation. And if he saw you in Diller's, and he knew me, it's only a simple question."

"I thought he was hinting that I was Jewish. I didn't like it, and I left."

"You thought he made an antisemitic slur? asked Daniel.

"Why else would he comment about you being Jewish?"

"What am I going to do with you, Estelle? We've been friends ever since you moved to the Fillmore, and maybe we are more, so what does it matter if he thought you were Jewish?"

Daniel leaned over and kissed her. It was longer than it should have been – sweet, loving.

"I hope that was all right with you," said Daniel. "I've wanted to kiss you for years."

"I felt the same way."

"Please then tell me why you're angry about being Jewish." Daniel asked. "Why do you feel so slighted that someone asks you?"

"I feel the person asking is being accusatory," said Estelle. "You can tell by someone's tone of voice that there's something wrong with being Jewish. There is a stigma."

"I pay no mind. I live my life the way I want to, no matter what anyone thinks. Besides, you know that San Francisco is the least antisemitic city in the country, except maybe New York. You lived in New York so you should know. And German Jews were accepted in San Francisco way back in the 1800s. Jews are everywhere in our city – not just the Fillmore – and nobody thinks anything about it. People live where they want, but business is business."

"Still there's no reason to point it out, saying 'I'm a Jew' or 'He's a Jew,'" Estelle said. "That identity will always catch up to you, and nothing good will come of it."

"What will catch up to you? What could catch up to you or anyone who's Jewish?"

"The antisemitism. Always being the other. I don't want to be part of it."

"The truth is that some aspects of identity are always with you. They travel with you no matter how much you hide behind your protective fortress."

"It's too late, Daniel. I've made my choice. I choose to live in the hands of fate."

Daniel took her in his arms and held her so close she could hardly breathe.

"Will you ever love me, Es? Will you ever feel comfortable with me?"

"I will always love you, Daniel, but I can't live a Jewish life with you."

She stood and took his hands. "The sun's coming up, and we need to catch a streetcar."

CHAPTER 13

THE JAZZ AGE

Estelle found it difficult to go back to work after the holiday. She missed Daniel, his arms, his words, his patience, his generosity. But she made plans to move her family to another district, out of the Fillmore, which was crowded with new immigrants, with too many bars and restaurants around O'Farrell Street. They needed a quieter neighborhood, not too far from Commerce High School where Mildred was in her sophomore year, although it would make Rose's commute to Schlage Lock and Key one streetcar stop longer.

Estelle and Lucille were finally exploring San Francisco as adults. They picked up new friends at work and frequented restaurants and dance clubs, and they took up tap dancing. Tap was all the rage. Estelle knew it was the most important preparation to be a good dancer. The tap teacher was Joey Papp, a young man in his early twenties. Estelle thought Joey could tap his way across America. He was six feet tall, slim, with a straight mustache that was barely coming in above his lip. He wore slacks that showed the outline of his legs and argyle sweaters in bright colors. He was the first gay man Estelle met, and once Joey groomed Estelle to be a fabulous dancer, she and Joey fell in together as a dancing duo.

"You must come to my apartment in the hills above North Beach," Joey said to her one night after dancing. "I've got a small place, but it's perfect for intimate parties with the gang. I bet you've never met these kind of people before. But you must know that we are not all homosexuals. There is a mix of men and women who are artistic and fun. They smoke cigarettes, drink bathtub gin, and dance the Charleston and foxtrot until dawn. And you'll learn from the gang what ballrooms to go to and where the best speakeasies are located around town."

"I can't wait to go to one of your parties, Joey," said Estelle. "

"Let's go tonight. My roommate is throwing a soiree at midnight."

"Are you sure it's kosher, Joey? I mean what about the cops and all?"

"Being queer is forbidden everywhere in the city except North Beach. It is a beacon of queer life. The cops look the other way. Why put queers in prison? It's too much trouble to write it up, take us in, and then we get out with a queer lawyer. Would you believe that some of the cops are homosexuals? Everyone knows who they are."

Estelle and Lucille loved North Beach and often hung out at the Saloon at Columbus Avenue and Broadway. They saw men and women go in and out of dark doors or eat at establishments that offered alcohol in the back rooms. Joey told them that there was a loose arrangement with the owners of the speakeasies and the cops – mainly, the purveyors of alcohol paid off law enforcement.

"Now, listen up you gorgeous ladies," said Joey, "I must give you an overview of the best hooch establishments around town. The best one, of course, is the infamous Hotel D'Oloron on Columbus Avenue in North Beach. It's hidden behind fake signs in the Financial District, in the basement of the Café du Nord in the Castro District, but everyone knows about it. I must take you to the Amocat Club on Turk Street. This is a kick because it's behind mirrored glass in a barbershop. The most fun is Izzy Gomez's Café on Pacific Avenue. Everyone wants to catch the Poo-Bah – the biggest man you have ever seen – wearing his black fedora, brim turned down, holding court with his customers at his place in North Beach. I will take you to them all."

One night, Estelle and Lucille ran into a friend from Commerce High School, Margaret Richmond, at the Hoffman Grill Market Street. She matured into a pretty woman with deep brown eyes and dark curly bobbed hair, and her dress was hovering above the knee.

"Well, this is old home week," said Margaret. "I wondered what happened to you two. Still palling around together, I see."

"We're still together," said Lucille. "What are you up to?"

"I work at Roos Brothers in notions," said Margaret.

"That's such a swanky department store," said Lucille. "It's owned by a Jewish family from France, right?"

"A hundred years ago. It's all custom men's clothing, and sometimes I help the tailors with alternations. Where do you girls work?"

"I'm a seamstress at City of Paris, and Estelle is a stenographer for the City Council."

"Good jobs, ladies. I guess we turned out alright after all. Listen, I'm waiting for my boyfriend, so I have to powder my nose. Wait here and I'll introduce you to him."

Margaret left and Estelle and Lucille walked to a nearby table. A handsome man sat down in their booth.

"Excuse me, ladies, but I saw you talking to my girlfriend, and I thought I'd introduce myself. I'm sure she'll be back in an hour. John Quinn's my name."

John was a bit older than Margaret and as handsome as the day is long. Obviously, he was not Jewish. Estelle was fascinated.

"I'm guessing you went to Mission High," said Estelle.

"You guess right. Did you go to Commerce with Margaret?"

"Yes, indeed," said Lucille.

"What do you do, John Quinn?"

"I'm in sales for properties in the Fillmore. That's where the action is."

Margaret came up to the table and hugged him. "I see you all met."

"Where did you two meet?" asked Lucille.

"At a YMCA dance," said John.

They talked for a few more minutes. Margaret was all over her boyfriend, and obviously, it was time to leave. They stood up, said their obligatory goodbyes, and left.

"Let's go to the movies at the Castro," said Estelle. They're playing *Cocoanuts*."

"I love the Marx Brothers, and now that all the movies are all talkies, it's divine."

For the past year, Estelle was aware that any day in the Fillmore she could run into Daniel. New Year's morning was the last time she saw him. She still felt the pain of their parting. That feeling of love, or whatever it was, made her heart feel tight. One night at the Majestic Hall Ballroom on the corner of Geary and O'Farrell, Estelle was hanging out with Joey Papp on the second floor where the dances were held. They were standing in a corner, watching the dancers when she spotted Daniel dancing with a pretty girl. She was not able to take her eyes off him. Estelle thought he was having too much fun with his date.

"Come on, Joey, let's dance," said Estelle.

They walked out onto the crowded floor and danced the Charleston to the popular song, "Varsity Eight," a combination of jazz and big band style. Since Joey was a first-class dancer, and probably the best on the floor, Estelle was sure she would be featured as one of the best female dancers as his partner. Joey showed her off to perfection as Sid LeProtti's Jazz Orchestra played. The next song was a foxtrot called "Get Together," which got everyone on the floor. That was when Daniel almost bumped into Estelle and Joey. He first looked at Joey and then at her, realizing Joey was a friend, and he smiled at her and nodded. She lost her step momentarily, recovered to acknowledge him, and the two couples danced by each other.

Estelle was a foggy mess when the song was over.

"We're going to have a tango, Estelle, so let's get our practice in," said Joey, taking her hands. "Oh, darling, you are cold as ice. What's wrong?"

"Nothing, darling. We need to practice our tango. I hope Sid gives it a jazzy rhythm."

The orchestra began to play "La Cumparsita." Joey waited for a space to enter the floor. He held Estelle's hand and they began to dance, but she did not have the heart to continue.

"I'm sorry, Joey, I'm distracted."

"I can tell. Let's go home."

The pain of saying goodbye to Daniel on New Year's morning in Golden Gate Park was ever present in Estelle's mind. She was convinced that it would be the last time she would see Daniel. Her heart was broken. To ease her loss, she threw herself into hunting for a larger apartment. Spring was coming, and she wanted Rose and Mildred settled. Evelyn had a good idea about finding an apartment close to Van Ness and Hayes, where Commerce High was located. Mildred would be closer to school for her last two years."

"Darling, we're perfectly fine where we are," said Rose. "There is no rush to move."

"Maybe not, but I want us to have three bedrooms and two baths. It's time we lived well."

"Mildred is too much to handle, Estelle. You know that. And if I have to take more time to travel to work, she'll have no supervision. It's eight o'clock, and she's not home."

"I'll have a talk with her, Mom. Why isn't she working after school?"

"You tell me. I have talked to her about it."

Mildred had no aptitude to work or study. Her interest was music, particularly the piano. Estelle talked to her music teacher about her progress in class. What could she do with her talent? "She could teach," said her music teacher. Estelle thought about encouraging her to give piano lessons in the neighborhood.

After another month of walking the streets near Van Ness, Estelle found the perfect apartment on Fell near Franklin Street. In addition to having three bedrooms, two bathrooms, with a small room that could be a sewing room or a cubby hole to sleep in, it was neat and clean with painted white walls and a little balcony outside the curtained front window. Estelle was just able to put down the first month's rent plus a security deposit. And then she was broke. They have a month to organize the move.

Two happenings gave Estelle hope. Louie Blum offered to pay for the move, and Mildred wanted to give music lessons, maybe in the neighborhood or maybe in the music room at Commerce High School. Estelle decided to find a music store that had a piano she could rent out by the hour for Mildred's piano lessons. Having a piano teacher on the premises might bring new people into the music store to buy sheet music or take lessons.

On moving day, Louie organized a van pull up in front of their old apartment building. Aunt Anya was already in front, ready to help.

"I hate to see you go," said Anya. "We don't get a chance to socialize except on Friday nights and Jewish holidays. I hope we won't be strangers."

"Don't be silly," said Rose. "We're only a couple of streetcars away. This is not goodbye. We're family, and we'll always be so."

The move to Fell and Franklin was relatively smooth with Joey and Lucille helping.

Before Estelle left the Fillmore, she took a walk down to Diller's Strictly Kosher Restaurant and hung out across the street to see if she could see

Daniel – just see him, not talk to him, not engage him in any meaningful way. It still hurt her. Daniel was moving on and courting a proper Jewish girl who would give him the life he needed. Estelle knew she was not going to be the typical stay-at-home Jewish wife who had children immediately. She was driven to succeed. She would succumb to marriage only if she found a man who was willing to go along with her plans, a man who was also creative in his own right, a good worker, and funny and bright. For the time being, children were not in the near future.

"You're so sad," said Lucille one night after they attended *The Broadway Melody* at the Lyceum Theater. "Even the music didn't make you smile."

"I think I'm still not over Daniel. I made the choice, I know. He's traditional and close to his religion, And that's not for me. My parents tried it, and it was not for them. - an atheist and a Jew."

"Well, I can't figure why it won't work since he's handsome and going to make something of himself. Besides, you love him."

"His way of life isn't mine. The Jewish life is set in stone. I want to build a life with a man who shares common interests and creates future plans that are exciting and not someone who adheres to the dictates of a religious tradition that is all-consuming. "

"You're anything but just a married woman, Es. You're modern and I admire that."

"Well, then let's plot and plan out our future better. Now that I'm moved and closer to you, we need to go to other places in the city and explore our options."

"Let's go to Dreamland. I've never roller skated, have you?"

"I thought it was a boxing arena."

"Not in the daytime. But I'd like to go to the fights at night, too."

"Smashing, Lucy. Let's do it."

Estelle and Lucille's circle grew to include many young men and women in the neighborhood around Van Ness and Franklin. There were groups of people who they went to school with, and their proximity made it easy for all of them to get together and ride trolleys anywhere in the city or take ferries to Sausalito, Vallejo, Richmond, Berkeley, or Alameda. Estelle's favorite activity was riding the ferries to Oakland and to the Richmond train terminal, which brought people into the city for work or pleasure, or to the University of California in Berkeley. Finally out in the world with time off on the weekends, Estelle loved to get aboard the Northwestern

Pacific ferry with knapsacks and rented bikes and go across to Sausalito for the day. Sometimes it was just as exciting to ride the passenger ferry boat operations, like the Southern Pacific and Santa Fe, with their colorful boats with splendid vistas from the open decks. Hearing the cacophony of whistles, bells, and horns that blew from the tops of steamboats and tugs was magical.

The largest and most populous ferry terminal in San Francisco was at the Embarcadero. Estelle and Lucille spent little time inside the classic Beaux-Arts style ferry building situated on a long boulevard that ran along the eastern waterfront complete with piers and numerous ports. Every trolley in San Francisco began and ended its route in the Embarcadero.

"The Embarcadero is intimidating," said Lucille. "There must be over fifty streetcars on the loop, and the view of Alcatraz looks like it came from a movie."

"Look how many people are coming out of the terminal. It's a stampede. How do they stuff them inside with all that baggage and freight and mail?"

"The waiting room is stuffed with people and reeks of the smelly stink of cigars. I read in *The Chronicle* that the ferries land 170 times a day, back and forth across the Bay."

"Come on, it's time we bought a ticket to Berkeley and looked at the campus," said Estelle. "It's Saturday and it won't be too crowded."

They bolted into the crowd and pushed their way to the ticket office and joined a line of men reading newspapers – wearing wool suits, smoking cigarettes, and sweating profusely under their bowler hats. Estelle and Lucille looked at one another in horror.

"I hope it's worth the trip because this place smells, and you can't breathe," said Lucille.

"Let's go to Larkspur next time. There's dancing under the stars at night in a redwood grove. Maybe we'll meet some nice boys from the city. And there's a half-acre of dance floor. But best of all, we can see Alcatraz up close when the boat passes the island."

"We'll do that next time, Lucy. I just have to see Berkeley. One day, I want to go to college, maybe not Berkeley, but some college somewhere."

Winter turned to spring and Estelle's workload increased and she had to stay longer at the office in order to meet deadlines and not fall behind. It was seven o'clock on a Friday night, and she was ready to put in her resignation.

"You don't have to finish," said Evelyn. "Take a break. Come out with us tonight."

"Where are you going?" Estelle asked.

"North Beach to hear jazz at the Saloon and then we're going to the Black Cat."

Estelle picked up her coat and purse. "You're right. I was thinking of quitting, but having fun is what I need."

The evening group was mostly from the city council's office, and the guys and gals were drinking like Prohibition was over. San Francisco was a city without alcohol borders. The Saloon was crowded, and Estelle found it difficult to have a conversation.

Evelyn yelled at her. "Hey, Es! Kid Ory and his band are playing tonight. Let's get a front-row seat."

Kid Ory was a legend, and his bandmates were the finest musicians around the city. They finished off the evening at the Black Hawk, where Jelly Roll Morton was playing. It was an evening to remember. Estelle didn't know much about jazz, but she thought the scene was engaging with a racial mix of musicians and fans who made the evening exciting. The jazz scene in San Francisco in the late 1920s made Estelle the happiest woman on earth.

Afterward, Estelle asked Evelyn if she wanted to see the Arcadia Dancing Pavilion. "It's the most elegant dance hall - high ceilings and a shiny hardwood floor. All the best dancers go there."

"I'd love to see it one night, Estelle. Promise me you'll take me."

"Of course, I promise."

At the end of August, Lucille asked Estelle if she wanted to go to a dance at the YMCA.

"I know it's not as fancy as where Joey takes you, but it's fun with all kinds of men there who are pretty good dancers. They don't play much jazz, but you can hear standard foxtrots and some Charleston. Some kids even dance the Lindy."

"Sounds good, Lucy. We haven't done much together lately so it's our time."

Estelle got home from work at six, and saw Mildred crying on the sofa.

"What's wrong? Where's Mom?"

"She went out with Louie for dinner."

"You're upset about something, Millie. What is it?"

She began to cry again. "I'm pregnant," she said through her tears.

"For Christ sake, you're sixteen and you're having sex? You don't listen to anyone, least of all me. I told you about this when you were fourteen, and you brushed it off. Now what? Does Mom know?"

"Please don't tell her. My friend told me where to go. But I need you to help me."

"No, Millie. This is something your friend has to help you with. Better yet, tell the guy whose child it is that he should pitch in."

"He's gone. I need to borrow money from you."

Estelle was angry. She was beside herself, furious that she did not succeed in holding Mildred on a tighter leash. She left Millie's and went to Lucille's home. She was waiting outside.

They took the streetcar to Mission Street between 23rd and 24th streets. Anyone who did not know it was there, could easily have missed the YMCA entrance; it was between a hardware store on one side and beauty shop on the other. They entered and climbed the stairs to the second floor, where the offices and the dance floor blended together to form what looked like a basketball gym minus the hoops. Couples were already dancing to the slow rhythm of "Ain't Misbehavin'." They sat at a long bench and watched the dancers.

"Tame stuff," said Lucille. "It needs a little jazz."

"It needs more than that."

A young man came up to Lucille and asked her to dance. He took a look at Estelle, smiled, and nodded. Another man, very handsome, tall, over six feet, with curly black hair and a devastating smile approached Estelle. He held out his hand to her. She looked at it, then looked into his eyes. Hazel. Irish, she thought.

"Would you like to dance?" he asked. "I'm not very good, but I bet you are."

"I'm pretty good," she said. "I've been trained by a great dancer."

"My name is John."

"I'm Estelle."

"Stella by starlight. Sweet sound."

The music stopped. Estelle stood. John engulfed her in his arms before the music began again. They held each other and waited until "When My Baby Smiles at Me" began.

"It's a little fast for me, but I'll try," said John.

Estelle guided John through the music as she counted out steps. "You have potential."

"I hope you stick around to teach me."

John led Estelle back to the bench and sat down next to her. "Do you mind?"

Lucille appeared in front of Estelle without the young man who asked her to dance. "He's a real jerk."

"This is John, Lucille. He's not a jerk. He's an up-and-coming dancer."

They shook hands. "My pleasure," said John, "I think I know you from the Mission."

"Sure. Probably," said Lucille. "Is your last name Moran?"

"Yep, and yours is Flynn. Your dad is Bill."

"Right. Do you still live at 1578 Noe Street?" asked Lucille. "You have some brothers and a sister that I remember from St. Paul's grammar school."

"My mom and dad still live there with the two of us and the goats."

The same young man whom Lucille called a jerk came up to her and asked her to dance again. Lucille did not take his hand and turned away. He looked confused.

"Lucy, he doesn't know he's a jerk," said Estelle.

"What do you mean?" asked the young man.

"What's your name?" asked Estelle.

"Peter," he said.

"Peter what?" asked Estelle "Full name, please."

"Peter Burrows."

"Lucy said you were a jerk, Peter. Did you say something rude?"

"I don't know," said Peter.

"You see, Lucy," said Estelle, "he doesn't know why he's a jerk, so why don't you teach the young man how not to be a jerk?"

Lucille laughed at the incongruity of the situation. So did John. Lucille and Peter walked off together and began to dance. John and Estelle followed, and their embrace persisted until closing time . Lucille left with Peter sometime after midnight because she still had a curfew. John walked Estelle to the last streetcar of the night. He wouldn't let go of her hand.

"I want to see you again, Stella by Starlight," said John. "You're beautiful and I love the way you move and dance."

"I'm flattered, and it would be fun to go on a picnic with you or take a ferry to Sausalito."

John kissed her on the cheek. "How do I find you?"

The streetcar was beginning to move. "Fillmore 8779. Or call me at work. City Hall. Councilman Crowe's office. I'll pick up. What's yours?"

"Western Pacific Railroad offices near the Embarcadero." John blew her a kiss.

CHAPTER 14

BACK ALLEYS

Estelle was dreading the conversation with Mildred. There were many questions to be answered: How long was she pregnant, what did her friend have in mind to accomplish the abortion, where was she to go, and who was going to do the medical work. It was going to be complicated and secretive, with no guarantee of a positive outcome. Estelle heard stories at work among some of the women in the stenography pool who had abortions or knew where to get abortions. The whispered conversations took place at lunch and in private places around the building. Estelle overheard many of the stories, but never asked where to find a back alley where abortions took place. None of the women admitted to getting a back-alley abortion, but they all knew about their availability around the city. It was a secret never revealed.

The next morning, Mildred came into her room, crying. She was completely distraught and mumbling incoherently.

"I'll take care of this, Millie. Don't worry about the money. That's the least of it. I need to meet your friend and find out the details. How far along are you?"

"Two months," Mildred said, catching her breath.

"We have to do this fast. It has to be this weekend. Take me to the girl now."

"I don't know if we can get an appointment. And where am I going to stay after? I can't come back home."

"Let's not worry about this. I can tell Mom that we are going for a ferry ride over the weekend, and we want to start our trip today after work. We need to make an appointment tonight. Pack some clothes and towels in a bag and anything else you can think of. I'll meet you here at home after around six tonight."

Work that day was unbearable. Estelle had difficulty focusing. She didn't know how they would manage the aftermath of the abortion. Where would they go? She left her desk on the pretext of going to the ladies' room, but veered into the administrative offices and asked the receptionist for a telephone directory. It took her a few minutes to find the offices of Western Pacific Railroad.

After the third try, she found the number and jotted it down on a scratch of paper and headed back to her desk. There was lunch and another five and a half hours of work. Evelyn came by and asked her if she wanted to go to North Beach with the gang. Estelle said she had plans for the weekend with her sister. They were going to take a ferry ride to Marin County.

When Estelle came home from work, Mildred was in shock.

"Mildred, we have to go to your friend's house now if we're going to get a late-night appointment. Come on. You can't fall apart."

Mildred took Estelle to her friend's house in the Mission. She went around the house and knocked gently on her friend's window. They knocked again and waited impatiently for her friend to open the window. After the third knock, her friend appeared,

"Carol," whispered Mildred. "We have to talk. It's urgent."

"Hi, Carol, I'm Mildred's sister, and I would like you to give us the information about the woman who will help my sister, and it needs to be this weekend. Can you help us?"

"I don't know if I can go with you that fast, but I'll give you the information. Wait a minute."

Carol came back to the window and handed Estelle the name and address of the woman who would perform the abortion. Mildred hugged Carol through the window, and she and Estelle ran to the sidewalk to find a streetcar that went to the Tenderloin, which bordered the Mission District and Market Street. The instructions were written down, but Estelle was momentarily stuck because she was unsure what streetcar to take. The Tenderloin was not technically a district – it was a section of downtown bordered by Geary Street to the north and Market Street to the south. The address of the apartment building Carol gave them was in the western part of the Tenderloin, the seediest and most dangerous part of the area.

Estelle and Mildred got off at Larkin Street and began to walk the five blocks to the address. They passed sketchy vagrants and drunks, men in tattered clothes dragging other men into hidden speakeasies, prostitutes walking the streets, pimps hanging out in front of dirty hotels, and sick people shivering under thin blankets. Estelle heard the neighborhood was notorious for its gambling, billiard halls, boxing gyms, speakeasies, and other forms of indecent nightlife. They reached the address and stood before a dilapidated building. Estelle rang the bell.

"Don't say a word, Millie. Leave it to me."

Minutes later a man in his early sixties opened the door. He was wearing a dirty brown cotton robe and his face was covered with stubble. His hair was gray and unkept. Estelle figured he rarely showered considering the smell coming from his extremities.

"What'd you want?" asked the man.

"Is Delores in?" asked Estelle.

"She's busy."

"I'm sure," said Estelle, "but I'd like to make an appointment for tonight."

The man pulled Mildred and Estelle inside. "You have to be crazy coming here asking for something you have no business asking for."

"I've got money. I know I don't have an appointment, but my sister is beside herself and needs the operation."

"No can do. We're full up."

"Ask Delores anyway. We'll be ready tonight and can pay. Please, Mister."

He turned away from the sisters and walked slowly up the creaky stairs, which appeared to be close to crumbling under his weight. He disappeared into a dark hallway like Bela Lugosi in Count Dracula. Five minutes later an older woman, haggard, with matted, stringy gray hair that fell to her shoulders, came down the stairs escorting a young woman who was obviously a client of Delores. Mildred squeezed Estelle's hand as they watched Delores guide the young woman to the last step. Estelle pulled Mildred to the back wall of the entry to let them go by. Delores opened the door for the young woman who walked out without a word. Delores waited a minute before she looked at the sisters. "I'll do it after hours. It'll cost you more."

"How much more?" asked Estelle.

"Another twenty," she said. "Plus the thirty."

"I've got it."

Mildred tried to hold her tears back. "I've made a mess of this."

"I have to be in the room with her," said Estelle.

Delores climbed the stairs as if it was the tallest mountain in the world.

"What's after hours?"

"Eleven tonight," said Delores without turning around. "Let them out, Tony."

The doorkeeper narrowly opened the door for the sisters as they walked outside into the cold night air. The darkness was broken by a gaslight on the corner across Larkin Street.

"Hi, girls," Rose said. "I'm just leaving some food for you."

"I thought you were going with Louie somewhere," said Estelle.

"I'm just about leaving. You have fun over the weekend."

"We're leaving on the last ferry to Marin. About nine o'clock."

Rose hugged her daughters. "I'm on my way. Take care."

The sisters looked at each other with momentary relief.

At eleven, Estelle and Mildred rang the bell at the Larkin apartment building. Tony opened the door, let them inside, and indicated they should walk up the stairs. Delores was standing beside an open door on the left. She motioned for them to walk into the small room. Sharp instruments were precisely placed on a high table. The room was stuffy and cold. There was no chair for Estelle to sit. She pulled a handkerchief out of her purse and held it to her nose.

"I've got to get hot water," said Delores. "Take your clothes off. Leave the bra on and get on the table. Pull the sheet over you."

Estelle helped Mildred undress. She was shaking.

"I'm cold," Mildred said to her sister. "And scared."

"Remember this next time you fool around. No more mistakes."

Delores came into the room carrying a large bowl of hot water and an armful of rags.

"How long?" she asked Mildred.

"I think about two months."

"Let's hope," said Delores. "Any more time after that and it gets tricky."

"You mean difficult?" asked Estelle.

"You could say that. The farther along, the more complications."

Delores picked up a long, sharp instrument from the table. She dipped it in alcohol and wiped it with one of her rags. "It may not look clean, but it is. I'm going to scrape inside the womb then cauterize the cervix to help stop the bleeding afterwards."

Estelle looked away, closed her eyes and hoped that nothing would happen to her sister.

Delores spread Mildred's legs and put a piece of wood in her mouth. She inserted the instrument and Estelle looked away waiting for Mildred to scream. It came like a bolt of thunder, at first sudden and loud, then long cries brought about by the intense pain. It went on for five minutes. When the long instrument came out slowly from Mildred's womb, she began to moan and breathe heavily. At that moment, Estelle felt bile coming up from her throat and her strength evaporated. Dolores stuffed towels against Mildred's vagina in order to stop the bleeding.

"It was more than two months. I'm leaving the towels there until I'm sure there is no bleeding. But it won't go away for a while, maybe a day or two. Use old rags to catch the blood. If it continues to bleed, take her to see a doctor. Leave when you want. You're the last one."

Delores washed her hands in another bowl and left the room. Estelle held Mildred's hand for the next twenty minutes and made sure the rags were absorbing. Delores entered the room again and checked her blood flow.

"Better. Give it another half hour or more if you want," said Delores. "You can pay me now. I won't be back. You take her downstairs. Tony will be there to let you out."

Estelle took out fifty dollars in bills and paid Delores. She was out the door in seconds. Not another word, not a wish you luck – nothing. She stood by her sister and watched the red blood leak out between her legs. The clock moved slowly, and the half hour passed.

"Are you ready to leave, Millie?"

"I have stomach cramps, Es."

"You are going to have them for a few days. We have to keep Mom away from you. Say you have the flu, but I don't know how to get rid of the rags – getting them in and out of your room. I have to be with you in case something goes wrong. I didn't have a good plan."

"What would I have done without you?"

"Please, Millie, let's get you over the next few days. Do you have a friend, someone older with an apartment where you could stay? I'll stay with you, I promise."

"I have a place to wash up but not to stay. These cramps are awful."

"Help me get you to a sitting position."

Estelle took the rags from between Mildred's legs and helped her sit up. Blood was still trickling out, but it was not a heavy flow. She helped her out of bed, dressed her, and adjusted the rags so her sister would be able to walk. Mildred was unsteady as she descended the stairs.

Tony was a fixture by the door. Mildred clutched Estelle's arm as Tony let them out the front door into the inky darkness of night. Estelle pulled away from Mildred's arm and ran to the curb and threw up. She could barely manage to stand.

"I don't know where to go, Millie. All I can think of is a hotel nearby, but I don't have any money left."

"Not too far, Es."

Two doors down on Larkin there was a brothel. Only men were walking into the ground-floor bar. She caught a glimpse of couples in amorous embraces. Another man passed by and Estelle stopped him. "Sorry, sir, but can you tell me where the nearest hotel is?"

"End of the block on Eddy. It's called the Crystal Hotel. Got to warn you that the second floor is a brothel, but there are rooms on the third floor. Ignore the bar. You kids are too young for that stuff." He took a look at Mildred and walked on.

They entered the Crystal Hotel and witnessed men fondling women as they drank at the bar. The proprietress of the hotel, a tall redhead in her late forties, wearing a white crochet dress, walked up to Estelle.

"Honey, are you sure you're in the right place?" she asked.

"We're not in the right place, but we need a room to rent for the night."

"We don't have any left tonight, but we have an annex on the third floor. Will that do?"

"Yes, and I could use a bowl of hot water, a couple of towels, and a pitcher of water."

"I can do that."

The madam led the sisters up two flights of stairs. Mildred was close to collapsing. Without a word, the madam disappeared into an annex. Estelle followed, carried her sister to the bed, and laid her down gently. The madam picked up the pitcher and left the room.

Mildred was sweating and the pain was palpable. Estelle removed Mildred's top garments, pulled her shoes off, and pushed back her hair from her eyes. The madam returned with two pitchers of water and a pile of towels and put them on a table.

"I'll pay you extra for everything."

"Don't you worry, honey."

The madam put her hand on Mildred's forehead. "She's running a fever. I'll get you something for this. Change the rags and clean her up. I'll be back."

The night was long. Mildred slept intermittently. Estelle tried to stay awake, but dozed off, then she woke up with a start. Whatever the madame gave Mildred, it was working. She didn't call out in pain. Estelle was sure that the madam was familiar with what was happening to Mildred. After all, she ran a brothel in a hotel under the guise of managing a bar.

Sometime in the early morning light, still awake, Estelle worried that Mildred might have an infection, or worse. She rolled her over and checked to see if her blood was still flowing. To her relief, dried blood stuck to the towels. Several towels stuck to her legs. Estelle wet extra towels to remove the areas where dried blood coagulated. Mildred was deep in sleep.

The madam came into the room and examined Mildred.

"It looks good. Whoever did this knew what she was doing. Stay as long as you need to, but leave the name and address of the woman who did this."

"Of course," said Estelle. "Do you have a phone downstairs?"

"There's one in my office," said the madam, as she walked to the door. "You can use it."

Several hours later, Estelle left the room with her purse and went downstairs to the bar. There were few customers in the early morning. Several ladies were slumping at the table, sleeping. The madam walked out of her office.

"Do you need some soup? I'll bring it to the room."

Estelle nodded yes and walked into the office. She called the operator and asked for the Western Pacific Railroad office just to make sure she had the right number. She was too nervous to trust herself. The clock on the wall indicated that it was seven in the morning. It was too early to call. No one would be there. And it was Saturday. Did John work on Saturday? She went upstairs and slept. The soup would be cold when they woke up.

Mildred was doubled over when Estelle got up.

"Millie, you must have some soup. It's cold but probably okay to eat."

"I can't eat. I don't feel right."

"Part of it is hunger so drink the soup. You must be needing water. Let's get your liquids back. I'll get a new pitcher of water."

Estelle went downstairs and found the madam behind the bar.

"This is awkward," said Estelle. "I have no more money left. The woman who did the operation asked above the price because it was done after midnight. But I'm going to call a friend, and if I can get ahold of him, he'll bring the money. Could you please give us an hour or so?"

A smile crossed the madam's face. "Do you think I am worried about you paying me for the use of the annex, for some towels and a pitcher of hot water? Listen, honey, every once in a while, we make mistakes. You did good for your sister. And you remained calm. Stay as long as you like. I'm not worried about money. I'd let you walk out of here without paying, but I'm sure you'll come back and pay."

Estelle let her breath out and then took three more deep breaths. For the first time in twenty-four hours, she knew Mildred would be safe. The madam gave her a perfumed hankie. It smelled like heaven.

"Keep it," said the Madam. "Go make your call."

Estelle went to the phone in the madam's office and stood by her desk. She wasn't sure what to do. Maybe call Evelyn. But she was a work contact. What would she think? Louie was away with Rose. She was sure that Louie would have given her money for Mildred and would not tell Rose. The night before, with John, was magic. He was not just a man who you could trust, but he was kind and giving. Yet, she hardly knew him. But if John was a man who could be called upon to rescue, he was her man forever. It was a test, but not the final test.

Estelle called the Western Pacific Office. Someone picked up.

"Hello, I'm calling for John Moran," she said. "Is he in today?"

"No," said the man. "He wasn't scheduled."

"Do you have his home phone?" she asked.

"Who are you?" he asked.

"I'm a friend. More than a friend. I need to find him."

The man put the phone down. Estelle could hear him ask someone if they knew John's phone number. Someone answered. The man came back to the phone and gave her the number. She hung up and called John's home. A woman answered. She was cautious in her response and wanted to know who was calling. After telling her that she and John had become good friends, the woman said she would give her brother a message.

"I'm his sister, Hannah," the woman said.

"Tell him to please come to the Crystal Hotel on Larkin," said Estelle.

"Are you in trouble?" Hannah asked. "He's good at rescuing. Is that it?"

"Yes. Thank you. Thank you for your kindness and trust."

Estelle hung up and cried from relief. The madam entered with a plate of eggs and toast and gave it to Estelle, and set down a pitcher of water.

"I'm hungry and didn't know it. Thank you. I'll bring the pitcher of water to my sister.

CHAPTER 15

JOHN

John came to the hotel several hours later. When he entered, he noticed a few men at the bar drinking hooch and a few women lounging in scanty clothes. Estelle rushed to him and gave him a hug. Her scarf was dislodged from her goiter, and John saw it briefly. He embraced her again.

"Thank you, John. Thank you. This is so kind of you to help out. I am in your debt."

The madam indicated that Estelle should take him into the office. She kept an eye on Estelle and John in a protective gesture and watched as Estelle recounted the story. John pulled out his wallet, gave her money.

"We have to stay another night for my sister's health," Estelle said as she put the money in the madam's hand.

"Please, honey, don't insult me," the madam said.

"It would be our pleasure to pay you for your help," said John.

"I'll take it on the condition that you'll come back and visit me. Drinks on the house."

John walked Estelle out of the office, with his arm around her. On the way up the stairs to visit Mildred, John stopped Estelle and kissed her.

Less than twenty-four hours later it was all over. Mildred was looking better and feeling better. She tried to distract herself by doing homework in her room. Rose was in the kitchen making dinner. Estelle was sitting on her bed, thinking that a beautiful romance was about to begin – it was the culmination of Estelle's dream to fall in love with a handsome, smart, funny, and caring man, especially one who was as far from the traditions and symbols of Judaism as was possible. As an Irishman from the Mission District, John was Catholic not Jewish, and he did not care where she came from, her history, her need to disidentify from being born Jewish. She was sure she was falling madly in love with him.

On the way home from the hotel, while sitting next to her on the streetcar, John was worried how Estelle felt after the ordeal with Mildred.

"I'm very happy you came to my rescue, to Mildred's rescue. It was exhausting and scary, but it had to be done. And thank you for not judging us."

"It's not my place to judge. I think you are a strong woman, besides being beautiful and exotic. But you probably get these compliments all the time."

Estelle laughed and kissed him on the cheek.

"Would you like to spend more time together? I'd like to see you as much as possible."

"That would be lovely, John."

Estelle and John decided they needed more time together. They would leave introductions to the Lanch and Moran families for later.

"Mom, Estelle has a boyfriend," Mildred announced at breakfast a week later. She's going out on dates."

"It's for me to tell, Millie, not you. But yes, I have a new boyfriend. He's from the Mission, and he's Irish."

"I'm not going to faint, darling. I always figured you would not marry a Jewish man. When are you bringing him around?"

"In a few months. I have to get to know him better."

"What about his family?" said Rose.

"What about it?" asked Estelle.

"You may not be welcome with open arms."

"We'll deal with that later, Mom."

On a Saturday night in October, Estelle and John met up with Lucille and Peter at the YMCA for an evening of dancing and bar hopping. The foursome became inseparable on their travels throughout San Francisco's dancehalls, bars, and speakeasies. John fit right in the scene with his sense of humor and his natural ability to tell witty stories. His green Irish eyes were always smiling.

"Let's cut a rug, Stella," said John. "I'm getting good at this."

The first song was the "Sweet Georgia Brown," and John was barely managing his awkward feet and locked knees. The wild exertions of the Charleston caused Estelle's scarf to fall. She was unaware, and John did not want to embarrass her. The classic "I'll See You In My Dreams" began to play softly, and John held her close.

"Stella, my love," he said. "When we're married, I can put you on my insurance, and we'll use it to remove the goiter. No more scarves. No more hiding. It'll be over."

"I'm going to love you forever, John Moran. There will never be a day when I won't love you, even when we find it impossible to live with each other. When we are finished with each other, I will still love you. But you must know I will never be finished with you."

"Marry me, Stella. Maybe it isn't the proper way to do this, but I want to marry you."

One night they decided to go to North Beach to Izzy Gomez's dilapidated loft on Pacific Avenue. Estelle thought it was a scene right out of a movie – Izzy was a barrel of man, rather dark, but fully kind and regal at the same time. The black fedora he never took off was part of his mysterious allure. The bar was on the second floor of an old building with a narrow, rickety staircase that had not been cleaned since the 1906 fire. It had dark, dirty floors with cigarette ashes sprinkled around the edges. When Estelle saw Izzy for the first time, sitting on his perch with a cigarette dangling from his mouth, dropping ashes and pouring drinks, she knew she was witnessing the greatest show on earth. Every once in a while, he was known to cook a steak for someone too drunk to leave.

Without warning, the carefree days of the Jazz Age suddenly came to a halt. On the morning of Tuesday, October 29, 1929, the stock market crashed. The bottom of the American economy opened up to reveal the egregious, corrupt, and unregulated financial activities prevalent during the Roaring Twenties under President Calvin Coolidge. Upon his death, Herbert Hoover pursued the same kind of malevolent cronyism.

The next day around lunchtime, Estelle rode the trolley to the Western Pacific building at the end of Market Street, close to where the ferries and freight ships were docked. It was the tallest steel structure west of the Mississippi, designed in the style of the Italian Renaissance, complete with Roman brick and terra-cotta designs.

On the sixth floor, Estelle entered a plain office space that was well laid out with desks and chairs and no frills. This was an office for men only. John guided her back to his cubicle. He removed a brown paper bag from his desk drawer and pulled out two sandwiches. Then he went to the coffee station, poured two cups of coffee, and brought them back.

"There we go. I hope you're hungry."

She was ravenous. Anticipating meeting up with John made her nervous, but being with him calmed her down. They ate in silence until lunch was finished. He pulled out two cookies for dessert.

"This is wonderful, John. Thank you for lunch."

"Nothing to it, honey."

"Are you worried about your job?" she asked John.

"Why would I worry about that?" he said. "People still take trains – maybe not as many riders if more and more people are out of work, but trains will operate no matter what."

"I don't understand how we got into this position," she said. "One day we are on top of the world with money to spend and food to buy. The next thing we know people are jumping off rooftops and standing in food lines. People have lost their wealth, and ordinary people have lost their jobs. What happened?"

"The Roaring Twenties were just that. Roaring with prosperity for people in the middle class and especially people with wealth. And what did the rich people do?"

"I don't know. I never had money. I worked and saved."

"Then you're one of the few savers. When people have money, they want to make more money anyway they can. It's called speculating. They take risks."

"Where do they do that?" she asked.

"In the stock market. Companies issue stocks from a variety of companies, and people invest in those stocks. If the stocks are good and increase in value, they will sell them when the value of the stocks increase. If they don't sell the stocks, they will hold on to them hoping they will rise even more in value. And they'll make even more money. That's the risk."

"Did people think this prosperity would go on forever?"

"When people see they are making money, they take more risks," said John. "They feel safe, but it actually isn't safe because the banks take risks, too, by loaning money to investors and offering easy credit for land speculators. But remember, money can flow into bad deals; then people can't pay their debts. Banks lose money on their loans, and they can't pay back other customers who cash in their loans. It's a vicious circle. This situation will end badly with a run on the banks."

"And no one saw it coming?"

"Maybe some did, but that was a train no one wanted to get off. More important, my little star, what's our plan going to be?"

Estelle wrote down an address. "Right now, the plan is to meet my mother first and then my father. Come for dinner on Saturday. The other decisions can wait for another day"

On Saturday, Estelle spent most of the afternoon cooking dinner. Mildred was excited to help, since they would be entertaining Estelle's boyfriend. She set the table and arranged flowers she acquired from the market two streets over. Rose relaxed with Louie at the park and stayed out of the way.

"Thanks for helping, Millie. I appreciate it. I want everything to be perfect."

"I want everything to be perfect, too, Es. You and John have done so much for me, and you deserve all the happiness in your lives."

Estelle hugged her sister. "You're growing up fast now. I'm proud of you."

"That means a lot to me, Es. So, when do you think Mama will marry Louie?"

"When she's good and ready," said Estelle. "It's the longest courtship on record."

"What about you and John? Any plans?"

"It's way too soon. We're only a few months into knowing each other. John is jumping the gun a little about getting married, but with this crash, no one knows what's going to happen. I say we keep an even keel. Louie will have a thing or two to say about this banking situation."

"Who's going to want to splurge on prunes?"

They both broke out in laughter simultaneously. It was a cathartic moment, letting go and having fun. They had their struggles and disappointments, but they were still a family and looked after each other.

"We're lucky, Millie. I work for the city and John works for a big railroad company. We have to put our nose to the grindstone and save some money along the way – keep expenses down, see you through high school, and in a couple of years, you'll get a job. It might not be easy, but we'll find something for you."

Rose and Louie came into the apartment holding hands and accompanied by Aunt Anya. They were all laughing.

"Dinner is almost ready," said Estelle. "We're just waiting for John."

"Speaking of the devil …" John said as he entered.

"Is this the famous John Moran?" asked Aunt Anya as she gave him a hug.

"There you are, Miss Rosenbaum. I thought I'd never meet you."

"Call me Anya. And it's a mitzvah to meet you, dear John.

"Sit down everyone," said Rose, "and let's offer a prayer of thanksgiving for our food."

Barukh ata Adonai Eloheinu, melekh ha'olam, hamotzi lehem min ha'aretz.

"Blessed are You, LORD our God, King of the universe, Who brings forth bread from the earth."

It was a lively dinner. Estelle managed to get a piece of meat, origin unknown, and potatoes and carrots. John was a meat and potatoes man – Irish to the core – so she wanted to make a good impression. The conversation was mostly about the stock market crash.

"The banks were the culprits in this crash," said Louie.

"Banks aren't regulated for how much money they can lend," said John.

"And let's not forget that the money sitting in banks is not insured," said Louie. "People have been lining up for days to get their money out of banks. But the truth is that it's already gone. It was gone the minute they gave out speculative loans to customers. To quote from the New Testament, a book I never read from cover to cover, it was borrowing from Peter to pay Paul. That's a Ponzi scheme if I ever saw one."

"Did you take out a loan, Louie?" asked John.

"I took a couple of loans back in the early days of my prune farm around '22 or '23. I secured the money, paid it back, and took out a few more loans to buy rental property in the city. By 1925, my borrowing from banks was a thing of the past. But I'm not out of the woods yet. I've got tenants who won't be able to pay rent. It'll catch up with me by next year unless I can think of a way to utilize the space."

"There might be a few companies who have the means to stay in business with less overhead and would need less space," said Aunt Anya.

"Not a bad idea. I'd have to advertise in the neighborhood where I have my apartments. Want to help me figure it out, Anya?"

"I would if I could, but I'm otherwise engaged with some work and a very nice man," she said. "What about Estelle?"

"I took another civil service test before the crash. I'm now the head stenographer for the president of the city council. I get a bump in salary and one week of vacation."

John stood up and kissed Estelle on the cheek. "I've got an early meeting at the railroad tomorrow morning so I'm off. But I want to thank you Rose and Anya and Estelle and Mildred for a wonderful dinner. And it was very nice to meet you, Louie. I look forward to more conversation with you because I think our country is in trouble."

Everyone said their good-byes and Estelle walked John to the door. There was silence at the table. When Estelle walked back into the room, there were smiles and nods.

"He's a good man," said Rose. "I know he's not Jewish, but it doesn't matter at this moment in time. We like him a lot."

"I second that," said Anya. "I hope he becomes part of our family."

There was no such thing as disposable income in those days. Every penny was spent on rent or food. Estelle and John both lived with their parents to conserve money. But they managed to court by meeting after work or on weekends with picnic baskets and anything that resembled alcohol. Golden Gate Park was a favorite place on the weekends. During the week, if they could manage it, Estelle took the trolley to the Embarcadero and met John on the docks with her picnic basket. They sat on benches facing the water while the cool salty sea air washed over them. They talked for hours.

"I want you to meet my family," John said. "It's been four months since I met yours."

"It's going to be awkward, honey. You'll be bringing home a Jewish girl. Even though I don't practice or believe, I'll still be a Jew in their eyes, and I always will be. This may not go well with your parents. And what about Hannah and your younger brother?"

"We can put it off for another few weeks, but eventually, we'll have to do it. I rarely eat a meal at home and my mother is asking questions."

"It doesn't matter when you introduce me to your parents. They're straight from Ireland. I have a bad feeling that your mother isn't going to be smiling at me with her Irish eyes. The Mission District is tight, and they don't let in strangers. I know this culture from Lucille."

"I've got a better idea. I'd like to meet your old man first," said John.

"He is a tough one, John, but you'll probably get along with him. I don't think there's anyone you don't get along with."

"Probably. But I can't think of anyone. What happened the last time you saw your father?" asked John.

"I haven't seen my father since the day I left his fur store after realizing that Jake was not going to pay me fairly for selling his hat designs. My mother warned me about his devious ways, always trying to make a buck off other people. I didn't listen. I wasn't like other people. I was his daughter. All I wanted from him was to learn to make hats – he was a haberdasher among other talents and a couture designer. And did I mention he was the union president of the Ladies International Garment Union when we lived in Canada?"

"That's impressive. So what's wrong with him?"

"He's a bastard and an abuser. If anyone becomes his enemy, if anyone crosses him, including my mother, he will bully and abuse that person into the ground. If he saw my mother lighting the Friday night candles, he would rage, and I would hide."

"You're still hiding, honey, but I don't mind. You can be what you want, believe what you want. It makes no difference to me."

CHAPTER 16

MEET THE FAMILY

Estelle opened the door to her father's fur shop on Geary Street. She and John entered and waited for several seconds for Jake to come out of the back room. When he saw his daughter, he showed no surprise and no curiosity about the man standing next to her.

"The prodigal daughter has returned," Jake said with sarcasm.

"Hi, Dad. I'm sorry I didn't give you notice that I was coming by to see you. It was a spur of the moment idea. This is John Moran. I wanted you two to meet."

John extended his hand. "It's good to meet you, Mr. Lanch."

"What's this about, Esther?"

Estelle rolled her eyes. "My name is Estelle, Dad. I'm introducing you to the man I'm going to marry."

"That's a good one. By the look of him he's not a Jew. How did your mother take it?"

"Mom has already met John, and I thought you might want to meet him, too," she said. "If not, then we can leave and let you get back to work."

John explored the room, examining the individual furs and jackets, hats, and neck warmers. "You've got some good-looking merchandise here, Mr. Lanch. The hats are snazzy."

"What do you know about furs and hats?" asked Jake.

"Nothing, but I can appreciate the designs and see your talent. Your daughter makes her own hats. I believe you taught her to do that."

Jake puffed his chest out and started to look for something in his fur pile.

"Nice to meet you, Jake. Good luck in your business."

Jake had no response. John disarmed him and calmed the bully.

"Good-bye, Dad."

Estelle and John left the store without another word. They did not talk until they got on a trolley that ran in the direction of Fisherman's Wharf.

"I'm sorry, hon," Estelle said once they found seats. "That's just the way he is. He was born that way, trapped in his anger."

"He liked me, Stella," said John. "He'll be back for another round."

"I hope not."

"Why did he call you Esther?"

"That was my birth name. Aunt Anya changed it. She thought it sounded too biblical."

"I like the name. Anya was perceptive about you."

They hopped off the trolley at the bottom of the hill that ended at the Wharf. There were few restaurants, mostly shacks, opened for the customers wandering around the docks. John grabbed Estelle's hand, and they walked about a mile in each direction, enjoying each other's company, holding each other against the winter wind and talking of nothing and everything like all young people do when they are in love.

The economy worsened after New Year's. Winter blustered in. People grew hungry. When Estelle got off the streetcar to go to work each morning, she was emotionally challenged. Every day, more and more people sought shelter near the entrance to City Hall. She gave the coins she carried in her purse to the women with children before entering the building.

Inside City Hall, the composition of the workforce seemed to change daily. For those who ran the government, it was not only a matter of recognizing that there was less funding for the various agencies, they wrestled with the obvious problems of how to cope with the wretched fallout from the economic collapse of the country. City Council meetings and problem-solving sessions went on for weeks and months.

John was also experiencing serious issues at the railroad. Trains were not running on time. Layoffs occurred frequently. Ridership worsened.

On a cold winter morning, John and Estelle walked silently, hand in hand, up the steep steps to 1578 Noe Street. Estelle noticed the stained-glass window to the right of the door.

"Ma, I'm here with Estelle," he said as he opened the door and walked inside.

Mary Moran walked out of the farmhouse kitchen in her apron, wiping her hands on an old blue dish towel, gray hair tied in a knot on top of her head. She had a sturdy body and a scowl on her wrinkled face. She did not greet Estelle.

"Good, you're here, John" she said in an almost unintelligible Irish brogue. "Your father's working, and I need you to look at my stove. I can't get the wood to burn."

"Ma, this is Estelle. She's my girlfriend."

Mary turned and walked back into the kitchen. There was no exchange of pleasantries, only silence between Estelle and Mary – not a hostile word spoken, but not an acknowledgement that they existed in the same universe. Estelle knew it was a sign of things to come.

John entered the kitchen behind his mother. Estelle followed. "The wood is wet. Dad could have handled this."

"Don't you know, he works seven days a week," she said, or at least that's what Estelle thought she said. "He's working himself into the grave."

The paint on the old wooden cabinets was peeling, and the linoleum floor was cracked. Estelle walked to the back of the kitchen to see the backyard. Well-worn stairs lead down to a concrete patio. In the upper section of the yard, four goats grazed on the grass. Estelle could not imagine that scene in any backyard in San Francisco. She was rendered speechless. Between his mother's incomprehensible brogue and her animosity toward Jews, it seemed impossible that Estelle could make things work with John. But she loved him, and that was that.

"Ma, the wood needs to dry. And with rain in the air, nothing is going to dry. When Tim gets home from school, have him get you some dry wood."

John reached into his pocket and pulled out some change. He left it on the kitchen table.

"Have a good rest of the day."

The holiday season of 1930 proved to be difficult for John and Estelle. After the disastrous meeting with his mother, John made sure that she met his siblings. He needed to have some back up in the family regarding Estelle. Not being Irish was one thing; being Jewish cast a larger shadow.

Two days before Christmas, John's siblings – Hannah, a sweet woman in her early-20s, Tim, a teenager full of energy and fun, and Tom, the oldest brother, late 20s, another good-looking Irishman but lacking John's charm, and Tom's wife, Margaret, a pleasant but nervous woman who said little – met John and Estelle at the Blarney diner in the Mission, a neighborhood meetup for most of the Irish families in the Eureka Valley.

"John told me you work in city government, Estelle," said Tom. "What's that like? I want to get into city politics someday."

"I'm just a stenographer, Tom, but from what I see and hear, there's never a dull moment. Something is always going on, what with making new laws and trying to get the city agencies to work efficiently."

"Yes, that's exactly what I want to get into." Tom replied.

"Hannah, what about you? John says you're studying to be a school teacher?"

"I want to teach in the neighborhood at St. Paul's grammar school," said Hannah.

"And Tim here is still in high school," John added. "He goes to Mission High."

"When I grow up, I want to be the life of every party I go to," Tim said with a wild laugh.

The table went quiet. "I think it's time to order," John announced.

"You realize our mother will never accept you into the family, Estelle," said Tom. "She's one of those strict Catholics. No other religion exists except Catholicism."

"Hush," said Hannah. "Why are you saying this?"

John said forcefully, "Don't go there, Tom."

"Go where?" asked Estelle.

"I'm guessing you are not of the faith," Tom said. "It's going to be a tough road."

"If you mean, I'm not Catholic, you're right," said Estelle. "I don't have a religion."

"You come from the Fillmore."

"And I went to Commerce High. So what of it?"

"And I went to Mission High," Tom said.

John got up to leave. "Sit down, Johnny," said Hannah.

"You are out of line, Tom. No one has a right to address Estelle as anything but a smart and beautiful woman."

Estelle got up and stood beside John. "You don't have to defend me, John. I can stand up to your mother or be as sweet as apple pie to your family. And Tom, if you have any issue with me, keep it to yourself. And with that, we wish you a Merry Christmas."

John put some money on the table, and they walked out of the Blarney.

"I love you, Estelle Lanch," he said. "And I'm going to marry you."

The Lanch and Rosenbaum contingent gathered at Aunt Anya's for Hanukkah dinner. Louie included. As much as Estelle would have liked to have John included, they decided that they did not need any more complications. The menorah was centered on the table. Rose lit one candle as she began to say the first prayer of the eight-day celebration:

Baruch atah, Adonai Eloheinu, Melech haolam, shehecheyanu v'kiy'manu v'higiyanu laz'man hazeh.

"Estelle, how is it going with John lately?" asked Louie. "What's happening with the railroads?"

"Aren't those railroad jobs pretty secure during hard times?" asked Rose.

"John tells me that there are ups and downs but if they can keep to scheduling, then the trains can run on time. And that's John's job. Scheduling is crucial."

"Any talk of marriage?" asked Anya.

"It won't happen for a while," said Estelle.

"Things don't look good," said Louie. We're in trouble everywhere, and it will get worse."

Anya got up from the table and signaled Estelle to help her in the kitchen.

"Aren't you going to John's for Christmas?" Anya asked.

"I'm sure I won't be going. What can I expect from the Irish? His mother knew I was Jewish and scowled at me when John brought me over. And was also insulting when we met at dinner one night. I'm an outsider and always will be."

"Let me give you some advice, honey," said Anya. "It's not important to be understood or liked by those people. They wear their prejudice on their sleeve. You don't win them over. You don't change their minds. Put your blinders on and remember they can't hurt you. If you marry John, it's only a once-a-year dinner or maybe one of his siblings will take on the holiday. But in the long run, you're free to do as you like. They can't hurt you."

Estelle gave her Aunt Anya a hug. She was always ready with sound advice. She understood more than anyone how Estelle felt about hiding her identity.

"Now, let's go back in and finish dinner. Why don't we plan Mildred's graduation party in June and give her some joy?"

As Anya started to walk out of the kitchen, Estelle noticed she was slightly limping.

"Auntie, why are you limping? I never noticed that before."

"Oh, my dear, I'm fine. My hip is sticking and I need a jump start. I am seeing a doctor about it. Maybe he will give me something."

New Year's 1931 was not a happy holiday. It was over a year into the Depression, and still, there were no solutions to America's economic problems. Prohibition was still part of the landscape, but it did not have much effect on the economy. On her walk to work, Estelle saw even more people in the streets begging for food and shelter. All they wanted was relief from the government, and that was not forthcoming. Estelle thought about her father's political world. Maybe Karl Marx was right when he said, "From each according to his ability."

Estelle thought that celebrating New Year's Eve with Lucille and Peter would pull her out of her funk about what was going on with John's family. The couples decided to go to the Castro District to see *Mata Hari* and eat dinner at the Cove close by the theater.

"What do you think, John, about this bad economic situation forced upon us?" Peter asked John over dinner.

"I'm no economist and I don't have a crystal ball, but if I were a betting man, I'd say we are just getting started. Watch the breadlines, and you'll get a good understanding of how long the Depression will last."

"That's bleak," said Peter as he reached into a pocket for his flask and took a long swig.

"Do you have investments in the market?" asked John.

"Afraid so. And I can't get my money out of my damn bank."

The line was long going into the theater, and there was some pushing and shoving among those who already had too much to drink. The couples could not sit together. After the movie, on the way out, people were more physically aggressive.

Peter said, "The Jewish rabble are taking up too much space in the theater."

Lucille let out an audible gasp. John clenched his fists. Estelle stopped walking. "Too many Jews in the theater for your taste?" asked Estelle.

"That was uncalled for, Peter," said Lucille as Peter walked on, leaving the three of them standing in front of the theater. "He is a pig. And a jerk. And I told you that, Es, the night I met him."

"I almost punched him," said John, "except he's drunk. Won't do any good."

"Watch out for your Irish temper, John." Lucille said. "He's not worth it."

A few weeks later, after work, John wanted Estelle to meet his father, Dennis. "He's rarely home, so we have to catch him on his schedule," said John.

"Dockworkers work too long and hard and get paid nothing. I know this from working in City Hall. Lots of complaints and injuries. and their union is bad. The situation is criminal."

"Sounds like it's a job for Jake," John said. "He loves a good union fight."

"Wrong union. Jake only has love for the ladies garment union."

"Dennis was born a teamster," said John. "He always worked on the docks at the Embarcadero. He fits right in – a big Irishman who drinks too much. If there is a bar fight, you can bet he's in the middle. I've spent more than a few evenings hauling him home."

"I don't want to meet him, John," said Estelle. "I think I've had plenty of dirty looks in your house. Except for Hannah and Tim, the rest can go to hell."

"You don't know him yet, Estelle. He's not like my mother or Tom. He has a heart of gold. Give him a look-see and then tell me he's a bastard."

John was hurt and walked away from Estelle to hop a streetcar. She didn't chase after him – she had enough of the Irish clan.

Rose was still at work when Estelle got home so she took time to do some thinking. How much longer would her mother be working at Schlage? Would she get laid off? How was her health? She heard Rose open the door.

"Hi, Mom. How was work?"

"Good. Schlage cut some staff and I've taken on additional administrative work.

"That's great, Mom. I'm so proud of you."

"Well, Louie wants to marry me, and I guess that's good, but I'm not ready to quit.

"The question is do you want to marry Louie? Are you ready to settle down."

"Don't get me wrong," said Rose. "I'd like to marry him. He's a good man. But right now, I can build up my bank account with the extra work."

"You're as pragmatic as I am, Mom. I'm glad you're waiting a while longer until you marry, Mom. I'm also waiting to marry John. Too much going on I don't like. He wants me to meet his father."

"And you think you'll get the same response as his mother gave you?"

"Unless he's in his cups. Then he won't notice."

"I think we need to have John over for dinner more often. It's got to be tough for him. For everyone in our families."

Estelle called John at work the next day. He was busy and tried to get off the phone.

"Please, honey, I'm sorry. I got off track with all of this talk of marriage and the financial situation. I do want to meet your father. I'm sure he's all that you say he is."

"Thank you for staying with me. We're only doing this as a formality like we did with Rose."

"You see how ridiculous religion is," said Estelle. "It's defining us and it shouldn't. We're walking a tightrope, and we have to go through the motions to make sense of our lives."

"I think you're saying our identity should be each other."

"I could not have said it better, John."

"I'll let you know when it's a good time to meet my Pa."

John hung up the phone and called his mother.

"What time does Pa get home from work?" asked John. "I need to talk to him."

"About what?" Mary asked.

"It's between me and Pa. When does he usually get home?"

"Five in the afternoon if he doesn't go to the pub and start drinking. That's all I know."

John called Hannah to ask her when the best day was to see his father. "Thursday," she said.

"Why Thursday?" asked John.

"It has to do with his drinking," said Hannah. "The first two days of the week, he hits it hard, then he rests on Wednesday. If he doesn't rest, he'll never make it to work on Thursday. And if he misses too many days of work, he will get fired. So he behaves himself on Thursday to show he's a team player, a good worker, and then he drinks hard on Friday after work."

"Are you sure he's home Thursday afternoons?" John asked Tim.

"Yes, sometimes he comes to the gym to see me play basketball after school."

On the first Thursday of March, Estelle and John walked into the house on Noe Street.

Dennis was sitting on a dark gray loveseat in the small living room, smoking his pipe and reading the newspaper. He did not notice Estelle at first, but when he saw her, he stood up to greet her properly.

"Pa, this is Estelle, my girlfriend," said John.

"You're a pretty little thing," said Dennis. "Come sit on the sofa."

Estelle and John sat down next to each other. A bay window let in late afternoon sunlight. Dennis moved to one of the two heavy greenish armchairs with white doilies covering the arms that sat on opposite sides of the brick fireplace. On the mantel, two candles were lit on either side of a painting of Jesus hanging from a cross with blood coming out of his sides. Three lamps with green shades dotted the room. Estelle thought it felt like a séance was about to happen.

Dennis was a strongly built Irishman with a ruddy complexion either from drink or the sun or both. He was the picture of a teamster. His hands were rough, his fingers thick, dirt caught under his fingernails. His eyes were green, but they appeared more like slits when he smiled. Although his teeth were brown from smoking cigarettes, his smile was a winner.

Mary came around the corner to listen without acknowledging Estelle.

"Nice to meet you, young lady," he said in his Irish brogue and a warm smile. "You are a beauty, not in the Irish way, thank God – but are you in the movies?"

"It's good to meet you, Mr. Moran," said Estelle. "No, I'm not in the movies."

"I'm Dennis, young lady," he said. "Don't go formal with me. I came from County Cork where all Irishman are friendly and down to earth. Mary, who you met already, is from Kerry. They're all nasty. Now, we got that out of the way, are you sweet on my Johnny?"

Estelle smiled without answering.

"We got that out of the way, I see, and now what do you do?"

"I work for the City Council in the stenography pool, Dennis," she said.

"She's a keeper, son. At least she doesn't clean houses like my Mary."

Mary turned around and walked into the kitchen.

"Most people are poor in Ireland, you know, and we came over in waves in the 1800s – when the potato famine hit us hard in Ireland, and that's when we left on the boat for America. Not all of us Moran's. Some are still there."

Dennis looked around the room, then went behind the sofa where John and Estelle were sitting and put his hands behind the pillows.

"Pa, what are you doing?"

"Damn, Mary. When I'm at work, she collects my hooch from my hiding places."

"Pa, we'll go now, but thanks for meeting Estelle," said John, rising up. "See you later."

Dennis kissed Estelle on the cheek. "You'll be good for my son, lass. Take care of him."

Mary came back into the living room. "Stop it, Dennis. You've already been drinking today. And they'll be no wedding between those two."

"Who are you, Mary Moriarty?" asked Dennis. "You're not Jesus, although you act like you've been hanging on the cross your whole life."

"You don't know the whole story, Dennis," Mary said. "You don't know who she is."

John took Estelle's hand. "Watch what you say, Ma."

"Johnny, what's she talking about?" Dennis asked.

"Don't listen to her, Pa. We will do what we want." John hugged his father and he and Estelle left the house and went to a streetcar stop. Neither spoke until they reached the tracks.

"I can't go through this again, John. She's tough and it's not worth me trying to make nice with your mother. If we marry, we'll never find the glue to make us stick with all the hate."

"I'm not going back. And what do you mean, if we marry?"

John got down on one knee. "Estelle Lanch, will you marry me?" She did not answer.

"Will you marry me?"

Estelle pulled John to his feet and wrapped her arms around him. "Honey, I don't want to pull your family apart."

"You can't and won't. In time we will be civil with each other and get along once a year when we meet. We will be fine."

The streetcar was coming toward the stop. "Hurry up and answer me, Stella. Marry me."

CHAPTER 17

TYING THE KNOT

John turned twenty on February 21, 1931. There was no time for a birthday party. Estelle and Rose gave him a little dinner celebration, but it was brief since he was overwhelmed with work. Railroad life was in his blood, but administrating the details were getting more difficult to manage with all of the firings, rescheduling, and overtime. It was a challenge to keep accurate records. The binder system in theory worked, but implementing the paperwork and keeping up the with rapid scheduling changes put a strain on him – it felt like it was 1900 and the trains were never on time. He did not see much of Estelle for the first six months of that year.

Estelle was working overtime every day. With poverty increasing everywhere, City Hall was in a frenzy trying to take care of the poor by providing housing and establishing food pantries and soup lines. It seemed impossible to handle the volume of needs. Cars sat parked in the streets. There was no gas to buy and no people to drive them. City projects stalled. Restaurants, bars, and even some schools closed. Taxes were reduced, and payments were nonexistent. Where was the money going to come from to pay city workers and employees, School teachers, judges, and organizers? Everyone in City Hall put their heads down and focused on their work. They were exhausted.

There was no talk of marriage between Estelle and John. They got through the summer with early Sunday morning road trips in Tom's borrowed car – even though gas was harder and harder to get – driving along El Camino Real and picnicking in San Jose parks. They stocked up on cold meats, kosher dill pickles and herring, which John loved. He was not used to Jewish food, but he fell instantly in love with the tastes and smells. Irish food had no flavor and was mostly overcooked. Often, they drove so far south that they caught a glimpse of a gigantic airplane hangar called Hangar One at the Naval air station on the Bayfront at Sunnyvale.

South of San Francisco was farm country. Driving along The El Camino Real highway they saw a plethora of orchards of apricots, peaches, pears, and cherries.

"Someplace around here must be Louie's prune farm," said John. "See those white blossoms? They're from the prune tree orchards that are spread over the Santa Clara Valley. These farms have seen better days. They're all dried up."

Sometimes Estelle and John went to The Rose Bowl on Saturday night to dance in Larkspur. It was not as crowded as it was during the late 1920s, but it still drew people who caught the ferries either from the Ferry Building or from Sausalito, or from the Hyde Street pier where they drove their cars onto to the auto ferry. Tickets cost fifty-four cents one way for the thirty-two minute ferry trip to Sausalito. The ferry ride was always a great adventure, invigorating and a bit cold and windy. It was too expensive to eat or drink on the ride, but John always brought some hooch. If he was clever and funny enough, one of the guys offered him a cigarette, bought him a beer for fifteen cents or a mixed drink for twenty-five cents.

Estelle's favorite dates were when she and John spent the day at Fleishhacker Pool or even better, when they drove to Neptune Beach amusement park and resort in Alameda on the east shore of San Francisco Bay. It had two swimming pools with filtered salt water pumped from the Bay. Every spectacle conceived by the owners of amusement parks around America were on display – death-defying stunts, entertainment acts and free concerts, beauty contests, fireworks, picnic areas, flashy dance halls with mirrors and chandeliers, big dining rooms, a stadium, and even a movie theater. The good old days were ending.

By the end of 1931 Americans fell deeper into the doldrums. There was not much of a Christmas or a Hanukkah. Separate celebrations and family meetups continued. Estelle got to know Hannah better and they became friends. Hannah was rather stern and studious, but Estelle liked those characteristics. Tom was aloof, but he was sickly and spent all his time with Margaret. Tim was the youngest trying to grow up. For years, Dennis struggled with worsening health issues. He worked himself to the bone on the docks, spent too much time with the teamsters in bars, and fought the dead end battle of making a decent living to support the family.

"I think we should marry, Stella," said John one evening as they were getting a bite to eat at Compton's Cafeteria. "Life has become too complicated living in two different places."

Estelle threw her arms around him and hugged him for a long time.

"The timing is right, honey. I'll let everyone know. Whoever can come, will come. You take care of your family. Ask everyone, even your mother. What do you think about the day after April Fool's' Day at City Hall. I'll make all the arrangements."

"I'll ask for the day off and make it up later. I'm sure my Pa will be working. I'm sure we will surprise no one. They all expect it."

On April 2, 1932, John and Estelle went down to San Francisco City Hall and took out a marriage license at two o'clock in the afternoon. Lucille was with them, as was Hannah and Tom and his wife, Margaret. They seemed to be happy about the marriage. Anya came – she will not miss it – but it was a weekday and Rose had to work. Mildred cancelled her piano lessons while Tim stayed in school. They were married by a justice of the peace in a plain, windowless office on the ground floor. The justice of the peace had too much to drink at lunch – his Irish eyes were twinkling. John kibitzed with the judge, and they shared a laugh while John provided information about himself and his fiancée. The ceremony took four minutes. Without fanfare, without champagne toasts, Estelle and John kissed and began their exciting and creative life together.

John arranged for a honeymoon trip on the Western Pacific line to Canada when one came available with extra seats. Estelle wanted to see Montreal again, and Canada turned out to be the first of many trips riding the rails together. John was a skillful traveler, and it was easy for Estelle to have him take the lead. Traveling together gave them the opportunity to solidify their interests and passions, their love of art and architecture. Estelle was surprised that John seemed to be a natural historian. He read history any time he got the opportunity.

Estelle and John lived with Rose for a year after they were married. Rose wanted them to stay longer, but Estelle did not feel right accepting.

"Stella, Rose knows money is tight for us, but on the other hand, we're contributing to her cost of living. She gets to save some money, too. It won't be forever. And someday she and Louie will get married."

To break the monotony, Estelle and John spent time at Aunt Anya's. She was always thrilled to have them stay for a weekend. Anya had a boyfriend by then – against her better judgment – and most of the time, she was not in residence. It turns out her boyfriend was the doctor she saw for the pain in her hip. He fixed her right up and then some.

John was adamant that the Western Pacific Railroad should take care of his wife's goiter and assign a doctor to perform the operation. It took months to handle the insurance paperwork. Estelle never brought up the subject. If anyone could make a miracle, it was her husband. At the end of 1933, John came home to Rose's apartment, looking for Estelle.

"Rose, where is she?" he asked. "I have great news."

"She's not home from work," Rose said. "It's Friday. Sometimes she has a drink with her office friends."

"Do you know where she went?" he asked.

"She's mentioned the Little Shamrock, but it doesn't mean that's where she is."

John left the apartment in a hurry. He wanted to tell Estelle that he got permission from his insurance to allow her to get her operation. He started at the Little Shamrock but Estelle's gang wasn't there. He then headed over to the Saloon and Shotwell's. He finally went to a dive bar called the Elixir. He had a shot of gin and lit a cigarette.

"Different than the rotgut bathtub gin, eh?" asked the bartender.

"This stuff is beyond my budget."

"Well, have one on me, man." The bartender poured another glass.

The gin went down slowly this time. It was smooth and John felt the release of stress. "One more and then I will get out of here."

John made it home late and tipsy. When Estelle saw him in that condition, she was furious. He tried to explain, but she cut him off.

"You can sleep on the couch, John," she said as she marched into the bedroom.

Estelle got up early and left the apartment. She refused to look at her husband. He heard the door close and bounded off the couch. Rose came into the living room.

"Good morning, John," said Rose. "How about some coffee?"

"Morning. Yes, please. Where did she go?"

"Maybe a walk, coffee with a friend. Were you a bad boy last night?"

"I went to three, maybe four bars and never found her. And then I stopped off at the Elixir and had a couple of drinks."

"A couple too many," she said. "Estelle will be back. Be patient."

"I have great news. Insurance will cover the operation on her goiter."

"That's wonderful, John. She'll forget all of this when she hears that. I'll fix you a breakfast fit for a king."

"Some king. More like a clown."

John picked up a newspaper and drowned his sorrows in the bad economic news: "1933: The First Hundred Days and the New Deal." He could not focus and closed the paper.

That afternoon Estelle and John accidentally met outside the apartment building. They looked at each other with solemn faces. John took her hand and squeezed it gently. Estelle threw her arms around him and wept.

"I won't do that again, Stella," he said.

"Yes, you will. You're an Irishman. It goes with the territory. But I love you anyway. Come on, let's take a walk."

They went down O'Farrell and looked in the windows. Few people were out at 5:30 in the afternoon. Restaurants were empty, as were shops and stores.

"It is sad to see everything so empty," said Estelle.

John stopped walking. "Stella, I have something to tell you. You can schedule the operation on your neck any time you want. It'll be covered by insurance."

Estelle could hardly speak. "John Moran, I'll love you forever for this. I will be grateful every day for the rest of my life. Nothing will ever compare to this gift."

She kissed him deeply, her face full of tears. "I think it's time to get out of my mom's apartment. What do you think?"

"We might be able to swing it. What about our savings?"

"There's about one hundred dollars in my cookie jar. Thank goodness I didn't put it in a bank account. We could have lost it all. What do you have?"

"I did a few favors for my boss – there were several schedule discrepancies, and I fixed them so they made sense – meaning he screwed up. He's not very good at what he does, but when that happens, I help him make it right. There's a fifty in it for me, and sometimes a few Jacksons. I used to stash them in a locked drawer at my office, but since the crash, I don't leave cash at work. I got a locker at one of the train stops until we could get our place."

"You should have been a cop or a criminal, darling," said Estelle. "I think we need to move out, and besides, I'm tired of my job at City Hall. They're letting people go, and that makes more work for me without a pay increase. I heard that Canada Dry has an opening so I went over and took a test. I got the job. I was going to surprise you with it. I get two more dollars a week, but if I prove myself, I'll put another buck in my pocket, as you would say."

"Who did you hear about Canada Dry from?"

"Evelyn, the woman who took a chance on me at the city council, told me about it. She thought I deserved more money when I got promoted to the mayor's office. Canada Dry, here I come. I'm giving a week's notice,"

"First things first. In between jobs, get the goiter off."

"And then we will figure out where we're going to live, what location is good for both of us. We have enough for the first month's rent and more. Let's try the Mission first. I wish we could afford the Avenues. Maybe someday we'll get closer to the beach."

"That's my Stella." He stopped, twirled Estelle around, and kissed her.

Estelle had her goiter removed after more than twenty years. It was a two-centimeter raised bump, multi-colored, white and red nesting an inch to the right of the front of her throat. The biopsy indicated it was never infected. The removal of the goiter left a scar in its place. After the bandage was removed, Estelle could easily cover it with makeup, but in time, it would fade. The doctor told her she need not have waited so long to have it removed. Two months after birth, it could have been done.

The first Saturday after the operation, with a bandage covering her wound, Estelle and John walked the streets around Mission Dolores. They went into the mission and admired its old Spanish style. After getting serious about finding a place to live, they viewed several apartments – most were old but livable.

"Don't worry, honey," Estelle told her husband. "I can make any place look marvelous – curtains, rugs, I can even upholster furniture."

By the end of the day, exhausted but excited, they selected a large second-floor apartment, which was five dollars more in rent than the ones on the third floor.

"No elevator, John. Good exercise."

John took her in his arms and felt relief that they had taken a step to independence. He paid for the first month and told the landlord they would move in within the week.

"Where do we get a truck?" asked Estelle as they walked into the street.

"Hey, honey, this is the Mission, and I have friends. It's time you met them."

As the depression took its toll, life began to change for the Moran's and for all Americans. Estelle and John read the newspapers incessantly. After dinner most nights, their discussions centered on the over twelve million people who were out of work and those who were working but experiencing drastic wage cuts.

As usual, John was able to sum up the state of the country after Franklin Roosevelt was sworn in as president in 1933: "We are in the middle of the worst economic disaster in American history. Add to that, a drought which could go on for a decade, and there is hardly any affordable housing, soup kitchens, everywhere. And long breadlines. It's a catastrophe."

"Jake always said that the myth of the rugged individual was a fraud. A man needs more to work his way up the economic ladder to provide for their families than a pick axe. The old communist spent years talking about how America needed to get rid of capitalism. He believed everybody should be treated equally."

Suddenly, Estelle felt the need to see her father for no reason than to tell him she married John and to ask how he was doing. "Want me to come with you, Stella?" asked John.

"I know he likes you because you pose no threat. It's one of the great things I love about you, darling, so the answer is yes, come with me."

"I'll bring him a carton of Camels," he said.

CHAPTER 18

TO LIFE

As they walked inside the shop, John hollered. "Jake! It's John here and Estelle!"

Jake appeared from the back, wiping his hands on the bib apron, making it look like an abstract painting.

"Well, isn't this a surprise." Jake peered at his daughter. "No scarf. No goiter. I hardly know you."

"How are you, Jake?" Estelle asked.

"How do I look? The goddamn city is taking a nosedive and bringing all of us with it."

John held out a carton of Camels. "For you, Jake."

"That's nice of you, Jack," he said as he greedily took the carton from John's hand.

"We wanted to tell you we got married a while back and thought you'd like to know."

"No surprise. I figured." He held out his hand to John. "You both did well."

He looked at his daughter as if he wanted to give her a hug, but Estelle did not move toward him. John put his arm around his wife.

"Estelle got a new job, Jake. She works for Canada Dry." "Good for you. Out of the bowels of city government and into the dark side of corporate greed. I'm not sure it's a step up."

"You pretty much summed up my work history," Estelle replied. "How are things going for you?"

"I make a living with what I have. The few customers that come around pay up."

"What's going on with the unions nowadays?" asked John.

"We're active. Half my time is about my meetings. We've got a few cells around town. The union doesn't like the commies, but they let us in anyway to hear about our ideas."

"I'm glad you're alright, Jake. I'll probably drop in from time to time."

"Are you still sewing, Esther?"

"I will always sew."

"Well, you look good. By the way, if you've got a free night, I sure could use a ride to one of my meetings in Petaluma. It's the best cell meeting in the area."

"Sure Jake," said John. "When we have nothing better to do, we will take you to a few."

After Estelle and John left the shop, they started to laugh in unison.

"John, tell me you didn't mean that we'd give him a ride."

"Why not? It's just another adventure, and the old man will be thankful. Come on, Stella. I think Jake has softened a bit. He even called me Jack!"

"You're incorrigible, John Moran. Have I told you lately that I love you?"

Dennis died a month after Estelle and John got married. No one knew how he died. "Maybe cancer," said John. "No one knew if he was in pain. Ma never thought to ask."

"He masked the pain with alcohol," said Estelle. "But I liked him – his thick brogue and Irish antics. I would have liked to get to know him better."

"The funeral is in three days at St. Paul's church. My old elementary school. You don't have to come."

"I won't let you go alone. I want to pay my respects to those Irish eyes. And I'm sure your father did the best he could under the circumstances for his family."

"The best he could was trying to survive. Off the boat at Ellis Island, working his way to San Francisco – a city he loved – marrying a strong woman who worked her hands to the bone and raised four kids."

"I'd say that is a decent legacy," Estelle said. "He will be remembered."

Estelle was not looking forward to the funeral. There would be plenty of dirty looks. The Irish tribe would be in attendance, probably in their cups before the priest read his eulogy at the altar. Or maybe he would be still hungover from the wake the night before. She would put on a black veil, and Mary Moran would not recognize her if luck was on her side.

Most of the male mourners were shuffling their feet in the early morning cold by the front steps when Estelle and John arrived. They were smoking their last cigarette until the funeral started. It was a neighborhood church, small compared to the many cathedrals throughout the forty-seven districts in San Francisco. Designed for the residents around the Noe Street neighborhood – a stone's throw from the Moran house – its architecture was simple and without decorative carvings. Estelle did not expect much, although she was surprised at the beauty of the tall steeple.

"My elementary school is on the left next to the church," said John. "Looks like they fixed it up with spit and elbow grease. Behind the church is where the diocesan priests live."

"How much did you hate it?" asked Estelle.

"I don't have fond memories – I got slapped on the knuckles and kicked out of every class I was in. The nuns were angry, and the priests were horny. Great environment to grow up in while you learn your ABCs."

Estelle walked into a church after decades of familiar smells and bad memories. It was well taken care of – clean and smelling of burning candles. The church was half full, and she almost turned around and bolted outside. John suspected as much and clasped his wife's arm and walked her into the foyer. By habit, John made the sign of the cross. Then he smiled at Estelle who was none too pleased. Estelle lost the rituals long ago. In the light of that day, she considered it pagan. The call and response inside, the singing of hymns, and the priest mumbling something about God carrying Dennis Moran's soul up to heaven gave Estelle chills. There was no heaven and there was no hell – only ashes to ashes, dust to dust.

The women sat in the pews toward the front, whispering quietly to each other, no doubt gossiping. Mary, Hannah, Tim, Tom, and Margaret sat in the front row with eyes straight ahead. Estelle wondered if any one of them shed a tear.

"I should go up and sit with the family," he said.

Estelle said nothing as John walked down the aisle to the pew where his family sat and nudged his youngest brother so he could squeeze into a seat. When Mary saw him, she turned her head to the back of the church. Her eyes searched for John's wife, but Estelle already left the church. She stood by the front steps several feet away from the few men who passed a flask of alcohol back and forth.

"Do any of you men have a cigarette?" she asked.

One of the men handed her a cigarette and lit it for her. She usually did not smoke, but she felt she needed to relax. She inhaled deeply and found a bench to sit on as she waited in the cold for the funeral to be over. Estelle would not give Mary the satisfaction of being seen in a church, even with a black veil covering her face.

The ordeal was not over yet. There was a gathering at the Moran's house. Hannah met them at the door with a warm greeting. She gave her sister-in-law a quick hug.

"You know Tom is sick," Hannah stated to John. "Margaret is worried to death."

"Slow down, Hannah. We just buried Pa."

"Sorry. I have to help, Ma. It's crowded there." She walked off to the kitchen.

"Who are all these people?" asked Estelle.

"Mostly friends and workers from the docks. The relatives died off years ago either by working or drinking themselves to death. Come to think of it, I never knew an Irishman who did not die of drink."

"The Irish have the black gene, John. It's your curse."

"I'm afraid we do."

The dining room table was full of food – sandwiches with corned beef, salads, potatoes, and a few pies – along with silverware, plates, and water pitchers. Estelle was starving. She skipped breakfast because she was meeting John in the Mission at nine in the morning. He had an appointment to confer with the priest conducting the ceremony. That same priest was piling food on his plate. One of the men walked up to the priest, put his arm around him, and whispered something in his ear. Another man brought the priest a glass of white liquid. With a little too much vocal force, the priest said, "Now that's good gin, fellows."

Tim stood next to Estelle, shifting from one foot to the other. "Is this the first time you've been in a Catholic church," he asked.

"No, Tim. I went to Catholic school in Canada and New York, and we all had to go to Mass. The hymns were nice."

"Does the Jewish religion have singing?" he asked.

"Yes, It's in Hebrew. In the Catholic church, Latin is spoken, but you know that."

The conversation awkwardly ended, but Tim tried. Estelle liked him. His brother, Tom, was of a different demeanor. His illness was a constant burden.

Hannah came over and took Estelle by the arm and walked her to Tom and Margaret.

"We are a family now," she said, "so let's put our grievances aside and celebrate Pa."

"How are you, Tom?" asked Estelle.

"I have my days," he replied.

Margaret looked down and was silent. She was holding her emotions in so as not to make a scene. Hannah hugged her. John came over to join them.

"How's your treatment going, Tom?" John asked.

"Doctors want me to go back to the sanitarium," said Tom. "I guess that tells you how I'm doing with this TB."

"I'm sorry. Please let me know if you need anything."

"Margaret's going to drive me to Santa Cruz. Thanks anyway."

John impulsively hugged his brother. It was a difficult moment for the family. Estelle was saddened by the revelation that Tom was not getting better. He did not look well.

"I think Rose is getting married," said Estelle to John while they were getting ready for work shortly after the funeral. I'm not sure of the date or time or even where. I hope it's not in a Jewish temple. Louie does not seem that religious. But you never know."

"The wedding might interfere with our trip to Mexico in the spring," John said.

"John Ambrose Moran. What trip to Mexico? You can't spring this on me."

"It's your first anniversary present. We'll leave on April second and stop in Los Angeles for two nights. Then we'll go to Guadalajara. I've planned it so we can cross into Tijuana – there's nothing to see there except the bullfights – and then spend three days in Guadalajara before heading home with no stops. You will miss five days of work."

Estelle's eyes lit up. "I want to go to the bullfights."

"Just braid your hair on top of your head and do your Carmen Miranda look, Stella."

Estelle arranged the marriage of Rose Lanch and Louie Blum in February of 1934. They were married by a justice of the peace at City Hall where Estelle and John were married the previous year. Mildred brought her boyfriend to the wedding – a dubious sort with dark eyes and lips that could not muster up a word or a smile. Aunt Anya and her doctor boyfriend also joined them. Anya whispered to Estelle that her doctor friend wanted to marry her. Estelle was not aware that Louie had a married daughter until they made up the guest list. His daughter was a lovely dark-haired woman named Sarah, who was married to a rabbi in a Conservative temple in San Jose. He wore a disapproving face throughout the ceremony. They brought along their two teenage children who also wore long faces. Estelle was sure they would have preferred their father to be married in a temple, but Louie was not a member of any temple in the Fillmore.

Estelle noticed a lovely woman leaning against a wall during the ceremony. Her naturally curly shoulder length light brown hair was perfectly coiffed. She was elegantly dressed in gray tones with soft yellow accents at the neck. Her eyes followed the photographer most of the time. And the photographer was a dashingly handsome man with movie star looks and salt and pepper hair. He moved around the room like a dancer or an animal stalking his prey. When he saw Estelle and John standing next to Rose and Louie, he quickly took a photograph, blinding them with his flash.

After the ceremony, he asked Estelle and John to pose for another photo and placed them against the back wall of the chapel that the city used for weddings. He never asked them to pose, but rather, he let them talk and laugh with each other as he snapped photos. For a moment, they forgot where they were and why they were there.

John turned to the photographer. "Sorry about our gabbing. We were married in this room a couple of years ago and now my wife's mother is marrying in the same place. I'm John Moran, by the way, and this is my wife, Estelle."

The photographer shook John's hand. "I'm Ray Kosta. Nice to meet you. I have taken a million pictures already, but hold it there. The light is great. Put your heads together and smile at me." Estelle and John were more than ready to pose, and Ray snapped several pictures. In fact, Ray took more photographs of Estelle and John that day than he did of the newly married couple.

"Meet my wife, Mel," said Ray, gesturing to the woman leaning against the wall.

"It is a pleasure to meet you, Estelle," said Mel. "You have great hair. Your dark eyes and black hair are camera ready. You're a perfect subject for Ray – and both of you are so photogenic."

"I have an idea," said Ray. "Let's get together. We'll make a perfect foursome."

"I was just going to say that," said John. "I cook up a mean batch of bathtub gin."

"Please come to the reception at Louie's," said Estelle. "There's room for everyone."

"Your mother was kind enough to ask us to join in the celebration," said Mel. "And then we can exchange our information."

"Next week, we are having a party," John said. "We'll invite our gang, and you both will come."

Parties and get-togethers at the Moran's apartment became part of a young, popular social set – the cool cats. If the Moran's were throwing a bash, everyone wanted an invite. John's hooch was famous all over town. He was noted for making the best bathtub gin in San Francisco, and the crew from Canada Dry always carried bundles of ginger ale and Collins to add to the gin. Estelle's forte was her ability to throw a jazzy party with nibbles and invite a cross-section of friends – alternative individuals who were stylish, funny, and creative. Besides Lucille and her new boyfriend, Robert, and Ray and Mel, Estelle extended invitations to Evelyn and some of the City Hall gang, co-workers from Canada Dry, shopgirls whom she befriended on her excursions to the Emporium or other fabric stores in the city, and friends in the gay life like Joey and his gang and a lesbian contingent. John made friends with everyone, but he preferred his gang from the Mission District, the high school kids who were on the football team with him. They all danced, and drank until dawn. Ray and Mel fit right in, and Ray became the deejay, playing jazz mixed with the most popular songs in the

1930s – 'Cheek to Cheek,' 'Jumpin' Jive,' "In the Mood,' 'Puttin' On the Ritz,' 'It Don't Mean a Thing' (If It Ain't Got That Swing)." After a night of partying, the guests dragged themselves into the streets and the cold morning air.

Sometimes on the weekends, Estelle gathered together her favorite couples to picnic in Golden Gate Park. Estelle put on a spread with sandwiches and flasks of gin or bourbon, and everyone brought their favorite nibbles. The men would play football, and the women would take naps or gossip about the latest movie, if any were lucky enough to have extra money to attend.

"What movie have you seen lately?" asked Lucille one Saturday afternoon in early spring as the girls were lounging around.

"Last night we saw *It Happened One Night* with Claudette Colbert and Clark Gable," said Estelle. "It was so romantic and funny, and is Gable ever the hunk."

"That's exciting, Es. You and John seem so happy."

"We are. He's so much fun, and I'm so serious that I think we make a good pair. And we have so many interests in common. We're talking about moving next year and fixing up a place. I hope our jobs hold out. But what about you and Robert? "

"It's been about six months. I like him – at least my parents like him."

"What's that supposed to mean?" asked Estelle.

"They made me break off with my last boyfriend, Patrick, because he was not a practicing Catholic. And the one before that was not even a Catholic. I'm so tired of dating. Maybe that's why so many countries have arranged marriages. It's easier. Just meet the guy on your wedding day."

"I'll second that," said Evelyn. "Dating is impossible today. Where are the good guys?"

"They have been snatched up," said Mel. "I have my man, thank God."

"I thought you liked your guy, Evelyn," said Estelle.

"There is a big difference between like and love, as you know, Es. I have a long road ahead of me if I want to declare love in my relationship. By the way, my newest guy is Jewish."

"I was lucky John never took his religion seriously," said Estelle, "but everyone else in the Moran family did except for Dennis, whose God was alcohol and the Irish Sea. He was Black Irish to the core – moody, a little dangerous, and a man who drank heavily."

"I don't know what to do," said Lucille.

"If you like Robert, but he is not perfect for you, don't worry too much. In time, he will grow on you. He's got a good job at the post office, so together you can make a good life. You can even work when you're married if you want. For all that, we're not perfect, Lucy."

The girls giggled and hugged each other and poured hooch into their cups, toasting life.

With her uncanny discipline, Estelle continued to save her money in a cookie jar as Rose taught her to do. Two months after Rose married Louie, Estelle took half the money out and left the rest inside the jar. She and John were packing for Mexico, their second adventure by train.

Estelle did not have a clue about what it was like in Mexico, even though she took out a few books from the library on Mexican history. It was John who was the real traveler, and he demonstrated his skills early on in the marriage. He was always fascinated by the exotic, the unusual in travel. And he was a practiced researcher. Guadalajara was a good fit for his interests because of his fascination with Spanish history.

Before traveling to Guadalajara, they would be traveling through the California inland desert. It was "God awful ugly and boring. But just when Estelle thought she was about to enter California paradise, they got off at the Los Angeles train station. She was shocked to see uninteresting buildings and taco stands.

"Don't judge a book by its cover," John said "We haven't seen Hollywood yet."

Estelle was skeptical. But she had not yet seen the Art Deco facades of the Hollywood studios or the brilliant blue of the Pacific Ocean, or experienced the joy of walking along the Santa Monica Pier and listening to ocean waves or taking in the lush beauty of the surrounding Santa Monica Mountains. John served as the tour leader and saw to it that they visited everything that was on his list by cleverly riding streetcars from point to point without backtracking. Santa Monica became her favorite. Their only overnight stay was spent in Santa Monica in a small hotel on Ocean Avenue facing the Pacific Ocean. Hotel Shangri-La was a mecca for Estelle and John. They returned to the hotel whenever they visited Los Angeles.

John made sure that they were able to get off the train in Tijuana to experience the bull fights. As soon as the train stopped, they rushed to get to the bullring. Estelle wore her Mexican outfit and braided her hair on top of her head. She was so excited, she couldn't breathe. She loved the bull ring and the excitement and skills of the toreadors. She exuded happiness.

Getting off the train and walking into the city of Guadalajara was like entering a movie set. The city was established four hundred years ago and it was still picturesque. As they walked through Guadalajara's historic center, dotted with colonial plazas and landmarks such as the neoclassical Teatro Degollado and a cathedral with twin gold spires, the landscape became more elegant. Once they saw the Palacio del Gobierno's famous murals by painter José Clemente Orozco, Estelle was convinced it was not a dream. Its boldface reality was magnificent.

"Let's keep going, honey," she said. "This just gets better."

They spent three days in the colonial city, exploring its beautiful temples, monuments, and plazas. Experiencing the visual takeaways, eating authentic Mexican food, and listening to mariachi music was inspirational.

"We'll return, Stella," said John. "You'll have more scrapbooks from Mexico than you can count."

On their return, Estelle and John went back to work and back to reality. The Depression continued to deepen, but whether it was due to the luck of the Irish or the tenacity of whatever propelled Estelle to persevere in her job, it did not matter because the Moran's survived and did better than most. And after her marriage to Louie, Rose was finally able to leave her job after working for thirty years. It was time for her to enjoy life. Louie heartily agreed.

One weekend, Estelle and John saw a duplex in the Golden Gate Park on Fulton Avenue near Stanyan. It was adjacent to Haight-Ashbury, and they both thought the area would be a good place to live. There were two drawbacks – the duplex was not in great condition and the owner wanted to sell both units together.

"We have the down payment for one unit, but there's not much left over," said John.

"I think we should take the upstairs unit if your credit union could handle a small loan," said Estelle, "and maybe I can squeeze a bit more out of my cookie jar."

"Let's sweeten the deal by adding another thousand dollars to the purchase price."

While they waited for the duplex to close escrow, Lucille married Robert. Her parents were over the moon. Lucille was still uncommitted. There were no signs of happiness.

Estelle found Lucille in a room off the church as she was getting ready for the ceremony. "Lucy, what's wrong?" she asked as she hugged her best friend.

"I'm just going along for the ride," she said. "My parents pressured me to marry Robert. I felt I had no choice."

"Is there more? I know you don't love him like you want to love a man."

"I'm not pregnant if that's what you mean. I don't want to sleep with him, Es. I don't want this marriage. You'll be with me at the altar, right?"

"I won't let you marry him without me by your side. I'll be there."

"I love you, Es. You're my rock. And I have to talk to you about sex. I don't know how."

"Just remember not to have a gaggle of children that will tie you down forever."

Estelle hugged her, dried her tears, held her hand, and walked with her to the door of the church where her father waited. Estelle noticed that the people in attendance only took up about seven pews on the bride's side and ten pews on Robert's side. It was a simple ceremony. Estelle hoped for the best.

On a Friday afternoon, two months later, the escrow closed, and the loan came through for the duplex. The next day, Louie once again provided a moving truck, and Tim, Ray, and some of the bathtub gin gang showed up, and the move to the upper duplex on Golden Gate Street was completed.

"It'll take work to get in shape," said Louie as they walked through the duplex. "I'll give John a list of workers who can do the bigger jobs. And I'll cover the costs. Get your sewing machine out, Estelle. You'll need drapes for the windows to keep out the cold. It's a meat locker here."

Their first remodeling project was a nightmare. At one point, Estelle stood in the middle of the living room and sighed. "Maybe we bit off more than we could chew with our limited resources."

"Louie's offer to pay for the remodeling was gracious," said John. "But we have to pay him back."

"He told me he was in no hurry. But he should know it'll take us a year at least to complete."

"He knows that," John said as he took her in his arms. "I think we're doing just fine. It's the Irish luck."

CHAPTER 19

CRACKS IN THE BUILDING

Estelle worked herself to the bone to finish the remodeling of their flat within the first year on Golden Gate Street. It was early 1935, right in the throes of the Depression, but the gang came around for the housewarming party because it was at least something to celebrate: Rose and Louie, Ray and Mel, John's gang of railroad workers, Lucille and Robert (Lucille was pregnant with her first child). The congratulations and accolades were effusive, except for Louie.

"I hope you don't mind an old man's opinion," he said, "but I think you put too much effort and money into this flat. The place below your duplex was rented by the owner without doing a thing to it."

"He couldn't sell it, and someone was desperate enough to pay to live in that crap," said John. "Don't worry, Louie, we'll make it up on the sale and move into a better place."

"By the way," said John as he pulled a check out of his jacket pocket. "Here is the first installment on what we owe you."

"Don't insult me, Jack. You owe me nothing. Consider it a wedding gift. You don't know about what the Jews do for their kids. After education, we make sure our children live in a nice house. And if we can, we buy it for them. It's tradition."

"I don't know what to say. Thank you. Thank you again."

"Remember tradition, Jack. It brings you luck."

During the previous six months, Canada Dry had taken on two new executives, and Estelle started working for one of them in addition to Mr. Evans, who hired her. Mr. Costello was tall, commanding, and not even a little pleasant. After the first few weeks, he acted as if she worked just for him. He was insensitive to time and how long a project would take to complete, and he was prone to inappropriate remarks about the way Estelle dressed – her body, lipstick, even her hats. Estelle was smart enough not to complain; at that time, human resources departments did not exist. It was a man's world, and Estelle knew how to play it. She told Rose about the situation and why she wanted to leave.

"Do it quietly and without confrontation," said Rose.

"I think he's antisemitic. He studies me like I'm keeping a secret, watching me all the time, and his hostility to me personally is out of proportion to how bosses conduct themselves with employees. I recently saw propaganda newspapers on his desk. I know the war news is everywhere, but you don't bring it into the office."

"I trust you, darling, so do what you have to do."

Since the new flat was almost complete, Estelle decided it was time to leave a resignation letter on Mr. Evans's desk. She thanked him for a wonderful experience at Canada Dry and gave him a two-week notice.

One night after work, while Estelle was packing up her things in the steno pool, she heard Mr. Evans raising his voice at Mr. Costello. "Who do you think you are, Bob, running one of our best girls out of the company? She could run circles around you if she were a man. I'd fire your ass and give her your job."

"That Jew. You have to be kidding. Those people run too many businesses as it is. They have no right. We don't need these kind of people in our business."

"You're wrong, Bob. We don't need you in our business. You're fired. Now get the hell out of here."

Mr. Costello stomped out of Mr. Evans's office and saw Estelle packing. "You can't hide it, Mrs. Moran, even with your Irish last name. Everybody can see you for who you are."

"Hide what, Mr. Costello? Which part am I hiding?"

"You know what I'm talking about."

"Is that so? Well Mr. Costello, and I'm sure Hitler and his Nazis would have a place for you in the Gestapo, and you'd be right at home enforcing the rules of the state."

Mr. Costello left and Estelle's boss walked out of his office.

"I'm so sorry Estelle. We made a huge mistake. Can I convince you to stay?"

"Things have changed in the office, but it's time for me to go, Mr. Evans. Maybe it is the inevitable war or Hitler's fascist propaganda machine stuck in our heads. Or maybe it's just me who has changed. Thank you for your kindness."

She shook hands with Mr. Evans and left the building.

Upon reflection, Estelle thought it was not the best time to leave a job. The economy was in a recession on top of the Depression. A year earlier, in 1936, it looked as if the U.S. could slowly come out of its economic doldrums, but suddenly there was a contraction of goods and services.

John explained it succinctly. "Look, Stella, the only way we can get out of this recession is for Roosevelt to expand fiscal policies. Our economy is contracting because the Federal Reserve is limiting the money supply. Instead, we need the opposite. With a recession on top of the Depression, limiting the money supply makes no sense."

Estelle wanted to go back to the Financial District. After taking a stenographer's test at Dodge & Cox – a small personal and professional investment management company founded by Van Duyne Dodge and E. Morris Cox in 1930 – she was interviewed for the job. She noticed that the office was bustling and looked as if it was ready to expand.

"Our growth in five years has been solid," said Mr. Dodge, "considering the country is still in a depression. It's taken almost six years to build our financial investments. It looks promising because new investors who have some extra money want to try their hand at investing small amounts, testing the waters so to speak. Of course, it's all about trust. We have to have the reputation of a trustworthy financial company. Goodness knows Dodge & Cox is not a big firm, but today it does not matter. Bigger is not necessarily better."

The firm hired her in three days. Both men were impressed with her interview and thought her stenography skills were first rate.

Estelle was disappointed to discover that her new salary was not noticeably more than her job at Canada Dry. It seemed that salaries in San Francisco were comparable across the board, unless you owned a company or were a president or a top manager. Certainly women did not command salary increases.

"I think this salary business is unfair," she told John one night at dinner. "It's difficult to save anything."

"Nose to the grindstone, Stella. That is the key. You're not going to change the way things are done in business by complaining. Make yourself invaluable."

"It is certainly not the time to raise a family anyway."

"Let's wait. I don't like what's happening in Germany now. Hitler looks like he's on the march. He's about to take over Austria. We get tidbits from the government regarding Hitler's military movements, and the trains have been moving war material from the West Coast to bases in the south since 1936. It looks grim." John got up and poured another drink.

"Honey, you don't need that before bed."

"What I need from you is to not monitor my drinks." John took his drink into the living Room, and Estelle went to bed. He slept on the couch as he did frequently.

The quarrels over alcohol were not helping Estelle's marriage. She noticed it affected his sex drive, and she was worried. She was fairly sure that after five years of marriage and using the rhythm method as a form of birth control, there would have been a surprise pregnancy. It occurred to her that she might not be able to have children. But the intimacy between them was sporadic. The intense passion they experienced in the early years had tempered somewhat, but both of them often used the excuse that work was exhausting. Dinner provided time to relax, but if John drank too much, he fell asleep on the couch. She missed talking about their plans and dreams more than anything.

Estelle's new job was comfortable because she finally worked for just one boss. It was luck that one of her bosses, Charlie Bartolo, claimed Estelle for himself. He was senior in the management tier, and the other men could not raise complaints. Charlie took what he wanted because he brought in more business than other financial advisors. He wanted Estelle exclusively. At her other jobs, the frenetic pace of working for three bosses and the demands of time-sensitive correspondence or detailed reports and charts wore her out. Most of the women in the steno pool did not have it as good as Estelle. They all complained to each other at lunch time about being tired; then they had to hurry back to their desks to catch up.

"I don't work late, Mr. Bartolo," she said. "I have to take three streetcars home. I don't like to travel after dark."

"That's fair," he said. "We'll keep overtime to a minimum, but just so you know, overtime is double your hourly rate."

"I appreciate that, but I'm a fast worker, and I hope to finish a day's work in seven hours."

"I'll have Agnus move your desk closer to my office," he said. "I do a lot of dictation."

Charlie Bartolo was a strikingly good-looking man. In certain lights, he looked like Rudolph Valentino with dark hair, a straight nose and high cheekbones. His suits fit him smartly, and his tie was always fashioned with a perfect knot. She tried not to notice anything personal about him, but she sensed his eyes following her whenever she walked out of his office. He was cautious about handing out compliments or mentioning her stylish clothes. One day he approached her as she was sewing a button on her jacket. She looked up at him.

"I'm sorry, Mr. Bartolo. The button unraveled. I'm finished."

"There's no problem," he said. "Your hands, well, they move so fast, like an expert."

"Years of practice," she said, turning back to her typewriter.

Estelle liked working for Mr. Bartolo. As far as she could tell, he was one of the brightest financial managers, succinct in his meetings with his clients, considerate about dictating correspondence, and gave impeccable instructions. Unusual for an executive, he also had a great sense of humor. Estelle's curiosity about him prompted her to listen to gossipy conversations among the other stenographers, who knew quite a lot about the men at the firm. One day a woman mentioned Charlie Bartolo.

"Bartolo is married with two small children," Jane said. "Did you know that, Estelle?"

"I haven't been here long enough to know much about the bosses."

"He was born and raised in North Beach. Quite a hunk, if I do say so myself."

"All I know is that he goes out to lunch with clients most days," said Estelle.

"That's how he builds his portfolio of investors," said Jane. "Smart man."

Every so often, Mr. Bartolo invited Estelle to join him for lunch with a client. He called it a learning lunch – a way to teach Estelle more about finance and portfolio management. He told her to take notes in shorthand of the important points in the meetings and later make summaries of the conversation.

Their daily proximity fostered a close familiarity. Over time, they could finish each other's thoughts and communicate in verbal shorthand. One evening, Mr. Bartolo asked her to dinner, and she surprised herself by saying yes. Curiosity got the better of her; she wanted to learn more about Mr. Bartolo. During dinner, it became clear that he wanted to learn more about her as well. Both of them felt the sexual tension. They both knew the dangers. He asked her about her wardrobe to deflect what they were both thinking about, and she expounded on her passion for design and sewing. She briefly mentioned her father's talent. They never spoke of their spouses – it would be upsetting to them both. After dinner, he put her on a streetcar and sent her home. Estelle vowed there would be no more dinners. When she entered the flat, John was asleep on the sofa with half a bottle of gin sitting on the counter. He had not eaten. She left him where he was.

The vow not to go out with Charlie did not last long. Another dinner occurred at the back of a restaurant on Bush Street. It was dark and half empty. He kissed her and lingered on her lips.

"I swear to God, Estelle, I didn't mean this to happen. I'm sure you didn't either. Goddamn, how do these things happen?"

"I would rather this didn't happen, Charlie," she said. "It muddies the waters."

They ordered but did not eat much.

"I'm going to drive you home and leave you a block from your place."

Estelle thought that was the end. But the kiss in the car said otherwise.

Estelle's relationship with Charlie became dangerous – with furtive meetings at hotel rooms during lunch and several dinners a week. On the outside, in the real world, no one noticed or suspected that they had fallen in love. Responsibilities were met. Work priorities were executed. They did not attract suspicious glances. It was both exciting and guilt-ridden. Estelle worried that there would be no good outcome.

Estelle and Charlie's relationship went on for two years. Then, she became pregnant. Estelle was shocked, but she believed things happened for a reason. She did not tell Charlie about her condition. It was not his business. She took care of getting the abortion herself, except she asked Mildred if she would be willing to be with her for support. Mildred was living with friends in the Haight area and supporting herself as a music teacher. Her sister was glad to return the favor.

"It's early," said Estelle. "It's not even two months yet."

"What happened?" asked Millie.

"I thought I could not get pregnant. I used the rhythm method and even used a calendar to chart every month."

"It sounds like this had nothing to do with John," said Mildred.

"John and I tried but it never happened. It was with someone else."

"Are you early?" asked Mildred. "Maybe they will give you a D and C like I did."

"You have been two months, Millie. It was more dangerous for you."

"Don't get mad at me, but I slipped again. Second time it was a D and C. I did not want to bring that to you again.

"Maybe we should both learn to read a calendar better. Never again."

Mildred suggested a woman that many of her friends had used. The woman did procedures in a better location – not Delores's back alley with a creepy greeter.

Mildred led the way down a dark alley reminiscent of the alley they had walked down the first time Mildred was pregnant.

"Are you sure we're not going to the same woman?" asked Estelle. "It looks familiar."

"We are turning up the block. It will look more respectable."

They turned right at the corner onto a street that looked like any other downtown street.

"We're headed toward Union Square. This can't be right."

"You'll see," said Mildred.

They stopped walking about two blocks away from Union Square.

"This is it," said Mildred. "The building has an elevator. When we go in, get into the elevator and press number four. I'll be right behind you."

Mildred walked closely behind Estelle, checking to see if anyone was observing. On the fourth floor, Mildred knocked on the door of an unmarked apartment. A woman in her late thirties answered the door. She indicated that Estelle should sit on a sofa. The room was painted in soft blues and appointed with knickknacks and pictures of nature. An area rug in violet and yellow was placed under a wooden coffee table with a glass top.

"Hello, I'm Laura, "she said. "Do you have any questions before we begin?"

"I'm not two months yet, Laura."

"That helps greatly. More than likely, you'll have a D and C rather than an extraction. You might bleed a little, so if you did not bring a pad, I have one for you."

"I have a few with me."

Laura got up and put warm water in a large bowl.

"You can leave the money on the table," said Laura.

Estelle placed an envelope on the table and walked into the bedroom. Mildred sat in a chair near the door to the operating room and leaned her head back.

A half an hour later, Estelle came out of the room, feeling tired and empty.

"Everything okay?" Mildred asked.

"Just some cramping," she turned to Laura. "This isn't about money for you, is it?"

"No, I don't do it for money. I do it to help women like you who have had an accident or found themselves in a difficult situation with nowhere to turn. This is an issue of women's health and emotional well-being. We have few places to go, but I am a place you can come to."

When Estelle returned to work two days later, she felt numb. Charlie was gone, and her desk was moved to another section. That was strange to her. She thought he would call to tell her what happened. She preferred to stay at Dodge & Cox rather than look for another job.

One of the women in the steno pool remarked on Charlie's departure. "I heard from upper management – or maybe it was Mr. Cox's secretary – that Mr. Bartolo got a job offer from Bank of America in North Beach."

In a whisper that Estelle overheard, another woman remarked how strange it was that Estelle was left with no boss. Everyone noticed that her desk was moved.

Estelle vowed to keep moving forward on putting her marriage back together despite the emotional disruption. More than anything, she needed to have a heart to heart with John.

Dinner was cooking on the stove when John entered the kitchen. She did not look up from the stove.

"Smells good, hon." John sat down at the kitchen table and set the newspaper down. "I've been thinking that we need to sell our duplex, even though Louie wants us to buy the flat below and rent it out for extra income. But the owner won't sell unless he gets his price and we're not going buy it at his price . Would you consider moving?"

"We could use a bigger place. And I'd like to be closer to the beach."

"So, Stella, what are we saying that we're not saying?"

"We haven't talked about having a family in ages."

"Where did this come from? I got the impression you did not care either way."

"We can't have a baby with your drinking," said Estelle. "I made a doctor's appointment to see if there was any reason why I could not conceive. I think you should do the same. If you want to have a family, you'll have to cut back."

"I'll do it, honey. I promise I'll get help."

Estelle and John started working two jobs – their day jobs and their after-work job of looking for apartments. They talked to Louie about one of his friends who wanted to buy their flat for hundreds of dollars less than they were asking. One of the secretaries in Dodge & Cox told Estelle that if she needed a real estate person, her cousin was in that business. Estelle considered it, but Lucille's husband was just getting started in real estate, and she thought she should contact him first.

Estelle and Lucille met for lunch at Compton's Cafeteria on Powell in the financial district.

"Robert has been selling real estate for about a year. He loves it and he's good. Now remember, there's a fee you have to pay when someone sells or buys a place. It's called a commission. It might be around three, probably four percent." Lucille repositioned herself in her seat with a frown.

"I think that sounds reasonable. Lucy, what's really wrong?"

"This pregnancy has been awful. I'm so fat. And Robert is still who he is, and I'm beside myself despite having everything I need and want. Oh, God, Es, I sound so pathetic."

"You're not pathetic. You're just unhappy and none of us is fully happy, you know that. We can't have everything. We have to make compromises in life."

"How come life doesn't come with a manual?" asked Lucille. "It might have been easier to study and take a test?"

CHAPTER 20

DANIEL

Estelle had fallen in love with The Avenues – a popular nickname for western San Francisco – the first time she went to Golden Gate Park. Technically called the Sunset District, it was the largest neighborhood in San Francisco. Estelle thought it was magical because it was near the Pacific Ocean. Before World War I, it was covered with sand dunes; after that, it had windmills, bison, museums, lakes, and a carousel. It was larger than New York's Central Park.

It took about six weeks to find a place that suited Estelle's criteria – a playground close to Golden Gate Park and a library branch nearby.

Underneath their domestic planning, both she and John were keenly aware that 1939 might actually be the year of impending disaster in Europe.

"John, are Roosevelt and his cabinet going to do something about Hitler? Louie told Rose that some of his relatives are in Poland, and it doesn't look good for them. Most of the Jews have read between the lines; some are leaving to get away from the laws against the Jews. His cousin closed his business in Warsaw because he heard Hitler is on the march."

"Hitler's hatred of Jews is not real to most Americans. It's on page six of every newspaper in America, but nobody reads page six. It's up to Roosevelt, and so far, he has not given the Jews any help. Roosevelt lacks urgency and is influenced by his cabinet who see no need to expand Jewish immigration to America. What's clear is that our government wants nothing to do with Hitler's war. I have no answers, Stella."

Estelle was deeply disturbed about the Jewish situation. She felt the world had abandoned the Jews to fend for themselves. Most countries allowed Hitler to have his way. Jews could migrate to Palestine, even though the British mandate made it difficult, or they could try to escape, forge papers, and call on relatives outside of Germany. She was horrified that the American quota for Jews was minuscule. Louie's family situation in Poland disturbed her. Nothing she read relieved her fears. Who could explain Hitler's killing machine? Who would help her feel safe?

Estelle took off early one afternoon from work. She rode a streetcar from the Financial District to the Fillmore and got off several blocks from Diller's. It was an hour away from the dinner crowd arriving. When she looked through the window, it was a sparse crowd. Daniel was nowhere to be seen. She walked through the front door and smelled the familiar Jewish food – dill pickles, coleslaw, pastrami, chicken soup with matzah balls. She asked the lady at the cash register for Daniel. She was a large woman in her mid-fifties, with curly hair tucked under a net, red cheeks, and labored breathing. Her name tag read Ruby.

"Daniel left several years ago. He went to college, I think. He wanted to be some big-time lawyer. Why are you looking for him?"

"I used to work here when I lived in the Fillmore. I went to Commerce and worked here after school for a while. Do you have any idea where I can find him?"

Ruby took a second look at Estelle. Beautiful clothes, perfect makeup, and black hair hanging to her shoulders in curls.

"The old man died about four years ago," Ruby said. "Daniel took over for the next two years. Then he left to go to school."

"Did he mention to you where he would go to college?" asked Estelle.

"We weren't that close, but I'm pretty sure he went to school somewhere in the area."

"Everybody does. Probably, he still lives with his parents or in a dorm. Are his parents alive? The rabbi?"

"He retired. He was not well."

"I forgot the congregation he served."

"Beth Israel on Geary Street."

Estelle thanked Ruby and walked to Beth Israel. The thought of entering a synagogue at that moment was dizzying. She stood in front of the massive carved double doors and tried to catch her breath. She entered with trepidation and saw a light inside a small office to the left. A young, attractive woman with straight shoulder-length hair sat behind a messy desk.

She wore thick glasses and no makeup.

"Excuse me, I'm Estelle Lanch."

"Hello, I'm Sara Ann. How can I help you"

"I'm looking for Daniel Goldfarb. I worked at Diller's for several years, and he and I were friends. I would like to talk to him. We lost touch."

Sara Ann wrote Daniel's address on an index card. "This is the law firm where he works.

You did not get this from me."

"And his father, the rabbi?" asked Estelle. "Is he around?"

"He died about two years ago."

"I'm sorry to hear that. Thank you, Sara Ann."

Estelle walked down Market Street and turned left at Third Street. It was muggy in the early evening. A light October rain had dampened the city streets. She did not realize how fast she was walking until a stream of sweat ran down the side of her face. She slowed down, looked up at the clouds, and took in a deep breath. As she stood in the middle of the sidewalk, she realized she was overthinking her next steps. Estelle was hesitant about seeing Daniel again.

There was bound to be unconscious emotions and unspoken feelings.

She stood in front of a nondescript building on Third Street. A plaque on the side of a plain, unassuming door read Weiss and Goldstein. She pressed a buzzer to be let in and a voice on the other side responded.

"Hello, I'd like to see Daniel Goldfarb. My name is Estelle Lanch."

"Do you have an appointment?" the voice asked.

"It's a surprise. I'm an old friend. I wanted to say hello."

The buzzer went off, and Estelle opened the door. She walked up three stories and entered a somewhat dark office with no windows. The walls were hospital white, which was pleasing in contrast to the brown wooden desks and chairs. The receptionist smiled and told Estelle to go to the back of the office where the interns work.

"He knows you're here," she said.

Daniel appeared next to her and took her hand and smiled. "To what do I have the pleasure of your company, Estelle?"

"I'd like to take you for a drink. Are you busy?"

"This is an event. Work is almost over, and I can take off a little early."

They walked out the door and onto Third Street. Daniel hugged her. "It's so good to see you! I'm completely surprised. I never thought we'd meet again. Let's go to the Tadich Grill on California. I feel like celebrating."

Estelle noted that Daniel had lost his awkwardness and developed a lanky walk she had not noticed before. He was more easygoing and engaged her with small talk as they walked.

The Tadich Grill was an upscale yet cozy neighborhood bar that was popular with businessmen in the Financial District. The décor was masculine in style – a contrast of dark colors that included a shiny mahogany bar already packed at five o'clock in the afternoon with men in fitted suits with felt hats or fedoras tipped back on their heads. She and Daniel settled in a red booth. She noticed his brown eyes were deeper than she remembered, but his gaze was still penetrating.

"Daniel, I heard that your father died. I'm very sorry."

"Thank you for your kindness, Estelle. I'm sorry you never met him. He was a brilliant man with a great wit and always drew his observations about life with a sense of irony. You would have loved that about him. I know how you feel about not recognizing your Jewish heritage. You made that clear from the beginning. I was shocked at first, and I thought your resistance was out of place. I'm still trying to understand and wrap my head around it, but that does not take away the respect I have for you."

Estelle put her head down and tried not to cry.

When the waiter arrived they both ordered gin martinis.

They laughed at the coincidence of the same taste for a drink. The ice was easily broken.

"I just want to look at you, Estelle. It's been so long," said Daniel. "You look good. Where are you working? I thought you'd become a journalist and forsake the business world."

"I worked in city government for years, and now I'm with a financial group. But what I wanted to tell you is that I am married."

"I saw your ring. It was the first thing I looked for. I'm happy for you. What is he like?"

"He's Irish and from the Mission. His mother hates me, but his siblings accept me as the wandering Jewess. John's funny and loving and smart and not religious and doesn't care a whit where I come from."

"I care where you come from." Daniel took her hand. "What is it you need from me?"

"I had to talk to someone who was honest and told the truth and saw what other people couldn't see. I don't have a list to work from, so what I'm about to tell you is scattered. I have learned there's another way to live my life untethered from traditions. I don't carry the burdens of being Jewish inside of me – not the rituals or prayers or rules. But there is evil in the world against the Jews. And when people are evil, as they are in today's world, I do not believe there is a God who rights the wrongs or protects the innocent. People have to do that. People on earth have to know that. There will be no God to save the Jews, because this war is mired in evil. I can read between the lines. There is an apocalypse coming and it will last a long time."

"You always read the news between the lines," said Daniel. "I'd catch you in the kitchen or in your office at Diller's reading *The Chronicle* and you'd say, 'It's between the lines where the truth comes from.' Are you scared, Estelle?"

"I'm scared of what's going on with Hitler. I'm trying to make sense of this. My mother's husband told us about his family facing the threat of Hitler in Poland. I worry that Germany will soon be in Odesa, where my family comes from. I never told you that my grandparents moved from Odesa to London because of a pogrom. My mother and father separately changed their last names when they left London, and my aunt changed my first name so it sounded more modern and less Jewish. I was born Esther. I use the E from Esther as a middle initial. Estelle E."

"Esther is a beautiful name. I'm sorry you chose not to keep it."

"I don't deny I was born a Jew, but I never wanted to live as a Jew. I don't want to stand out as a Jew, feel the discrimination, or be marked as other. It's complicated because Jews can pretend to be like Gentiles, but we're never going to be one of them."

"Why would you want to be one of them?"

"You know as well as I do that Jews are stigmatized. Antisemitic sentiment is growing in Europe and in America, too. Jews in Europe are stereotyped, barred from owning property in certain neighborhoods, subject to quotas at colleges, excluded from social clubs and places of employment. Why do you think companies ask your religion when applying for a job? So they can weed out the Jews. And this is in America. This chaos I'm feeling confuses me, and I thought you would be the only one who can help me understand the pending annihilation I feel is coming."

"You have been in denial your entire life. Denial does not make you safe. You think it does, but denial is irrelevant. Because you can't forget your family, where they came from, where you came from, how they were persecuted, how they assimilated."

"I haven't forgotten my family, and I haven't forgotten the fear I felt growing up with an abusive father who hated being a Jew. I feel that fear again. But I think more about the present because that's where I live. I want to look forward to another kind of life."

"I'm afraid you are right about one thing – the future will be more evil than you could imagine. Hitler is a monster. The Jews in Europe have a small window to make a choice to leave. They might be able to assimilate in England or America or settle in Palestine. But frankly, I don't think it looks good for them anywhere. The irony is that the Jews have always been about survival. And please, my wonderful friend, don't close your eyes to this or you will forget. You can't live without history. You can't live without memory. You can't live without identity."

"You mean the world to me, Daniel. I wanted you to know that."

"I know that, and I feel the same. A Jewish life together would have been wonderful for me but painful for you. None of us are truly safe. No matter who we are with, where we are, or what we do."

"What are your plans? Will you go to war? Will you fight the Nazis?"

"I don't know the answer to that. But even if America goes to war, being Jewish won't disrupt your life. You will be sad and worried about the future. American Jews won't have to hide, but it will be madness for the European Jews."

The silence that followed contained unbearable sadness.

"You're too quiet, Daniel. Are you hiding the rest of your thoughts?"

"I have to stop this conversation to protect my beliefs and mental and emotional stability. I'm the son of a rabbi, which renders me unable to say more. Your circumstances speak for themselves – your perspective of Judaism was never fully developed, and I'm sorry for that. Your family had already migrated out of danger, but your father put you in another kind of danger."

Daniel leaned over and kissed her softly on her cheek. "There will never be another you."

They drank their gin martinis in silence. Estelle wondered if she would ever see him again. He helped her pass this difficult moment of uncertainty as he had always done since he opened Diller's front door, took her in, and offered her a job. Estelle believed in fate and her relationship with Daniel was fate. Bashert. But war was coming.

It was late when she took a streetcar to her new home. She stared out the window as darkness descended and watched the lights coming from buildings and restaurants and the electric street lamps. She remembered when there were gaslights, and as a young girl, she found them romantic. Romantic was not how she was feeling. It was time to fully devote her energies to John and to her home. They were both doing well, and their salaries were providing them with a good life. The future looked bright, despite her uneasiness about the world.

When Estelle got home, John was already asleep on the couch with yet another bottle of half-consumed gin.

Estelle entered her sewing room and examined a pattern she was working on – a black suit that fit snugly at the waist, featuring a pencil-thin skirt. She planned to wear a pale yellow blouse she'd just purchased at the Emporium under the jacket for a splash of color. It always delighted her to lay out the pieces of the tissue paper pattern on the fabric. In doing so, she could escape her thoughts.

CHAPTER 21

THE WINDS OF WAR

Estelle was curious about a particular Jewish manager at Dodge & Cox who had a deeper understanding about the news of the war in Europe than even the newspapers. He was well read and had a master's degree in political science with insight into European politics and economics. Robert Rosen often talked to anyone who would listen about details in the European theater after the First World War – especially how the depression affected Germany's economy, referencing the rise of Hitler and the Nazi party as a popular path for Germans to regain their former status as a one of three great countries in Europe, alongside France and England. She often heard Robert's conversations with his co-workers, or anyone who would listen.

"Hitler began by closing all Jewish businesses across Germany to marginalize them," Robert said. "He invaded Austria during the Anschluss, then Poland. Where will he go next? Eventually, he aims to put all of Europe and Russia under Nazi control, leaving no Jews left to kill. That's Hitler's world plan."

"We don't see that in the newspapers or hear it on the news, Robert," said Sam, one of his co-workers. "Where do you get your information?"

"It's buried on page six, among news that nobody wants to read about the Jews and the coming war, Sam. What people don't read in American newspapers is the Jewish persecution, specifically the Night of Broken Glass, or Kristallnacht, which occurred at the end of last year and foreshadowed the official beginning of the Nazi extermination of all Jews."

"Why would Americans want to read that stuff?" Sam asked.

"You mean it's just another uncomfortable fact, along with the depression," said Robert. "Americans want to deal with the problems in America, not Europe."

"And rightly so," replied Sam. "We don't owe Europe anything after World War I."

Estelle and Robert Rosen did not converse much at work. He was all business except when he was talking about the coming war. When she caught snippets of his conversation with his co-workers, she wanted to hear his opinions on the coming war. He was Jewish and obviously had a deeper connection with what was happening with the Jews in Europe. Estelle worked for him on several occasions. He was fast and efficient and so was she. No small talk. No reference to him and her mother having the same last name. She needed to push back on the war information. It made her feel nervous and upset and vulnerable. It felt similar to the trauma she went through at an early age. The Jews and trauma. The Jews and struggle. Would it ever end?

One morning at the end of 1939, Estelle walked into work and noticed that Robert Rosen's office was empty. His desk was clean, his family photographs removed, and his extra hat and comfy office sweater were gone. But where was Robert Rosen? Was he on vacation or would he come back?

Estelle thought Robert Rosen seemed to be on a mission. He did not understand the world with the eyes of a journalist. He interpreted the world like a passionate warrior. Would he help the Jews leave Germany? Would he go to Roosevelt personally and plead the case of the millions of Jews being persecuted? For a brief moment, Estelle saw the irony in their world. Estelle and Robert, but for a stroke of luck, would be living in Odesa or Berlin or

Poland. If he believed Hitler would annihilate the Jewish population, would he be searching for a way to leave his circumstances, or would he stay and fight. Estelle thought Robert would stay – his passion was explosive. Estelle ran from that kind of passion. It was her way out of dealing with the ghastly state of antisemitism blanketing the world. Even America was in on it, too. Especially America.

In the spring of 1939, Estelle visited her doctor. She was still unclear why she was not getting pregnant. Maybe she had some scar tissue from the D&C. But the doctor said she had no scar, no blockage.

"Maybe your husband has an issue," said the doctor. The poufs of gray hair on his head made him look like a mad scientist. "It could be that he has low testosterone, a problem easily solvable with pills. He has to see a doctor for an examination."

Later that night, John was at the sink washing the dinner dishes. Estelle stared at his back and finally asked, "Honey, did you get a checkup with your doctor?"

"No, I forgot. We're so busy, and there never seems to be a good time."

"Please see a doctor and do it soon. I found out today that I'm not the problem."

"Good news, honey," said John as he embraced his wife. "I promise you I will get this done. And I'll cut back on the booze. You'll see. Everything will be alright."

John eventually saw a doctor who confirmed that he had a slightly lower testosterone level, but the doctor decided that the real issue was his heart.

"You smoke?" asked the young, athletic-looking doctor.

"For the past fifteen years or more."

"Quit. Quit or die. You have an atrial flutter. It's a condition that results from an arrhythmia that causes tachycardia, which is a fast heartbeat. That's about more than one hundred beats a minute. With an atrial flutter, you have a rapidly firing electrical circuit in your atrium, which causes your atria to beat quickly; that means your ventricles will beat faster than normal. You have a heart palpitation. You don't feel the flutters unless you are consciously focusing on your heart, but things like smoking, drinking too much, or carrying a lot of anxiety and stress will increase the danger of a heart attack. And watch your caffeine and fat intake. And limit any exertion in your physical activity. If you decide to do further tests, we'll know more information about your heart."

"I have no physical routine. I garden and fix up the house."

"Just be careful about how much you exert yourself."

"Thanks, Doc. I'll check in every once in a while."

Estelle never learned about John's arrhythmia probably because soon after the doctor's visit, John had a bout of pneumonia, and there was no more conversation about anything else except what to do to help him recover. With the amount of work he had to do at the railroad trying to create a new administrative system that would create an even more efficient railroad routes, his body was rundown and he developed a persistent cough, which developed into a deep chest cold, then pneumonia, and breathing issues. John never smoked another cigarette.

Estelle noticed that John stopped drinking during his recovery, or rather, he drank infrequently. He got his strength back slowly, rested, and he and Estelle found a new interest: Marin County, which was twenty miles across the Golden Gate Bridge. The bridge was completed in 1937, and millions came to view its high towers and long expanse over the turgid blue-black waters of the Pacific Ocean.

One chilly winter afternoon, after taking a bus to the bridge's toll booth to view the vista surrounding the magnificent Golden Gate, Estelle and John shared the same idea.

"We need a car to cross this magnificent bridge right in our backyard," John said. "Cousin Charlie sold his car right out from under me. I'll ask if Tom needs his car anymore since he's not driving it. His recovery from tuberculosis is so damn slow. It worries me."

"Let's hope for the best. He's too young to go through this illness."

"I think we should explore the other side of the bridge," said John. "I've heard good stories about a place called San Rafael. And did you know there is a Mission there established by Franciscan priests in 1817?"

"Of course, you would know that, honey," she said.

Tom's old 1930 Buick Roadster was parked in a neighbor's driveway on Noe Street and left to the elements of a damp climate. The Roadster was rusted on the outside with a corroded motor and alternator on the inside.

John worked on it for six months before he drove it. On a foggy summer morning, they stood at the bottom of 1578 Noe Street.

"You go up to say hello to your mother," said Estelle. "I'll stay here."

"You can go out back and play with the goats if you want," said John.

"Funny. Make it quick."

Ten minutes later, John came down the stairs. "Come on. Time to take a drive."

John drove the Roaster to the Golden Gate Bridge and drove down a dirt road to the bottom of the hill where there was a vista that overlooked the Pacific Ocean. It was a known spot for sweethearts who wanted privacy. Estelle cuddled with John forgetting for the moment that the world was about to drastically change.

The fog rolled in and covered the orange towers in whiteness.

"Fog has a mind of its own," said John. "We live with it daily, and we love it some days and hate it other days."

"Especially those three months in summer when it's freezing," said Estelle, snuggling.

The foghorns blew, and they both smiled in recognition of the familiar sound.

"Fog nourishes our city," said John. "It is a dripping system for water. How do you think the redwoods survive? Fog covers the tops of the bridge towers and settles just over the water to keep it pristine. It's nature's own way of protecting itself."

"How do you know all that, John? How do you know these little things?"

"I read anything and everything."

"I love you, John. You are full of surprises. But for a change, I have a surprise for you."

"I already know, Stella. You have a different glow. You're pregnant."

"Damn, hon, I can't even surprise you. How did you know I was pregnant?"

"Because you are more beautiful than ever," said John as he kissed her.

Estelle's happiness was always qualified by what was happening in Europe. Antisemitism was raging across the ocean. She was panicked by the incident of the German Jewish refugees who in May of 1939 sailed from Hamburg on the German liner, the MS St. Louis to Cuba. The ship put down its anchor in the Caribbean, waiting to disembark at the port of Havana. Even though the Germans gave visas to the Jews in order to enter Cuba, the Cubans refused entry to all but a few refugees. Estelle was not surprised that Hitler already knew they would be turned away – it was a set-up, the voyage of the damned. The captain turned the ship around in the direction of Miami, then on to New York. The passengers on the MS St. Louis were refused entry to any port city due to the U.S. Johnson-Reed Act's restrictions against Jewish immigration. Even Canada refused to let the Jews disembark. The Jew were on their own.

Estelle followed up on this story and was stunned by a later headline, "St. Louis Refugee Ship Forced to Return to Europe." To her horror, the 907 passengers on board the St. Louis were returned to Belgium. From there, the passengers spread out to unoccupied countries – specifically to Great Britain, France, Holland, the Nordic countries – and some even returned to Hamburg. Eventually, 255 of the 907 Jews who were returned to Europe on the St. Louis were rounded up and taken to work camps around Europe. Their names disappeared from history.

About this time, Estelle began to notice that American newspapers carried the stories of the roundups of Jews by the Nazis. After Austria, Poland was next where the so-called work camps were built. There was not much of a response by the American population since they thought the Jews sent to resettlement or work camps would be returned to their countries after the war. Some were pleased not to have more immigrants coming to America, especially Eastern European Jews. The quota system held firm throughout the war.

Estelle was increasingly curious about the whereabouts of Robert Rosen. Estelle wanted to ask someone where he was, where he went, or if he was working elsewhere. But she could not tip her hand, as someone who might misconstrue her intentions. She walked by several desks and listened to managers speak on phones, but there was no mention of Robert Rosen. She decided to ask his secretary.

"Hi, Jill," said Estelle. "I have a question. Is Mr. Rosen still around? He dropped a file on my desk a couple of weeks ago, and I forgot about it until I realized that he was not around."

"Where have you been, Estelle?" asked Jill in a whisper. "He left months ago. I thought he was going to join a political agency having to do with the war, but it looks like he headed straight for the war in Europe. He talked enough about politics around here to be president. But I bet he won't walk in Roosevelt's shoes." Jill looked around to see if anyone was listening.

"No follow-up address?" asked Estelle.

"None." Jill wrote down a name on a piece of paper. "Try this guy. He was a client and he might know."

"Thanks, Jill."

"And throw out the file on your desk because he won't be back."

Estelle began to notice that journalists around the country began to place stories leading up to a full war in Europe on the front pages. At the same time, Roosevelt's Secretary of State Cordell Hull, dismissed all talk of the Jewish problem as well as Hitler's plan to rule Western Europe and the Soviet Union. No American government official addressed the persecution of the Jews. No government official was outraged by the "camps," which soon became a euphemism for extermination. Louie continued to get news on the European front from family and friends detailing lives lived under the Nazis in Poland. Some family members were already in Auschwitz.

Estelle's rabid consumption of anything that had to do with Jewish immigration led her to discover in 1939 that President Roosevelt's closest ally, Henry Morgenthau, a Jewish businessman who was the Secretary of Treasury, exposed rampant antisemitism in the State Department that thwarted efforts to provide safety for European Jews. Morgenthau lost the fight because of strong opposition in Roosevelt's circle of advisors, particularly from Cordell Hull.

Estelle thought it had to be a rumor – Nazi spies had the ear of certain America First congressmen, senators, and businessmen who bought into Hitler's propaganda about embracing fascism and influencing politicians to destroy democracy. But the FBI had firm knowledge of a spy cabal through one of its agents, an American citizen who was a spy residing in Germany. The cabal consisted of principally eight homegrown U.S spies, radicalized by over fifty German spies who were cultivating people of influence to pursue Nazi propaganda.

She also found it shocking to learn about the German American Bund, a far right anti-war movement that embraced the Nazi Party and was influencing America's attitude about not entering the war. At the end of 1939, the Bund organized a pro-American rally at Madison Square Garden, where 20,000 American Nazis gathered to shout Nazi slogans and hate speech against the Jews – a vicious repeat of castigating the Jews for the ills of the world couched in the slogans of a pro-American rally. Robert Rosen must have known about all these seditious movements during 1936. Estelle wanted to know and did not want to know what he knew. But she felt compelled to find out if the annihilation of the Jews in Europe would be the precursor for a holocaust in America.

She called the number Jill gave her. A man named Stan Goldman answered and said yes, he was a client of Robert, and no, he did not know the whereabouts of Robert Rosen. Estelle told him she had a file he left at Dodge & Cox.

"I don't think he will be needing that file where he went," said Mr. Goldman.

"Where did he go? asked Estelle.

"You did not hear this from me, but the crazy guy probably went to England to fight Hitler and save the Jews."

She hoped Robert would survive his mission and come back and share the truth.

During Estelle's pregnancy, Estelle and John visited Rose and Louie. Rose basked in the glow of becoming a grandparent.   When they told Jake, he kidded John. "Welcome to the world of raising children."

"From what I heard, Jake, you never did much in that category."

"That's a damn lie, Jack," said Jake. "I was a good father until Rose kicked me out."

"You don't have to go deeper than that to explain your absence," said John. "Anyway, you're going to be a grandfather. Get to know my son because he's going to be taking over for me when I'm too old to bring you cartons of cigarettes or drive you to Petaluma for cell meetings."

Every weekend, Estelle and John went to Marin County, across the Golden Gate Bridge, and spent time in each of the burgs that spread throughout the county – San Anselmo, Corte Madera, Ross, Larkspur, Fairfax, Mill Valley – even stopping at several medium-sized dairy farms.

They spent time at Mission San Rafael and enjoyed walking along Lowrie Harbor on Point San Pedro, where boats were built and owners docked their yachts.

"This is where we are going to live, honey," said Estelle. "San Rafael is perfect. It's close to the freeway to San Francisco, and it looks like the area could use some creative building or at least remodeling."

"Clever girl, Stella. I'm just thinking the same thing. I saw some property that I'd like to get my hands on. Let's keep focused and put money in the cookie jar."

When Lance was born Estelle and John were beside themselves with joy. Estelle had one week off from work, and when she protested, Dodge & Cox gave her one more week, and then she quit.

"No thanks," she told her boss. "Consider the second week my notice."

She was tired of working for others – for men who were entitled with power and influence within their company's hierarchy. Thinking that the rest of her life looked like Dodge & Cox was unimaginable. At twenty-nine, life was more than being a member of the typing pool.

"Are you sure you want to quit?" John asked her.

"Don't worry, honey, I'll get another job. I need a change. Something more creative.

Anyway, you're getting busier with shipping even more orders of materials and supplies since the war expanded across Europe."

The baby cried, and John picked Lance up. "I'm glad you're not at work right now. You need time to think about what you want to do next. And at least, they'll never draft me. I'm too damn important to the war effort from where I work. So you can slow down and relax."

"We timed that right, didn't we, honey."

"With the baby and all, we're right where we should be."

"During the day, I've been experimenting with writing articles for a baby magazine. And I'm going to submit to others, maybe write an advice column. I'm going to take my life in another direction. I'm not sure how it will work out, but I have a few ideas."

"That's my girl. Always full of surprises."

CHAPTER 22

ON THE HOME FRONT

Estelle's knack for systems management and her organizational skills provided the foundation of her gift for writing. She wrote mainly for magazines. Her topics were about motherhood, working versus not working for the first two years of a baby's life, the role of the wife, tips for bringing up babies, as well as women in the workforce. Most of her articles were accepted, and editors always asked for more. In between writing, she took in typing jobs and contract work, both of which provided a nice income.

Estelle was perfectly happy for the next two years in between her stay-at-home duties and writing. She took a daily walk with Lance while looking for flats to buy, preferably flats that needed renovation. Remodeling was in her blood. She knew that hunting for houses in San Rafael was in the future, and she knew that the combination of finding properties with John and extending her sewing skills to include upholstering furniture, making drapes, and enhancing her decorative style, would be valuable assets in the remodeling process.

Estelle and the baby were waiting for the library doors to open. Lance was fussy. She worried he would start crying. He was two years-old and already showed signs of health issues. His nose was running constantly. It was not so much a cold, but more like an allergy from the dampness and fog in the Avenues. On top of that, he was teething.

The glass door to the library opened. An elderly lady with streaks of gray hair and small glasses that sat on top of her nose welcomed her. Estelle noticed how her well-worn gray dress, accented with a black belt, fit her small waist. It was warm inside, and Lance's cries turned to a soft whimper. "I'm Mrs. Shift. How may I help you?" asked the librarian.

"Nice to meet you, Mrs. Shift," said Estelle. "I'd like to research the newspapers we have in the city, especially the small papers."

"Come on inside where it's even warmer, and I can give you the directory," she said.

Estelle walked over to a comfortable chair, sat at a long shiny wooden table, and propped the baby on her lap. She gave him a biscuit to soothe his teething. Mrs. Shift brought a directory to her and set it down at the table.

"This is a list of all local newspapers in the city. Of course, *The Chronicle* and *The Examiner* have the most readership. They are the largest."

Estelle knew this because she worked at a newspaper for a short stint. This time she wanted to know the various sections of each paper, the names of the editors, and what subjects in the opinion section were covered. After an hour, which included a nap for the baby, Estelle thanked Mrs. Shift and went on her way.

The world changed on December 7, 1941. John was used to turning on the radio in the mornings. The dial was set to his favorite station – it had a good balance of news and music. He never set an alarm, so when he turned on the radio, immediately he heard the news.

"Stella," he called out. "Come here quickly. The Japs attacked Pearl Harbor."

"Oh, my God. Did anyone know that Japan was gearing up for a strike?" she asked.

"Where were our spies to alert us? Shame on our military. We were caught flat-footed. The death toll must be massive."

"I can't think what's going to happen with the railroads," said Estelle.

"We are only halfway ready to fight for the Allies. There's still more to do and we don't have the time to do it."

"How long is it going to take to get up to speed?"

"Within a few months, we might be ready to win the war. It'll be an all-out effort. No more lending and leasing war materials and airplanes to the allies. No more half in and half out."

John left after a long embrace with his wife, and Estelle put Lance with a babysitter and visited *The Chronicle.* She talked to the secretary of the editor in charge of advice columns and asked how to submit an idea for a weekly column. The young and attractive secretary was pleasant but skeptical and wanted to know what topics Estelle would like to write about. After giving the secretary her background in writing articles for magazines on the subject of babies and home management, the secretary was not interested.

"You realize we entered the war today, don't you?"

"All the more reason to distract a portion of your readership with other topics. People, especially women with children, need something to take their minds off the war."

"We won't be interested. Thank you."

Estelle promptly left and went to *The Examiner.* She received the same response – the war.

It was a discouraging morning. In addition to the numerous hurdles to overcome at a newspaper, payment for a weekly column was only five dollars. Magazine writing paid at least seven to ten dollars per article. Estelle knew better ways to make money. On her way out of *The Examiner,* she picked up a fresh copy of the newspaper, sat down in the lobby, and read the want ads.

The baby was napping when Estelle got home. After pouring herself a cup of black coffee, she realized she was not drawn to any of the open jobs that were posted in the newspapers. The work she liked the most was at Dodge & Cox – and she thought of Robert Rosen, the Jewish man who went off to war before there was a war to save the Jews. What happened to Robert Rosen?

Estelle's thoughts returned to the want ads and her need to keep up with her secretarial skills. She saw a few references to secretarial pools for the government and planned to follow up the next day. Maybe she would try to interview at a bank in North Beach. She decided to take the baby to visit her mother and get her advice.

Rose remained a comforting and warming figure in Estelle's life. She was steady and tenacious in a kind way. Estelle thought Louie was good for her, at least on the surface, but she knew that there were negative undertones in any marriage that had to be managed. But she sensed an honesty and closeness in their relationship.

Estelle rang the doorbell to her mother's apartment. She knew Louie would not be home.

Rose opened the door and was not surprised to see her daughter and grandson.

"I was expecting you," said Rose.

"Of course, Mama, we have that witchy connection," said Estelle as she entered.

Rose took the baby immediately. "Now, this is my baby boy," she said as she cuddled Lance. "He's getting so big."

"He's still got a runny nose all the time in this weather," said Estelle. "I don't know what to do with his cough either. I'm afraid the weather in the Avenues is not good for him."

They sat on the sofa. "Mom, you have to get a softer sofa. This is hard as a rock."

"Louie likes…"

"I know, Louie likes it this way."

"Don't be harsh, dear," Rose said. "You need to move to a warmer climate like Marin."

"That's true, but we can't afford it yet, and John's work is all-consuming. I guess I'm out of sorts because we're gearing up for a war. It's going to consume us for quite some time."

"I heard it on the radio this morning. I believe we should have gone in after the Germans ran over Poland. Stopped them right in their tracks. We've lost so much time. John is going to be up to his ears for the next several years. What are your plans?"

"I started writing for magazines, but I did want to contact a few papers that have a weekly column. I started with the big ones but didn't get a bite. Anyway, what I did find out was that piecemeal writing doesn't pay much."

"I'm afraid I don't have any advice for you in that area."

"I'm thinking out loud, Mom. Maybe I'll try to find a typing pool, that is, if I can get hired."

Rose stared at her daughter. "And why wouldn't you?"

"The war, Mom. The war is about German aggression and taking over Europe and destroying every Jew on the planet. Journalists are finally reporting on Jewish internment camps. You realize the camps are not really work camps. You know what they are."

"I don't know anything. I think people are just guessing at what's happening. And what does that have to do with you getting a job? This is San Francisco. They're not asking if you are Jewish before an interview."

"When you worked for Schlage Lock and Key, did they ask you for your religion way back in the day?"

"No. Why would they? This is San Francisco."

"Well, today they ask. They ask your religion, and I wrote Protestant."

"What does that mean? Protestant. What's that? You're Jewish."

"I have never been Jewish, Mom. Never went to temple. But I know that if I lived in Hitler's Europe in 1942, I'd be hauled off to a death camp like the other millions of Jews."

"Enough of this talk," said Rose. "We all feel for the situation, but the world has let this madman carry out his vile beliefs. Louie says our government never wanted to get involved with the Jews. They would rather wage war on the Nazis and deal with the Jews after."

"There will be no Jews left."

"If you cared, you would want to answer to our Jewish beliefs," said Rose.

"A long time ago, I chose to keep my head down and blend in with the others."

"I don't like that about you."

"I know." The baby began to cry. Estelle took the baby and walked the floor. "I want you to be safe, Mom. And I hope Louie makes you feel safe. Does he?"

"Most of the time he's good to me, although he's a bit gruff and gets on my nerves a bit."

"John's a rock. I'm lucky."

"John is safe and so are you with him. It's a terrible time for all of us, and we need to provide a safe sanctuary for all of us. Can you even imagine, there's not one square mile in Europe for the Jews? Not even for Jews who hide in basements or attics. We thought the Russian pogroms in the Crimea were horrid. It's always been the same for Jews."

"You never talked about those days with your family and leaving Odesa."

"You would not have liked the story. It would confirm your fears. And I never wanted to hold on to that horrible time with my family. The tragedy. The senseless deaths."

"Anya told me, Mom. She kept the secrets until she couldn't keep them anymore. They had to be told." Estelle embraced her mother. "We are safe with each other here."

"You have chosen your path, darling, and I hope it works out for you."

The bank in North Beach was small. Estelle noticed that no one was sitting at the reception desk. A man's voice interrupted her thoughts.

"May I help you?" he asked.

"Yes, please." Estelle held out the newspaper with the job notice. "I was inquiring about the job the bank advertised. I'm a typist. Is that what you're looking for? The ad did not specify."

The man was of medium height and balding. His face was slightly flushed, and he smelled of alcohol. "You have experience, I take it?" he asked.

"Over ten years as a stenographer," said Estelle.

"Is that so?" The man's voice slipped into a whisper. "But you won't do any job in this bank. Do you get my drift?"

"What is it you're trying to say?"

He took her arm and led her out of the bank's front door. He looked long and hard into her eyes without blinking. "

"We don't hire yids in this bank."

Estelle could feel the man's hatred. "Is that so? Tell that to Hitler and report me to the Gestapo because I'm reporting you to your bank. And for the record, I'm Protestant."

Estelle turned to go. The man caught her arm. "Why you disgusting kike – "

"Go back to Germany where you belong. You're a vile Nazi through and through."

Estelle pulled her arm out of his grip and walked away, shaking and crying. She was angry and humiliated. She needed to walk, to stop the pain. As she climbed the stairs to her flat hours later, Estelle realized the world would always have pockets of hate for the Jews. She vowed to guard against those who blame others, torture others, kill others to prove that their vile mythology was the only way to inherit the earth.

She walked into the flat desperate to see her baby boy. After letting the babysitter go, Estelle walked into Lance's room and sat down on the carpet next to the crib. The room smelled of baby. Surrounded by blue walls and blankets and stuffed animals, Estelle could hear Lance breathing. Her boy would not grow up in fear, and would never experience the discrimination and hatred of others. It hurt too much. That man at the bank had scarred her soul.

The phone rang. Estelle was too exhausted to answer, but she managed to walk into the living room and pick it up on the fifth ring. It was not John. He never called her from work.

"Hello," Estelle answered.

"Hello, Mrs. Moran, this is Robert Rosen. Do you remember me?"

Estelle felt her heart constrict. Breathing was difficult. "Why hello, Mr. Rosen."

"This is strange and odd," he said, "but I wanted to talk to you after I learned you were not at Dodge & Cox anymore. Jill told me you had a baby and left."

"I did leave, Mr. Rosen. And some of us wondered what had become of you."

"I joined the military and left for Europe." There was a long pause before he could continue. "You see, I wanted to work with the agencies that helped the Jews, and joining the military was one way to find out what was going on with the … with the roundups, and well, I'm sure you have read about it."

"Yes, I understand, but why are you calling me?"

"Are you employed?" he asked.

"I write articles for magazines."

"I see. I'm inquiring if you would like a job, Mrs. Moran."

Estelle took a deep breath. She was taken aback about hearing Mr. Rosen's offer for a job. Lance began to cry.

"I'd like to hear about it, but I'm afraid my baby is up from his nap and I need to take care of him. How about we meet?"

"Yes, good. How about lunch at Compton's Cafeteria? Noon tomorrow."

"I will see you then, Mr. Rosen."

Estelle hung up and walked into Lance's room. Her baby boy was standing, his hands gripping the crib, crying, screaming, until he saw his mother's face smiling at him. She picked him up and twirled him around the room. What had just happened? One minute she had no steady job, and the next minute she might have a job working with someone she respected. What kind of work did not matter as much as it was a job recommended by Mr. Rosen. It must be interesting and challenging.

When Estelle saw Robert Rosen after more than a year, she was surprised to see how he had aged. As they carried their trays of food to a table in the back of Compton's Cafeteria, she noticed his face showed the battle scars of war and felt his passion and abounding energy. It was crowded at the lunch hour, and she was certain that he wanted to get away from people so he could explain the job to Estelle.

Once settled at the table, once the first bite was taken, Mr. Rosen was ready to jump into his story.

"Before you begin, Mr. Rosen, I'd just like to say welcome back," said Estelle.

"Thanks, I'm grateful to be back. To begin, I had no real standing when I went to England. I was gathering information about Hitler's intentions and movements, and they all proved legitimate. We should have gone in sooner. Our government should have pushed back during the late thirties, at least after the incursion into the Anschluss and Austria. That should have been the moment. Poland was Hitler's next invasion because it was once part of German lands.

You know the rest, and then the pact between the Japanese and Germans. This is a war to preserve democracy and defeat Fascism, but more importantly, this is a war that stops once and for all, the madness of antisemitism.

"I don't know if you're Jewish or not, Mrs. Moran, and I am frankly not interested. I'm interested in your skills – and I assume you have some managerial skills. There is an office near the Haight that is connected to a government agency, the OSS, that collects intelligence information at home and abroad. Some information is sent by teletype. Some of it is in code, but if you come onboard, that won't be your area. You will be assigned to type information in various formats like teletype, fill out government forms, or take dictation depending on the sensitivity of what is collected."

Estelle had not eaten a bite of food. The information that Robert Rosen was giving her was uncomfortable. "What kind of information would I be reviewing?" she asked.

"Let's say troop movements, machinery transport, cargo, and keeping track of where the Jews go after the Nazis have occupied. This might seem fantastical to you, Mrs. Moran, but you will also be involved in tracking anti-democratic or seditious movements around the U.S. These movements, in essence, are internal threats that emanate directly from Berlin's spies and Goebbels's propaganda arm that are currently in the U.S. I am referring to groups like the Christian Front and Father Charles Coughlin and his disciple Father Francis Moran."

"Wait, Mr. Rosen. Is Father Francis Moran a real person?" she asked.

"I'm afraid so. He's from Boston where the revolution is being played out by two Catholic priests and their thousands of followers around the country. Father Coughlin has a radio show with thousands of listeners. Do you remember the Nazi rally in New York City at Madison Square Garden about a year and a half ago?"

"I saw an article in *The Chronicle*, but I could not imagine Catholics and Nazis in the same sentence, let alone the German American Bund. I wanted the image to go away."

"It's not going away. There are hundreds of people, maybe thousands, in our government supporting Hitler's Nazi party. They want their own American Nazi Party – their own American Bund, or a Christian Front with their own army dedicated to plotting the overthrow of the U.S. government. There are soldiers who are training right now for a war in America aimed against the Jews. Fascism is appealing to many people who need to point the finger against those they feel have wounded them, those who they think have taken away what belongs to them. The Jews manifest that for Hitler – that's his brand, his ever-present Jewish hatred."

"I'm not interested in this assignment, Mr. Rosen. It's been my life's focus to stay out of the way of antisemites. Hate has consequences, which makes it complicated. We both know the international Jew is not portrayed as an individual. Antisemites see Jews as one group, one identity – plotting to take over the Christian world – but why? Why would Jews want to do that when a fair portion of Christians deny them their basic humanity. It's vile, and Jews are not second-class citizens. But I still choose not to associate."

"Distance is always a safer place to be – away from those who blame, who single out differences, who make us the other. We don't have to defend our humanity against mainstream society. Our humanity is within us from the day we are born. Yet, the fact is that there will always be pogroms in order to cleanse and preserve the white race."

"Are you saying what makes us strong can't kill us?" asked Estelle. "Because in the case of Hitler, the Jews can be strong and defy Nazism, and they will still be killed."

"Remember, fear is a motivator. It is the basis for the hatred of Jews because it creates anger, and anger begets blame, and the Jews are convenient targets to attack. And then the hate snowballs. But they will never rid the earth of Jews. We have survived it all and more."

"How do you do it, Mr. Rosen? How do you keep the fight going?"

"If you're asking me why I fight for the Jews every day, it's simple. For me, being Jewish means to be a member of a culture and a religion that cherishes life and memory alike and believes that we live best, and understand best, when we remember well."

"I have to think about this, Mr. Rosen."

"Think of the job this way: Newspapers give you one perspective about the war, but now you'll be getting information about the war in real time. You won't be handling any material related to the Jewish issues. Others in the office will handle that. This is not a job for the rest of your working life. It's until the war ends. You can then make other choices for yourself."

"It will never be over, Mr. Rosen. Antisemitism will never be erased, the hate will never go away. I believe it is part of human nature. I will have to talk to my husband, Mr. Rosen."

"He's helping the war effort, isn't he, Mrs. Moran? Railroads are integral in fighting."

"How did you know what my husband is doing, Mr. Rosen?"

"The government is in the business of gathering information whether America is fighting a war or not fighting a war."

"I see," said Estelle. "I will get back to you if I'm interested."

"Don't take too long. Every day we don't gather our resources is a lost day. Believe it or not, Mrs. Moran, I selected you because you're smart and thorough, and I can trust you, "

Estelle left the table and her uneaten food. Her heart was pounding.

When John came home from work, Estelle was sitting at the kitchen table playing with Lance in his high chair. He was teething and running at the nose simultaneously.

"Hi, honey," John said as he hugged her and greeted his son. "How was your day?"

"Interesting. Let me get your dinner. You must be starving."

The kitchen was quiet as Estelle fried hamburgers and onions in the black cast-iron pan over the gas stove. It was a cozy kitchen, with light yellow walls and white counters. The window above the sink overlooked a small back yard. She put the patties and fried onions on buns and dressed them with tomato and lettuce.

"I don't suppose you're going to tell me about it," said John. "Or are you?"

"I don't know where to begin."

"Sit down and have a glass of wine."

She put a burger and potato salad on her plate. Estelle gave John a beer, poured herself a glass of wine, and sat down. She told him everything, including the encounter with the Nazi banker. She had not planned to tell John about the insult and stinging hatred, but she did. It was not something she would usually tell him because she preferred he did not know everything about how she hid her identity. At that moment, everything had to be on the table. And then she told John about Robert Rosen and the job offer.

"I told him I had to talk to you," she said.

"What about? It's your decision."

"Do you have any thoughts?" she asked.

"Maybe. But they're not important. It's not a job forever. It's interesting while we wait for victory. Same with me. When the war is over, my job is over. In the meantime, you will get firsthand information about the movement of troops and materiel and how the war is going. You might hear about the roundup of Jews in Europe. If that is too much, then don't take the job. If you get caught up in that kind of news, it will eventually affect you."

"Mr. Rosen said that it would not be my area," she said.

"If you can do what is required of you, minus dealing with Jewish transports, then help the government. No question you can do that job. Sleep on it. We'll talk about it at breakfast."

In the morning, Estelle told John that she would take the job.

"You're committing to fight the war, John. I want to do my part to destroy that madman."

CHAPTER 23

A DIFFERENT KIND OF WAR

Within a few days after the interview with Robert Rosen, Estelle contacted an older woman named Belinda in the neighborhood, who preferred to care for a child only until the age of three. Estelle did not want the sitter to bathe or cook for the baby – she made her own baby food, and she or John took turns with a nightly bath. The cost of childcare was reasonable and minimally cut into her new salary; yet, she made more money than she did at Dodge & Cox, and she now had her own government healthcare benefits. She hoped both salaries would get them to their goal of moving to San Rafael.

Estelle went to work at a small cubby-hole of a government office in Haight-Ashbury at the end of December, 1942. The bottom of the building that housed the government office sold fabrics. Mr. Rosen's office was on the second-floor. No one would notice it because it had no identifying features, no sign, no names, just like the other offices on that second-floor that were not rented. The office was hidden in a corner at the end of a long hallway.

Within the first few days, Estelle got her footing. The staff was small; she counted six full-time people who entered the office every day. The employees had quiet, low-key natures, which worked well, since talking interfered with the seriousness of the job. No one left for lunch. A pot of coffee was continually brewing. Mr. Rosen checked in and out of the office as he coordinated the information. She learned quickly that "need to know" was a euphemism for the government to disseminate information only when it was necessary. With Mr. Rosen's intimate knowledge of the quadrants of the war and the strategies of the Nazi regime, she was able to learn what data to look for, master a new vocabulary consisting of military terms and war terminology, and become part of a unique chain of command that went strictly by the book and tolerated few nuances. Essential to the information gathering of the office was the code-breaking operation run by a man and a woman whose names Estelle never knew. They were experts in breaking Nazi codes.

Estelle handled all correspondence for Mr. Rosen – typing reports and letters, reading teletypes, or answering telephones. She was not to go near the two cryptology machines. Her ears were covered most of the day, so she was not privy to any talk of the Nazis transports moving the Jews all over Europe. She was grateful that Mr. Rosen assigned others to gather information about the concentration camps.

Her duties focused on U.S. troops moving across the European theater and on fascist cells in cities around the U.S. led by Father Charles Coughlin's Christian Front nationalist movement. Estelle learned that these seditious underground organizations sent messages in code around the U.S. about the transportation of weapons, training facilities that taught weaponry with guns, ammunition, and bomb making techniques. Estelle confirmed information, previously rumored, that American congressmen and senators and wealthy businessmen were in the clutches of Nazi spies.

Mr. Rosen cautioned Estelle not to tell John or anyone what was going on with the war from her perspective at work. John as well told her little about what he was doing. The evenings were taken up with Lance and going for evening walks with him when there was no fog or wind. On the weekends, they sometimes rode the ferries. Once in a while, Estelle had to work a half-day on Saturday, but it never bothered her. And every now and then, she would see Mr. Rosen in the office, and he would say, "Great work, Mrs. Moran. Much appreciated."

At the end of 1942 and the beginning of 1943, there was an escalation in the movement of the Jews. Estelle overheard a conversation between two cryptologists: "They're picking up the pace of transports. Sending Jews to work camps until they can't work and then they go to a larger facility," said one cryptologist. "Treblinka to Auschwitz."

"Forty-three is the year it ramps up," said the other cryptologist. "They're filling the camps with women and children first."

Estelle felt sick and left the office to breathe fresh air. Outside on the street, she saw Mr. Rosen coming toward the office.

"Sorry, Mr. Rosen," she said. "I just stepped out for a break."

"What happened?" he asked.

"It was nothing, really."

"It was something. I'm sure you heard about Hitler's plan to escalate the number of Jews being sent to concentration camps. Himmler's work."

"I wish I had no knowledge. I wish I could live without history, but now the newspapers are reporting about the extermination camps on the front pages. It's like a foretold doom hanging over us. The Jewish plight is no longer on page six. Europe is in Hitler's grip, Britain is getting pummeled, and America is the only country that can do something about the Jews, and they won't. Or can't. It's like throwing a shadow behind you."

"I don't have answers for you, Mrs. Moran. Before I went to the European front, I understood that, for Jews, history has no hinge – the abyss is always open."

"What does that mean, Mr. Rosen?" she asked.

"A Jew can never be fully assimilated. They have been the other since they walked the earth – the Bible tells us this. The rationale for hating Jews is that they don't believe what Christians believe, that Jesus is the son of God. I don't observe Jewish customs except as a remnant of family ties. For the Christian, I'm always a Jew."

"Is the Jewish identity a curse, Mr. Rosen?" asked Estelle. "I have history in my family in Europe, my communist father and religious mother, and now the end result of the trauma is the extermination of all Jews? I'd rather not know any of this."

"Complacency is hubris. It is one of the most impactful conditions of all human experience. We are all unnerved by this war. What you should know for your job is that the military is trying to persuade members of the cabinet and the president himself, that it's best to stop the Nazis militarily first before America tackles the ravages of the holocaust. If we bomb the camps, there will be more Jewish deaths. We were late to the war, and this is the price everyone has to pay for those who obstructed the war effort."

"I will survive the day with earplugs," said Estelle as she walked inside the building.

It did not occur to Estelle that she might be pregnant. It was the beginning of summer, 1943, that she realized she must be pregnant. In her first pregnancy, she never threw up, never felt nauseous, or lost her balance. Although the beginning of her second pregnancy was discomforting – some morning sickness, which she took care of with saltine crackers – she had learned to successfully compartmentalize work and normal life. Obligated to Mr. Rosen and the American government, Estelle knew she would continue to work until delivery and perhaps until the war ended. John also had to stay at his job with the railroad until the end of the war.

The worst year of the war was 1943, with fierce fighting throughout Europe, especially the Soviet Union. Hitler's army had encroached on Soviet territory in 1941, but with the help of other Allied forces at the battle of Stalingrad, the German army was overcome in February 1943. Even though Stalingrad was a turning point in the war, there was still a long road ahead to recapture Western Europe.

Estelle delivered baby Joan Frances on November 11, 1943. It was ironic that in the midst of a second world war, Joan came into the world on Armistice Day – the day the First World War ended. Joan was a gift to Estelle at a time when she and John needed the joy of a baby – with curly red hair, hazel eyes like John, and an instant laugh as if Joan already knew what was funny in life. It was a national holiday, and John was at the hospital to see his daughter when she was born. Estelle insisted their daughter should be named after John – Joan was the feminine of John and also a tribute to Saint Joan of Arc, the heroine of France who helped her country win the Siege of Orleans during the Hundred Years' War. Estelle liked the idea of bringing a female warrior into the world.

Estelle returned to her government work three weeks after Joan was born. She was taking on more military information than at any other time in her job. By mid-1944, America and the Allies were winning the war. Step by step, they liberated Western Europe from the Nazis. Events in the theater of war were moving at breakneck speed. Estelle and John were busy fulfilling their responsibilities as fast as possible. Although they had no time for trips with the children to Marin County, something was becoming clear. Together they had saved enough money to buy a house in San Rafael. It would take another year and a half to wind down life in San Francisco and accomplish their dream.

Estelle quit her job the day the war ended on September 2, 1945. By then, the final tally of Hitler's murderous execution of six million Jews and other non-Aryan populations became known to the world. On her last day of work, Estelle said goodbye to Mr. Rosen.

"You're relieved, Estelle, I know. I don't blame you."

"You have never called me by my first name, Mr. Rosen."

"I'm not your boss anymore. You can still change your mind about leaving, you know."

"I believe it's my time to leave this work."

"It's surprising how little we talked over the years," he said. "I want to say you were a force of nature in this office. Our operation would never have been so successful without your passion and strength. Fortitude comes to mind."

"You're too kind. You are the real hero, Robert."

"How outrageous you are! And funny and brilliant."

"I know little, if any personal information about you, and I'm glad I don't," she said. "I know that the few times we connected, I showed my lack of courage about not acknowledging my identity. You gave me some understanding about my fears."

"Remember, Estelle, we all have our fears. It is part of how we live. The intention is not to give into our fears. That would be soul crushing, I'm afraid."

"Maybe I'm cursed to live with those fears for the rest of my life. For me, the war was a confirmation that those fears will always be with me."

"That is a profound recognition. I feel the same. Be well."

After the war, John left the Western Pacific Railroad. He audited the railroad cars used by the government, and was upset by the lack of organization he found. There was also no system for accounting. John had to use primitive binders held together by strings and canvas covers to separate his audits. Before he left his position, he asked his bosses if he could devise a better system of accounting to accommodate a new transportation paradigm that would occur after the war. The railroads would obviously not be dependent on military contracts. Railroad managers were not interested.

In the ensuing months after he left Western Pacific, John parlayed his knowledge of the binder business by contacting the McBee Company, a binder firm that sold mostly to the railroads. He backdoored his way into the railroad business all over the West Coast as a manufacturer's representative.

During the hiatus between Estelle's foray back into domesticity and John leaving the railroad, she and John went house hunting in San Rafael to start a new life. She had her eye on an older Craftsman house built in the early 1930s on a street in San Rafael called Linden Lane.

They had sold the flat in the Haight, put a bid on the Linden Lane house, and packed up their belongings. Their bid was accepted immediately. The new house was tucked away from the street. It had a huge backyard and two swing sets on about an eighth of an acre of property. It was clear that this old Craftsman needed work.

"How are we going to manage the remodel?" she asked John one night at dinner.

"We could hire subcontractors and you could be the general. I'll get the bids, and you can sub it out. It might just work."

The plan worked – from designing the interior, to getting Lance settled at St. Raphael's grammar school, to host a foster teenager to help with Joan during the day until Lance came home from kindergarten.

When Estelle was freed up after remodeling the Craftsman, she began to study for her real estate license. There was a method to her madness. Getting a real estate license and learning the ropes of buying and selling homes to clients in Marin County would give her a broad picture of the business and help her make contacts in the building trades.

"Someday, we're going to be our own bosses, John. In the meantime, your job with McBee will help us save for our future fixing up and remodeling like we did in the city.

"We are on a roll, honey."

Joan & Lance

PART 3
CHAPTER 24

JOAN

When I was three years old, my parents put me into nursery school at Dominican Convent. It was in an idyllic environment, surrounded by tall eucalyptus trees, fresh smelling scrubs, and beautiful homes set far back from the quiet streets. I was taken in by the immaculate school setting with a large and graceful nunnery where the older population as well as the recruits were housed. A classically styled music building situated to the side of the convent. There were miles of outdoor paths, tennis courts, and park-like settings. I fell in love with everything, including the Dominican nuns in their long, white robes and black habits. I could not get out of my father's car fast enough when he dropped me off in the mornings for school. I ran into my classroom with joy. The nursery school was situated to the side of the kindergarten and grammar school. The room was warm and cozy and Sister Patricia was an angel from heaven. My mother picked me up at the end of the day, but I did not want to leave my nursery. It was a torture for me when I turned five and my parents decided to take me out of the convent school and put me in kindergarten at St. Raphael's grammar school. I cried for days. Lance was already in St.

Raphael's so having both children in the same school was more convenient for my parents. But it was sad for me.

If my mother had negative reservations about a Catholic school education for her children, she kept it to herself. However, from the day my brother and I entered a Catholic school, my mother never went into a classroom or talked to a nun. She considered private school education, even with a religious component, to be preferable to public education. If religion was included as a subject during the day, so be it. If my mother had to endure the prayers and rituals of Catholicism, and she came out unscathed, then her children could manage the religious programs. However, the end result of Catholic education was mixed. Lance was bullied and kept his distance from religion for most of his life. And I was enthralled with everything about Catholicism and wanted to be a nun.

When I turned six and Lance was almost nine my mother decided that we should start taking tap dancing lessons. She adored tap dancing and told us stories about tap classes in the 1920s and 1930s in San Francisco. She told us about a man named Joey. "It was Joey's idea for me to take tap lessons," said my mother, "because knowing how to tap would make me a better dancer. Everyone should learn how to tap. It's good for posture."

"If tap is so special, why do I have to take ballet?" I asked

"One is not better than the other, darling," she said. "You must experience both. And by the way, I found a piano teacher across from the library where you both will take weekly lessons."

My mother took full control of my growth and development as I was growing up. Even as a little girl, I was her jewel. And I wanted to please her all the time. She used to say I was her doppelgänger – just like the doll my mother sewed clothes for when she was a little girl made to her perfect likeness. She wanted me to grow up to be a lady who was perfectly dressed with exquisite manners and top grades, who studied piano and ballet. She said to me when I was young that what is inside me is as important as what is showing on the outside. In time, she told me, I should develop several important qualities: discipline, a generosity of spirit, diligence, fortitude, self-awareness, and an attitude of authority about who I am. I wanted whatever my mother wanted for me, even though I did not fully understand those big words.

After kindergarten at St. Raphael's, my parents decided to sell the house on Linden Lane and move to another location.

"Don't worry, honey," my mother said to me. "We are moving in the hill behind St. Raphael's. The walk to school will be two blocks."

Little did my brother and I realize that this would be only the first of many moves taken by our parents. We did not know that we were going to be moving every two years.

"Mom, what did you and Dad do before we moved all the time?" I asked as we were moving into a rented duplex while we waited for another duplex to be remodeled.

"We always planned to buy and remodel the places we lived in. Later on, we hoped to build houses from the ground up. We would live in a house and then sell it for more than what we paid for it. That's how we make a profit. We'll always have a plan for the next project. For now, Dad has a job with McBee Binders, and I'm going to get my real estate license, sell homes, and look for good prospects to remodel or build."

"Why do you want to do that?" I asked.

"Because in time we are going to be in the building business."

In those years, I saw the strength of my parents, holding down two jobs each and managing their children's lives through solid organization. My parents were becoming a strong team with a clear future. The purchase of their first duplex after they sold Linden Lane was a first step to kick off something bigger and more lucrative. Buy a duplex, live in one and rent the other for extra income. Initially, most of our moving happened in the San Rafael neighborhood behind St. Raphael's grammar school.

My mother was a top earner at the real estate office across the street from St. Raphael's Church. She told my Dad that the men in the office were jealous of her. I overheard the conversation when my mother was fixing dinner one night.

"Behind my back they make snide remarks," she told my Dad – "'She thinks she's a hotshot' 'kind of talk. One of the salesmen, Bill, asked me if you and I had joined the Fairfax Cotillion. He told me it was a great place to meet potential clients. I told Bill we already were accepted to join."

"Honey," my dad said, "I don't think you're going to get a lot of clients from the Fairfax Cotillion. They don't talk business at these sorts of things. Mostly, they drink and tell bad jokes."

My parents were accepted. But it turned out that after several months of going, they were asked to leave. Although I did not know they were asked to leave, I was curious why they stopped going to monthly dances. Lance was the one who discovered the reason. He was clearing off the kitchen table after dinner one night when they started having the conversation about Cotillion, and noticed my parents had stopped talking.

"I'll clear the table, Lance," said my mother. "You have homework to do, I'm sure."

They waited for Lance to leave the room before speaking again, but he did not go to his room. He listened by the door.

"We were asked to leave Cotillion," my mother said.

"What happened?" asked my Dad.

"What do you think, John? They had suspicions that I was Jewish. I was out before we had our first waltz. That creep in the office, Bill Carson, probably had a hunch about me, and besides, I out-sold him every month."

"They're all jealous, Stella. The realtors in the office aren't your friends. You don't need these cotillion people to help you make a living. We've got our own moxie and some pretty good opportunities."

Lance did not tell me what he overheard in the kitchen that night until decades later. He did not understand the references at the time. What was Jewish? Why were they asked to leave the Fairfax Cotillon for being Jewish, which they were not, because his father is a Catholic? And so was Lance and his sister. He went to the World Book Encyclopedia to look up what "Jewish" meant. He read about Jewish holidays and traditions. He remembered the candleholder, the menorah, and a prayer shawl in Grandma Rose's dining room long ago during Thanksgiving dinners. He later learned that these items were part of the Jewish religion observed by Rose and Louie. He kept the information to himself because he was only beginning to understand what my mother said about someone suspecting her of being Jewish. He kept his secret.

There were unanswered questions about the family when it came to holidays. Lance and I never celebrated Christmas with our Grandma Rose, only with Grandma Mary and the Irish aunts, uncles, and cousins in San Francisco. Grandma Mary hardly spoke to us. But our aunts and uncles were kind.

We were much closer to Grandma Rose and spent part of our summers with her in Sonoma, where Rose and Louie had a small two-bedroom house not far from the hot springs pools where we swam every day. Lance and I rode bikes and played canasta and listened to the radio programs, especially detective serials. Our favorites were *Yours Truly, Johnny Dollar* and *Dragnet*, and, of course, *The Lone Ranger*. Religion was never mentioned. I worried about not going to church on Sundays when we were in Sonoma, but Lance told me not to worry about it. He said we could make up for church later. Suddenly, we stopped going to Sonoma when Rose and Louie divorced. No one talked about it. Lance and I went off to summer camp.

The other strangeness in my family was my mother's sister and her three children – two girls and a boy. She always came over to our house in San Rafael with her children but her husband was never with her. It was usually on a random Sunday. My cousins and I did not engage in conversation. I was frustrated because I wanted to know them. I noticed my mother didn't get along with her sister. Lance and I never decided what to make of our cousins who seemed to have no personalities. They did not speak much, except to say their mother forced them to take piano. Mildred still taught piano. Barbara, the oldest cousin, told me that her mother divorced their father. She did not seem to care. When I asked my mother about what it was like growing up with Auntie Mildred, she would say that her sister became distant and difficult to get along with as she got older. There was probably jealousy involved, my mother added.

Every now and then, we overheard my parents talking about bringing the kids to visit Jake. Lance and I had no idea who Jake was for the longest time.

"After all," my mother said, "The kids are old enough to meet him, especially Lance. Joanie is in the fourth grade now, so it's certainly time for her to meet him."

"Are you feeling guilty," my Dad asked?

"Maybe. I don't know how we should make the introduction. I mean, where has their grandfather been all this time? How do you explain that?"

"You explain it by saying that you and your father have not always been on good terms. Don't make too much of it. It's a good idea for the kids to meet him, except where do we visit him? At his fur shop or his hotel on Geary Street?"

My mother took Dad's advice and presented Grandpa Jake as aloof and distant and not much of a family man. Since Lance and I never gave a thought to having a grandfather, it was more strange than a surprise. After all, our parents and Grandma Rose had never mentioned him. He could not have been an important family figure.

It was at this time, I began to learn a little about family dysfunction regarding my mother's relationship with her family. Not that I knew at nine years-old what dysfunction was, but relationships seemed to show up out of the blue. Like my cousins who did not speak to me. Lance did not care, but I did. Lance pointed out that we did not have a grandfather on the Irish side, so we were not invested in having one, especially one we never saw.

"We're going for a Sunday drive to visit your grandfather," my dad said. "Your mother thinks it's time for you to meet him."

Lance looked at me and shrugged. He was resigned. He never caused trouble or opposed a request.

"I think it's creepy," I said. "I wonder why Mom and Dad waited so long to tell us."

It was a perfectly beautiful Sunday and a good day to take a drive across the Golden Gate Bridge. That was the way my Dad decided to tell us that we were on our way to visit Grandpa Jake.

"Grandpa Jake's furrier store is in this neighborhood, too," said my Dad. "You might find it interesting. A little rundown but interesting because it's an old neighborhood."

"It's not that interesting," I said.

We walked into an old, musty hotel on Geary and rode the elevator to the second floor. My Dad took the lead, knocked on Jake's hotel room, and walked inside holding the hands of his children. My mother was trailing him. He introduced us to our Grandpa.

"Good to meet you, two," said Jake. "You look healthy, and I bet you're smart, too.

"Hi, Pa," said my mother. "You look good." Jake ignored my mother's greeting.

My Dad gave Grandpa Jake a carton of Camel cigarettes.

"Thanks, Jack. Much obliged."

Grandpa Jake wanted to pay more attention to his grandchildren, but he did not know how to do that. He was old school, a man from another century with a slight English accent like Grandma Rose. He only talked to my Dad about unions and labor strikes and ancient history about communism and how Karl Marx was right: "Religion is the opiate of the people." My Dad and Jake got along because they liked to talk about history. When

Jake went on too long talking about the next revolution, my mother took us out to wait in the hallway.

"Grandpa Jake was nice, Mom," said Lance. "He was nice like someone from another time. I'll go see him again. And I'd like to see his fur store."

"Hold your nose when you do," said my mother. "It smells like another century."

"You have furs, Mom," I said. "Are they from Grandpa Jake? Did he give you some furs or did you buy them?"

"I bought them, honey. But I did learn about furs years ago when I saw him from time to time at his furrier store. He was a master at fur design. He knew every fur imaginable. And he was a designer of clothes and hats. He wasn't much of a father, but he was kind of a genius."

A year after my parents moved into a duplex they remodeled on Laurel Place in the hills above St. Raphael's, my Dad had a heart-to-heart with my mother at dinner one night. Lance and I were listening to *The Lone Ranger* on the radio, but turned our attention to what my Dad was saying. He told her that he had an offer from the McBee Company to move to St. Louis, Missouri, to work at their headquarters. He felt he owed it to the company to entertain the idea of relocating and see what they had to offer him.

"I think we should consider this move to St. Louis seriously," said my mother, "but I also think we might make an adventure out of it. Take a trip in summer and you can do business."

"You mean a vacation," said my Dad.

"Instead of only flying to St. Louis to interview for a higher up position, why don't we take a road trip around the U.S.? We could fly to Detroit, pick up a new Buick."

"Wait a minute," I said. "Don't we get to have a vote?"

"I'm afraid not," said my Dad. "First things first. I have to see if I want to take the job."

"This is about your father's business, and you kids don't get to vote."

School let out the second week of June 1952, and we did, indeed, make a trip out of it. We flew to Detroit. It was our first trip on a plane. My mother dressed like a fashion model in a chic suit, a dashing hat, gloves, and high heels. I walked beside her on the tarmac, looking like her twin except I wore Mary Janes with white socks. It was the quintessential 1950s look. My mother never met a fashion style she did not embrace, even false eyelashes, which she wore for the rest of her life, including the day she passed away. My mother dressed to fly.

In Detroit, my Dad bought a navy blue 1952 Buick for their trip. The first stop was St. Louis so my Dad could meet with McBee Binder Company to talk about the job and salary. He told McBee that he would have an answer by mid-August. While my Dad was in his business meetings, we ate lunch in a coffee shop next to the McBee Building. Finally, my Dad joined us.

"Don't keep us in suspense, John," said my Mom.

"It was a great offer. I was surprised. The problem is that there is too much of a desk job, too much public relations. I like the sales, you know that, honey. I hope you don't mind, but I decided that I'm not taking the job. I'm not telling them until mid-August." I jumped for joy. Lance and I hugged. We did not want to leave San Rafael. And my mother did not want to leave all those potential real estate projects behind.

"I like the freedom we are going to have, honey," said my Mom. "And you can go out on your own and work in the city, and I can help you, too. It is the best of both worlds."

Sightseeing took a back seat during the first week of July. My parents listened on the radio to the Republican National Convention, held in Chicago at the International Amphitheater. Lance and I listened, too. We were kind of fascinated by the nomination of Dwight D. Eisenhower. It got better when my Dad called Richard Nixon "Tricky Dick." Eisenhower was a "lightweight," my Dad noted. Both my parents were Democrats with a big D.

When the Democratic National Convention began its broadcast over the radio three weeks later, we were traveling in the midWest – Iowa, Nebraska and moving toward Colorado. I thought it was boring, so I was glad to listen to the convention on the radio. Oddly enough, it was also held in Chicago at the International Amphitheater. This was my political awakening.

"Mom, why do you like Adlai Stevenson so much?" Lance asked.

"Oh, darling, he's an intellectual," she said.

"The Republicans call him an egghead," John chimed in.

"Isn't Stevenson Jewish?" Lance asked.

This was the first time I heard the word "Jewish" in relation to anyone or anything.

"What makes you say that?" asked my Dad.

"I heard someone on the radio call him a Jew," said Lance.

"He's a Unitarian," said my Dad.

"What's that, Dad?" I asked.

"Unitarianism is a form of Christianity. They believe in God as a uniting force for all men, but they don't believe Jesus is God. And they don't believe in the Trinity, you know, like the God the Father, Son, and Holy Ghost as you both learned in school. They follow the Bible and believe in the Bible, more or less, except for Jesus being the son of God."

"The Jews don't believe that Jesus is the savior either," said Lance. "Their savior hasn't come to earth, so they are still waiting to get saved."

"The Jewish people have a long history on earth," said my Dad. "Over thirty-five hundred years, maybe more."

"I read that Bess Myerson – you know, Miss America – was Jewish," said Lance, "and I read that some of the pageant supporters pulled out because she was Jewish."

"She is a beautiful and accomplished woman," said my Mom.

"Did you know that she was Jewish?" asked Lance.

"Yes, I did know that. It was in 1945 that she got her crown."

"We were in San Francisco at the time," said my Dad. "And it was quite a scandal."

"You know a lot about history, Dad," I said.

"We learn more about ourselves and our country by studying history."

We came back from our road trip in mid-August. Our last exploration was in the northwest part of the country – some parts of Canada, Vancouver, British Columbia, the state of Washington, Oregon, and down into the northern part of California, and finally into Marin County. It was in time to prepare for school.

CHAPTER 25

THE CATHOLIC VERSUS THE JEW

I was never a teenage rebel. I believe it was because my mother let me develop my own ideas about what I wanted to do in life. I had one strong passion since I was a child – I wanted to study drama and be an actress. My mother embraced my interest. Above all, she never preached perfection. "Perfection should never be a goal," my mother would say.

Since I was a good girl, I did what was expected of me. I followed the rules, understood discipline, and was determined that I would get good grades and go to college. My mother taught me never to be afraid of failure – "Joanie, there's no such thing as failure, and remember to treat success with dignity." Most important was that my mother passed on to me her love of all art forms – theater, film, dance, music, classic sculptures and fine arts. Together we planned the plays and movies we would see throughout the year. My mother also built a superb library in her home – Hemingway, Faulkner, and Steinbeck, and the Russian novelists Dostoevsky, Gogol, and Tolstoy – so I could read the classics. I devoured them before I entered high school. I spent summers reading *Anna Karenina, The Brothers Karamazov,* and *War and Peace* on the diving board over our pool.

My parents never spoke of my mother's ancestry or religion. All I knew was that my mother did not have a religion or a belief system. She was self-contained. She followed her passions with conviction, choosing to spend her time creating a fulfilling life for herself and her family. My mother's essence was to assert that "We could be anything we wanted to be."

When I enrolled at Marin Catholic High School, my mother entered Marin Junior College as a freshman. The two-year college prepared my mother to enter San Francisco State College as a junior two years later. As a junior at State, she declared home economics as her major. She was already familiar with most of the areas required for her studies – expanding her sewing and designing skills long before she entered school. But her design skills were enhanced by learning how to design floor plans for homes, especially kitchens. This was her forte, and design excited my mother the most.

With my mother in college and I in high school, we studied together, wrote our papers side by side, and graduated after four years of academic work. I was inspired and excited to learn how to write from my mother. She was my primary inspiration for learning how to write my research papers and craft my speeches. My mother insisted on rehearsing endlessly for every speech contest. She was my coach – and she never missed a speech contest. My speech teacher, Father Ben Cummins, was always a strong presence in my life in high school. He was an excellent teacher and took care of his flock academically, as well as providing guidance for our maturation and personal development. Father Ben and my mother were good friends and enjoyed each other's company. I often saw them laugh when they were in conversation. I wondered what they said, what they had in common.

I was extremely proud of my mother when she was recognized as a summa cum laude at graduation from San Francisco State. Not only was she still working during this time for my Dad in the San Francisco office, but she also ran a household and looked after her family's needs. My mother never saw a football game, never saw her daughter cheerlead, and never talked to one of my teachers or interfered with the teaching process. And she never talked to a nun.

This was her way of fostering and developing my independence. And I never had a curfew. Living life with my mother was not complicated, not difficult, and always organized. My mother worked from the ground floor up – meaning, because she was an efficiency expert, her household had a code of conduct that was enforced without question. It simply made life easier. We never had a cleaning lady. I did the dusting. My Dad's job was to vacuum and garden, and Lance cleaned the pool, took out the garbage, and did odd chores.

My hideaway was my mother's bedroom, where I would study in the comfortable green chair with a side table and standing lamp. When I needed help with a test, my mother put her books aside and quizzed me.

One evening, I was studying with my mother for a religion test the next day. The Catholic catechism was on the end table. The format was call and response – questions like "Who is God?" "Who made you?" My mother read questions from the catechism: "What does the concept of the Trinity mean to Catholics?"

"Mom, what religion were you raised in?"

"I have no religion," she said. "I think I told you that a long time ago."

"If you had a religion, what would it be?"

"Protestant."

"You don't even know what that is," I said.

"It doesn't matter. It was easy to check off when I went for a job interview."

"Do you have any idea what the Trinity means?"

"In a way," said my mother.

"In what way?"

"I told you that I went to Catholic school in Montreal, then when we moved to New York, I went to a Catholic school in the Lower East Side. The closest school to our apartment was a Catholic school, and I was there for two years. Or three. I don't remember."

"Were you raised a Catholic, then?" I asked. "I don't know how you grew up."

"I wasn't interested in learning about a religion," she said. "I sat in class and memorized what I had to do for the test."

"And then you dropped it. You threw it away."

"I wasn't interested. Why are we having this conversation?"

"You don't believe in God."

"In the end, it's ashes to ashes, dust to dust as far as I'm concerned. You live, you die, and you're buried. That's it. It was strange to me that I had to check off a religion when I filled out a job application. The real question should be 'Why do companies ask about religion?' A job is a job, and it has nothing to do with religion, nothing to do what kind of person is being hired."

"Why didn't you put down Jewish as a religion?"

My mother did not respond.

"I always wanted to ask you about Thanksgiving when we went to Grandma Rose's house when she was married to Louie. There were a few candlesticks and a candelabra with nine tiny candle holes and a blue and white shawl in the dining room that hung over a chair. What were they for? It looked like something related to religion."

"Louie was Jewish," said my mother.

"Why didn't you go to his funeral?" I asked. "Lance said it wasn't in a temple, and Louie's children were not happy about that."

"Rose and Louie did not belong to a temple because Louie was not a religious Jew. He was not the kind to join a temple. Out of respect, Dad and Lance went to support Grandma Rose."

"But she was your mother. Shouldn't you have gone?'

"It wasn't necessary. I honored Grandma Rose in my own way, stood by her in the funeral home, and said goodbye to Louie with her standing next to me." My mother got up from her green chair and left the room. "I need a cup of coffee."

I suspected my mother was an atheist, but it took a while for me to get my head in that space. My mother left religious matters to my Dad. He was in charge. My mother was relieved from engaging in any of it. That was what she wanted.

My Dad was not particularly religious. Although he took Lance and me to Mass every Sunday, he did not have a deep commitment to faith. Going to church with my Dad was one important way we bonded. It was almost a ritual that only we understood. We had a way of signaling each other in church. I looked to the side pews to find him, and when he caught my eye, my Dad made himself pious, as if he was praying. That always made me laugh because he was never pious. Our play and banter had everything to do with how we related to each other – his Irish humor, the ironic way he looked at life, how safe he made me feel, how supportive and caring, and most of all, how he never judged.

I was the perfect Catholic girl. I followed the rituals precisely. When I had to go to confession to make my Easter duty, I would go with my Dad. We sat in a pew on the side of the church. Once I asked my Dad why he never went to confession.

"You mean talk to that guy in the box?" he asked, pointing to the confessional box.

"It's not a box. It's a confessional, Dad," I said.

"Why would I talk to the priest? He's just a man. He's nothing special. He's not God. Besides, I've got nothing to confess."

That made me laugh. Of course, he had no sins to confess.

"But you can't go to communion without going to confession," I said.

"Why would I want to do that? The wafer is not God because the ordinary man said so."

"When was the last time you went to communion?"

"Maybe eighth grade. I was an altar boy," said my Dad. "And then I left the church."

But my Dad never missed a Sunday Mass with his daughter. Even when I came home from college, we went to Mass together like old times.

In 1961, the year I graduated from Marin Catholic High School, my parents and I went to Europe as part of a group from Marin Catholic and a group from a school in Oakland, California,

Father Ben, my speech teacher, and his brother, Father John, led the tour. My mother was immediately enthusiastic about the trip. She thought it would be fun to have tour leaders who were lively and intelligent. Father Ben and my mother already got along splendidly, so it was the perfect trip for her. The only issue was that the tour visited all the Catholic shrines and cathedrals in Europe. We traveled by bus to thirteen countries in nine weeks. The tour didn't miss a cathedral, shrine, relic from a tomb, Sunday Mass, or a pilgrimage. My mother never went to Mass, but she did trek through Our Lady of Fatima Shrine in Portugal and went to Lourdes in France, all the time rolling her eyes. She would not kneel if she had a gun to her head.

My parents planned a side trip to County Cork, Ireland, to visit the Moran farm and meet the family. The Moriarty family, my Grandma Mary's people in County Kerry, had all died off. Before we left for Ireland, while we were in Rome, Italy, my Dad received news that his mother died. It was prescient that she passed while her son was about to visit her deceased husband's farm and deliver gifts. My Dad was more familiar with the Moran side still residing in Ireland and knew little about his mother's family. We couldn't attend Grandma Mary's funeral because there was no easy way to get back to San Francisco in time. When we got to the farm, my Dad went off for a time to walk the farm.

"What is Dad doing?" I asked my mother.

"Walking off his grief. He is stoic about his mother's death. He was a good son."

"What about you? How do you feel?"

"I feel nothing. Grandma Mary did not like me and was caustic and rude."

"It's nice that you brought a suitcase full of clothes for the cousins," I said.

My mother did not respond. I went outside to visit the goats.

After Ireland, we were to meet up with our group in Munich. There was a scheduled trip to Dachau concentration camp. I was getting ready to go when I noticed my parents were sitting on the sofa in the hotel room.

"We're not going to that place," my mother announced.

"It's not that place," I said. "It's Dachau. It's important."

"It's gruesome, and you are not going. We are not going."

"I'm going. Mom. The Nazis destroyed the Jews. Six million. It's important to give honor to those who died. Six million, Mom."

"I know the number. It's happened. It's over. We're staying here."

I stomped out of the room, furious that my mother wouldn't let me go to the concentration camp. I knew about the concentration camps – they were all over Europe, 44,000 of them. Most had been destroyed after the war. I ran to catch up to the group before it boarded the train, but it had left. I never forgot that day because of my mother's strong resistance to bearing witness to the past. I was frustrated and disappointed.

My father was no help. I pulled him aside and told him how angry I was that my mother would not let me go to Dachau.

"That is the way your mother feels. It is in the past. Let it go."

Shortly after returning from Europe, my mother and I drove to UCLA for sorority rush. She did not understand, nor did she care about the college ritual of pledging a sorority. During the first days of rush, I noticed there were two options listed on the information sheet for potential pledges.

"Mom," I said. "Take a look at this rushing schedule. I never noticed, but there are two columns to choose from: A and B. I picked Plan A because it has the most sorority houses to rush. I thought I'd have a better chance of getting into one."

"If you ask me, it's an entire waste of time. What was wrong with the dorm?"

"I decided to see what Plan B was about, and I found out it was for Jewish girls. This rush business is a segregated system."

"Can't say I'm shocked," she said as she walked to the balcony, pulled a cigarette out of her purse, lit it, and took a deep inhale. "That's the way it is. That's the way it always is."

"I don't see how that's possible. Practically the entire campus is full of Jews."

"You can always find people, even young people who hold those feelings, Joanie."

"What feelings are those?" I asked.

"Antisemitism. It's been around for a long time."

"It's the sixties," I said. "Free thinking and moving past the horror of the Holocaust will be our generation's mission. Dad was right. We learn more about ourselves and our country by studying history. He says history is where we learn the lessons of life."

"If you say so, Joanie. I'm glad your generation is more open in your thinking."

"How long are you going to stay with me? I know you want to visit Grandma."

"I'm going to see you settled, honey. And thank goodness it will be done by the end of the week. Grandma Rose and I planned to get together on Saturday. Best thing she ever did was move to Los Angeles ten years ago. The warmer climate helps her with her arthritis. She has easy access to the bus and to a dance club. She's already met a new friend named Harry."

"Is Harry Jewish?"

"I presume there is a group of Jewish seniors who are of like minds."

I lasted at UCLA for a year and a half. Sorority life was not for me. I was usually out of the house rehearsing for a play or scene work in class. It was all I could do to keep up in my class work.

There was the ritual sorority rush when I returned to UCLA for my sophomore year in September, 1962. A Jewish girl named Amanda wanted to pledge to my sorority. She was the famous daughter of a celebrity pianist. Most of the girls in the house wanted her to join. She was a perfect fit for the Kappa house, but the house mother vetoed it. The discrimination was palpable. I spoke up and told my sorority sisters that Amanda must pledge. She would be a valuable asset to the house.

"This kind of thinking supports the segregation of Jewish and Gentile sororities," I said. "It's time this kind of thinking is over."

Those in the room listened in silence and then voted to accept her. The house mother voiced her disapproval. I did not return to the Kappa house after the winter break.

My roommate, Bonnie, and I had discussed transferring to Berkeley for the winter semester. UCLA was more of a commuter school and did not foster the close relationships of people who live and breathe academic pursuits as Berkeley possessed. Bonnie and I wanted to enrich our experience at a first-class institution.

It was in the Berkeley '60s. John F. Kennedy was just elected president, and every student adhered to his progressive agenda. We never saw any president like JFK before. His youth and enthusiasm and hope prompted the freedom rides, the launching of the Peace Corps, and facing down Fidel at the Bay of Pigs. There was a flourishing of the arts and high-energy, philosophical discussions of the Beat Generation, a new kind of rock and roll music from the Beatles and the Stones. The Vietnam protests had not taken shape as yet, but the anti-war sentiment was palpable. The intellectual environment was intoxicating. I immersed herself in classes – styles of acting, theater history, and seminars about the Irish playwrights. I rehearsed scenes and performed in Shakespeare. It was a full year of the Bard. This was the best of times.

Cal Berkeley played UCLA in basketball in February of 1963. Cal won. The party was held at a bar off campus nestled in a wooded canyon. During a break in the music, the sound of a motorcycle blared. I was feeling no pain – having finished dancing on top of a table to "Be My Baby" by the Ronettes – when the driver of the motorcycle walked in. A cheer went up – "Hey, Jer! Jerry, my man!" There were a few embraces and he grabbed a beer. The second I saw him, I knew this beatnik motorcycle guy was mine forever. "Sugar Shack" by Jimmy Gilmer and the Fireballs began to play, and a mutual friend, Michael – Jerry's best friend since middle school in Los Angeles and also one of my best guy friends from UCLA – grabbed my hand to dance. Michael and I finished our dance with both of us almost falling off the table. I landed in the arms of Jerry the beatnik. I looked into his hazel eyes and held them firmly in place.

"Hi, I'm Jerry," he said. "You're Joan, right? I know about you, You and your roommate, Bonnie just transferred from UCLA. You hung out with my ZBT fraternity buddies. I bused tables at your Kappa house."

"Nice to meet you," I said, as I got up off Jerry's lap and climbed back up on the table.

Bobby Vinton began to sing "Blue Velvet." Jerry got on the table to dance with me. It became our favorite song.

"I want you to see my motorcycle," he said. "Come outside with me."

In the semi-darkness, I walked out with him to view his prize possession.

"I love it. It's gorgeous and sexy."

"It's a Norton. I'll take you on a ride tomorrow. It's Sunday. No classes."

"Sure," I said casually. My heart was pounding.

"Meet me at the corner of Telegraph and Bancroft at noon," Jerry said as he revved the motor and drove off.

I got on my bike and peddled back to my apartment. Real life was just beginning.

I began dating Jerry, but our schedules were intense. He was a second-year law school student at Berkeley. When he wasn't in law school, he was studying ten or more hours a day. And my classes were rigorous and time consuming with class work and rehearsals. Being a theater major was unrelenting in terms of time commitments. We had everything going for us in terms of interests, intellectual curiosity, and sexual attraction. Bonnie started dating a law school student from Hastings Law School in San Francisco. The other side of her bed was infrequently in use. That's when Jerry stayed over. If Bonnie needed the bed, I stayed at Jerry's house – sex, great conversation, politics, art – and life was good.

Four months later, I realized that Jerry and I needed to clear the air. "It's time to talk about the elephant in the room."

"What's that? I thought we're doing pretty good. In fact, I think I'm in love with you."

"Hold that thought. You're Jewish, and I'm Catholic. I still go to Mass when I can, and I'm sure you've got some religious obligations. And if we decide marriage is for us, then what?"

"The elephant in the room looks like this: I drink bourbon, and you drink scotch."

"Same thing: I'm Catholic, and you're Jewish."

"We're going to table the conversation until after the summer. I'm interning at a law firm in Las Vegas, and you'll probably be working. Let's play this out after summer."

At Easter, I invited Jerry to come home with me for dinner. My mother always made traditional food for my Dad. He loved ham with all the trimmings.

Jerry declined. "Second-year law school is a bitch, and I've got tests coming up. You know how I study."

"All consuming, I know."

Lance picked me up in Berkeley for Easter dinner.

"What's new on the home front?" I asked.

"It's official. Moran Construction is on the map."

"You guys work fast. What's going on? I haven't seen the property forever."

"The property next to 233 Laurel – you remember the eight rental units, the apartment complex – well, I manage the units, along with a fourplex on another property they bought, and would you believe, the place is on Laurel Street, too."

"How are the newlyweds doing? All good? It's been almost two years."

"We get along very well. And Carole is a big help managing the apartment building on Laurel. What about you? Seeing anybody?"

"I'm happy for you, Lance. Carole is a sweet lady. Let's see, my news is I'm dating a Jewish boy, and I'll probably marry him."

"Law school student?"

"Second year. Keep this to yourself. There's still time for us to screw it up."

Easter dinner was a fun affair. My Dad was almost in his cups.

"Be careful, John," my mother cautioned.

My new sister-in-law, Carole, was at the table. She and Lance got married right out of high school. They seemed well-suited. They were music lovers and met in the high school band. "Where's your boyfriend?" asked Lance.

I shot a look at Lance that was lethal.

"Okay, time to dive in," I said. "He's Jewish."

"Is he religious, your boyfriend?" asked Carole.

"Not so much," I replied. "He had a bar mitzvah and spent time in Israel on a kibbutz. He refers to himself as a cultural Jew."

"What does that mean?" Lance asked.

"It's kind of like you have some religion, but you don't have all of the religion,"

"It's a bunch of bull," my Dad said. "I left that damn church after eighth grade. Lock stock and smoking barrel."

"You went to church with Lance and me," I said. "Why did you do that?"

"You're my children. I had a personal obligation to go to church with you. Once you finished college, I was done. The Irish are half-assed Catholics anyway."

My mother walked outside on the balcony and lit a cigarette. I followed her.

"Listen, darling, I'm planning a trip around the world this summer. Pan Am has a deal.

Three weeks for $1,500 as long as you don't double back. I'm working it out now. Want to come with us? We'll put a cot in the rooms."

"You're full of surprises. Sure, I'll go. Three weeks is perfect."

"Check to see if your passport is good. When you come back, I've arranged a job for you at Draper Development. You know how much I enjoyed working there."

"What do I do about my boyfriend?"

"Let him pine for you. Besides, I'm sure he has to work."

"He mentioned something about working at the D.A.'s office in Las Vegas."

"I thought you said he's from LA," my mother said.

"He is, but he has contacts in Las Vegas from his father. I told you he went to UCLA."

"He's Jewish ..."

"Mom, practically all of LA is Jewish."

I went around the world in three weeks with my parents that summer. Lance and Carole were expecting a baby and they needed to be home and keep an eye on the business. The sophistication of my mother's planning and the selection of countries were breathtaking. From the Ginza in Tokyo to Singapore to drink a Singapore Sling with my Dad at the Raffles Hotel, famous for its history of first-class writers hanging out in the bar – Somerset Maughan and Rudyard Kipling. Then on to Bangkok and the thrill of riding a boat down the Klongs; to Egypt to see the Valley of the Kings and the Valley of the Queens, King Tut's tomb, and riding camels in Giza to see the pyramids; to India – Delhi, Bombay (now Mumbai), to Srinagar, the farthest northern province of Kashmir to stay with a Muslim family on a houseboat.

The next stop was Israel via Turkey and Jordan, because in those days, travelers had to walk from the Jordanian border, an Arab country, to an isolated kiosk known as No Man's Land and show their passports. I watched my mother calmly hand the soldier her passport.

"We're about to enter paradise," said my Dad. "Look at the contrast between Jordan and Israel. These Israelis sure know how to put together an irrigation system. Every inch of land is cultivated with a watering system in the middle of the desert. The farms must do very well."

"Dad, why did we have to enter Israel from Jordan?" I asked.

"Anyone entering Israel from an Arab country has to be checked through. This kiosk doesn't belong to either Jordan or Israel. It's No Man's Land. But Jews are not welcome in an Arab state. There is no reciprocity. No one wants another war."

My mother did not say much on this leg of the journey. Whether she was nervous passing through the kiosk or exhausted from the trip, it was difficult to tell. I did not feel my mother had a connection to the land, but my Dad was energized by Israel. History was still in the making for him. He loved the archeology and ruins, the old churches, and the pioneer feeling of the country. I also felt the history of Israel. It felt deep and special. I vowed to return.

When the trip ended, I went to work at the Draper Development Company as a typist and took two night classes at San Francisco State College. I loved riding into San Francisco with my Dad every day. He dropped me off at work on the way to his office on Market Street.

That summer, I felt like a grown-up – sophisticated, erudite, independent, and on the path to success. I met a second-year Harvard MBA student named Peter Solomon. He worked as a summer intern at Draper. He was tall, thin, modestly good-looking in a nerdy way. I went out with him to fancy dinners and saw him at work to talk about whatever Peter had in his brilliant mind. When I told my mother about Peter, my mother asked, "Is Peter serious about you?"

"I can't tell. He sure is sophisticated. He tells me stories about President Kennedy when he was at Harvard. He had a car and driver that used to pull up at Radcliff, an all girls' school where everyone was super rich. Kennedy picked up a different girl every night."

"Are you interested?"

"I don't know, but he wants to take me to Las Vegas for a weekend."

"We will see about that, darling. A chaperone is in order."

CHAPTER 26

MEMBER OF THE TRIBE

By the end of summer, I was considering going to Las Vegas with Peter and contemplating a potential future with Jerry. I was wallowing in self-doubt. After all, I would see Jerry in less than a month. I was in deep thought and did not notice my mother entering my room.

"I need to talk to you," said my mother. "I don't know how attached you are to the Jewish boy at Draper or to your other Jewish boyfriend."

"If this is about going with Peter to Las Vegas, I think I've already made up my mind not to go. I'm going to see Jerry when I get back to Berkeley."

"Either way I think there will be a Jewish boy in your life," she said.

"Is that so terrible?" I asked.

"I'm not sure how to answer that, but I think it's time to tell you something that might come as a surprise – or maybe not. You should know that your Grandma Rose is Jewish."

I inhaled deeply and tried to get my bearings. She looked into her mother's sad, dark eyes and saw her vulnerability, which confused her even more. At that moment, I did not know the mother who raised me. The mother I knew and loved would have told me she was Jewish years ago. She would not have hidden her Jewish ancestry.

"If Grandma Rose is Jewish, then you're Jewish, Mom. Being Jewish doesn't skip a generation. You can't erase that. You are Jewish. And now suddenly, I'm Jewish."

"Well, I'm not Jewish." She got up, but did not leave the room. "You can do what you want with what I told you. You can be Jewish or not."

"What does that mean? Don't be so pragmatic like you always are, Mom. You were born a Jew, but you don't consider yourself a Jew. But you are Jewish because being Jewish comes from the mother's side."

"How do you know such things?" my mother asked.

"It doesn't matter how I know. If Grandma Rose is Jewish, her mother was Jewish, and I'm sure back in the nineteenth century, her mother married a Jewish man, wherever that was.

"They came from Odesa, Russia, at the time, and then emigrated to London."

"That's interesting, Mom. But why am I finding out about this now? Why come clean at this moment? What's so special about now? Because I'm in love with a Jewish boy and am going to marry him? What if I never met or fell in love with a Jewish boy? Then you'd never tell me? Did you talk to Grandma about what was on your mind? And why did it take so long to tell me?"

"Of course, Grandma knew how I felt growing up, and she has lived with my decision in silence. I never wanted to be Jewish. As a young girl, I saw Jake abuse Grandma Rose for wanting to practice her faith. Growing up, I began to understand that prejudice against Jews is about being the other. I did not want to be the other. I did not want the struggle of being a Jew."

"How could you allow me to be raised Catholic, Mom? Was that a choice? Because I was not just any kind of Catholic. I was the I-want-to-be-a-nun kind of Catholic. What am I supposed to do with this? I'm not just surprised. I'm pissed. I'm angry. Now, Dachau makes sense. You did not want me to get near the effects of torture and suffering. You feared my response to the Nazi horrors against Jews. The Holocaust existed. But if I did not bear witness to it, if I did not see its relics, then I might not believe it existed."

"Something like that."

"And what about Dad? Where was he in all of this? Did everybody in the Moran family know about your being Jewish?"

My mother sat back down on my bed, exhausted. "Of course, they knew. But only Grandma Mary was hateful. The word Jew was never mentioned in her house. That's because John was so loved by his family. Hannah and Tim, and the cousins thought he walked on water. If they knew, they would never say a word."

"I remember Grandma Mary never talked to you. She never looked at you. The hostility was present at every holiday. Is that why I was raised a Catholic – to appease the Irish Catholic side of the family?"

"It just happened when we moved you kids to Marin County. We never talked about it before we had children. And I did not object to putting you in Catholic school because I knew you would get a better education than in public school. I went to Catholic school when I was young, and I got a good education despite the religious nonsense. Dad and I made decisions we thought were good for the family. It had nothing to do with religion. God knows John was a lousy Catholic. As far as I was concerned, you and Lance can make your own choices as adults."

"I guess it was easier for you to go along with Dad."

"Don't you judge me, Joanie. You don't know my circumstances. You have no idea how much I suffered growing up. All Jews have endured a history of antisemitism. You can't possibly imagine. You can read about the pogroms, the concentration camps during the war in Europe, and try to forget the marathon of horrors. But it happened in America, too. You have never known its reality. Many Jews hid and disguised their identity by developing coping skills like I did. I became a skilled survivor with distance and determination."

"You could have shared that with me, Mom. There is no shame in that. I can't believe you did not tell me. Did you think Lance and I would not find out?"

"Maybe I thought you would one day. Lance found out early, when he was in high school. He asked me about it and I told your brother I thought it would be too difficult to identify as being a Jew. Lance could choose his own path. But Lance never had much attachment to religion. Now it's your choice. Antisemitism is vicious and murderous. I lived through the twenties with the Klan and the thirties watching fascism spread not just in Europe but America. I worked for the government before and during the war. I knew what was going on with some senators and that traitor Lindbergh and the brutal Catholic priest Father Coughlin and his America First crap. They vowed to be more brutal to the Jews than Hitler. Hard to imagine, but antisemitism was in our government – in the Senate and the House, judges, governors. When these traitors were rounded up and charged with sedition, after two years of prosecuting the hateful American Nazis, there were no convictions, no consequences. Antisemitism is always on the rise. You did not need Dachau as a reminder of its pervasiveness."

"I'm truly sorry, Mom. I want to ask you a hundred questions about that time, but I don't want you to relive it."

"I did not want to be near the hate," my mother said. "I did not want to be the object of discrimination, but I still had my fair share of slurs. Most of the time, no one knew who I was on the inside. I was impervious to others. They were unable to identify me as a Jew, so I could protect myself. I hid behind a two-way mirror. I could see out, but the others could not see in. Then, when I fell in love with your dad – that he was an Irish Catholic was another shield, but that's not why I married him. He was the love of my life."

"Mom, I'm probably going to marry Jerry."

"You marry who you want to marry. You don't need my approval."

My mother hugged me and held me close. She was not a demonstrative person, except with her husband. She was of a different generation, but that hug was full of love.

"Bring him around when you're ready."

My mother left the room. I broke down – I was vulnerable, left with more questions than answers. Even though it was a confusing moment in time, it felt good to confirm what I already suspected – that she was Jewish. Lance knew it before I did. He kept the secret. I told Lance about my conversation with our mother. It felt like it was a confession. We talked briefly about their Jewish heritage and how my brother knew it to be true years ago.

"How do you know what you know?" I asked Lance.

"You just know," Lance said quietly. "I wish I was brought up Jewish."

Anger and sadness pushed up against the knowledge I had been given, because she, too, did not get the chance to grow up Jewish and learn all the traditions and share important rituals. The sudden impact of knowing I was Jewish gave me permission to be who I was born to be. At first I could not breathe another kind of air. Catholicism was there, but it worked through my system. I was beginning to feel liberated from an antiquated belief. And then, I was dazed. And then, I felt relieved. I hoped I was ready to be out as a Jew. It would take time – time to embrace the truth. I would make choices about the course of my life compatible with my Jewish ancestry. In time.

I went back to Berkeley and told Jerry that my mother was Jewish.

He smiled. "When you're in love, the whole world is Jewish. Welcome to the tribe." He seemed happy. His parents would be elated.

I never took happiness for granted. That time with Jerry at Berkeley was not to be a fairy tale. On November 22, 1963, I was rehearsing a play when I heard screaming and yelling outside as if the world was coming apart at the seams. I ran outside the theater and asked a random stranger what happened.

Kennedy was shot! It felt huge and momentous. I ran to the law school library and sprinted up three flights of stairs to the study carrels to find Jerry. I was the bearer of the horrific news: Kennedy was shot. Shock was slow to set in. Grief lasted for months. I was 19 and felt the world was never going to be the same.

Two months later I married Jerry at Mission San Rafael in a Catholic ceremony to honor the Catholic side of the family. And I was between religions – still Catholic and trying to discover what it meant to be Jewish. Father Ben officiated. It almost did not happen because Jerry told the parish priest he would not raise our children Catholic, nor would he take religion lessons. Father Ben smooth-talked to the pastor, asking him to waive all restrictions, because otherwise, I knew there would be no marriage.

As I walked down the aisle with my Dad, I glanced at a stained glass window dedicated to my grandfather, Dennis Moran. My Dad bowed his head, but made no sign of the cross. Jerry was waiting for me at the foot of the altar. My Dad let go of my arm as I stepped next to Jerry. I remembered the time I told Father Ben that I wanted to become a nun. He delicately told me that he did not think of a religious calling in my future. "Live life," he said. I loved that man!

Jerry knelt before the altar. He whispered, "You owe me."

Some of our friends and relatives on both sides did not attend the Catholic ceremony, including Jerry's parents, who never knew that the Catholic ceremony took place. Jerry saw no need to tell them. It would be confusing and hurt them. Jerry and I had already made the decision to have another ceremony the following month. Our second marriage was held at the Claremont Hotel in Berkeley. The justice of the peace who officiated forgot our names. This ceremony was for the atheists, Jews, communists, beatniks, and best friends from UCLA and Berkeley, and some childhood friends. We partied and danced at Fort Mason, a government facility overlooking the Marina. Jerry and I danced to "Moon River."

A month after our Claremont Hotel wedding, Jerry informed me that we were moving to Las Vegas, where he'd landed a job at the district attorney's office. Barely twenty years old, I argued that I had one more semester of undergraduate studies at Berkeley. I planned my curriculum for the next three years, including getting a Ph.D., with my college counselor. I would skip the master's degree and go straight for a doctorate in theater, and then I would be a college professor, teaching acting and directing plays.

"Why didn't you tell me this before?" I asked. "I want to be a theater professor. I need three more years at Berkeley. You can be a lawyer at a firm in the city."

"I can't. Jews don't make partners. I'll never get to the top of my profession working in San Francisco."

I remembered Jerry kneeling at the altar minutes before being married in Mission San Rafael: "You owe me."

It sounded all too familiar, as if my mother wrote that script for Jerry. There was an undisclosed undercurrent to his belief that he was not going to be as successful practicing law in a Gentile law firm across the bridge from Berkeley.

"How can you say that?" I responded. "It's 1964. Where's the antisemitism?"

"You can't see it, but you can sense it. I have studied white-collar law firms in the city since before I entered law school. They hire guys from Hastings Law or lawyers from the same clubs, sons of attorneys who work in the firms. My best shot is Vegas. Big fish in a small pond."

"It's a gamble," I said. "No pun intended. We should have talked about it."

"You will carve out your career. You are clever that way, and, if I know you, you're up for the adventure. That's why I married you."

Jerry was prepared for his adventure, but I was not. He gave me too much credit. It was easier for him. He was familiar with the Las Vegas law community and had contacts through his father, who had lived there with his family from 1948 to 1952. Jerry spent one summer as a law intern in the DA's office and another with a high-profile law firm whose lead lawyer was not Jewish. Las Vegas was half Mormon, almost half Jewish, and the rest were gangsters – from Philadelphia, New York, Cleveland, and Kansas City – who ran the casinos, plus a number of high-rolling Jewish gangsters who'd migrated from Los Angeles in the 1940s, including Meyer Lansky and Bugsy Siegel. They bought up land for a dime and expanded the casino business on the Las Vegas Strip. It was a time when the mob ran the town. Jerry and his law partner from Philly were ready to defend the gangsters and represent their businesses.

My entrance into Las Vegas in the summer of 1964 was a baptism of fire. Jerry told me that I had to get a job because he was studying for the Nevada bar. Jerry's friend was the slot manager at the Sahara. Vince told Jerry about an opening for a secretary to the catering director. But first I had to interview with the hotel president, a 36-year-old Jewish man who was a shill for the Kansas City mob. I went to his office in the executive office on the second-floor for the interview and encountered a packed room. A lone chair was situated in the middle of the room. It was my chair. The electric chair. No one introduced me to the catering director. The setup felt like a sleazy beauty pageant. The secretary to the president of the Sahara Hotel was a double for Cruella De Vil. It was June, over a hundred degrees outside, and I was sitting in the third rung of hell, sweating in a sexy polka-dot polyester dress that my mother made for me. The dress stuck to my back and bottom due to the heat. After the fake interview, for which I had to recite something from Shakespeare – I recited several lines from a soliloquy delivered by Ophelia from Hamlet – I stood to go, walking backwards out of the office into a freezing air-conditioned hallway. Cruella told me I had to take the test again.

Much to my surprise, I had the best summer of my life. Not only was my boss a funny character, a Jew from the Bronx, but I was assigned to drive comedians who performed at the Sahara, including Jackie Vernon, Allan King, Jackie Mason, and Buddy Hackett to and from downtown Fremont Street where they gambled. Since Jerry and his partner were buddies with Don Rickles, I got in on the action at the Riviera lounge, where Rickles performed. I also auditioned and starred in a Las Vegas Community production of Oklahoma. "The show must go on" was my motto.

My world was Jewish before I would raise my children Jewish. Beshert. It is Destiny – meant to be. After Jerry passed the bar exam, and we came back from our honeymoon – Mexico on five dollars a day – he took me to Temple Beth Shalom. It was my first Friday night Shabbat. We attended services with his law partner and wife. Carolyn and I became instant best friends forever. During the evening, Jerry introduced me to the rabbi.

"Rabbi, this is my wife, Joan. I have to ask you a question, Rabbi. My wife was born of a Jewish mother who denied she was Jewish, and she was raised Catholic, which was her father's religion. Is she Jewish, or does she have to convert?"

"You should know your Jewish history, Jerry. Your wife is Jewish, always was and will be. No mikvah is necessary. And always remember this: Jews feel they are born to make a difference, not to be a part of what everyone wants. That's more important than a mikvah."

It was an astounding moment at temple that night. I felt at home with the warmth and wisdom of the rabbi and meeting new friends. Even before the rabbi confirmed to Jerry that I was Jewish, even before my mother confirmed it, I had ruminated about an unconscious familiarity with being Jewish. I did not know why I felt an affinity toward Judaism, but I did. You just know. Thanks, brother Lance.

These early years in Las Vegas I was focused on finishing college, teaching high school, and moving forward with graduate degrees in order to teach college. While teaching high school in 1972, our son Jonathan was born. Jerry's parents had moved to Las Vegas the previous year, and Lance had already settled in that city with a mission to canvas the city for property for Moran Construction. Two years later, my parents moved to Las Vegas. I was pleased to have them involved in the Las Vegas community. The city was perfect for all of us personally in terms of making friends and professionally in developing my parent's construction business, Jerry's law firm, and my intentions to teach college at UNLV in the theater department.

After my parents moved to Las Vegas, my mother was concerned about Rose's health and suggested to her that she move to Las Vegas so the family could watch over her. Harry, Rose's last husband had died several years earlier. My Grandma outlived three husbands. Lance leaped at the chance to be of service. My family thought having Grandma around was a plus. Rose moved into an apartment close to downtown, and everyone helped out to make her life easy. At the point when her health began to deteriorate, Lance and Carole took Rose into their home to watch over her.

My second son, Aaron, was born in 1975 and brought joy to everyone. The family was growing with an understanding of a separation of religious rituals. It was understood that I celebrated Jewish holidays with Jerry and his parents. Christmas and Easter were celebrated with my parents and with Lance and Carole and their two sons. The elders understood the importance of celebrating holidays and the offspring were clued into the differences. After a few years, my parents invited Jerry's parents to the Moran's holiday table. Jerry's parents could not have been happier, more proud and loving during the holiday festivities. I was always secretly joyful that my mother-in-law taught me Yiddish slang over the years. I would use the words in sentences and as exclamations in my speech, and Anne would give me a knowing smile.

Joan & Mother Estelle

EPILOGUE

In 1980, my best friends invited me to go to Israel with fifty Jewish women around the U.S. from the National Council of Jewish Women. It was an overwhelming idea.

"Come on Joan, you've got to go on tour with us," said Charlene. "This is our time." Charlene, my wonderful friend, was right.

I felt it was time to visit Israel again – my last visit was in 1963 – and deepen my spiritual and emotional relationship to Judaism. I asked my mother to go on the trip with me to Israel with a different set of eyes.

"It is not for me. I did it once, and I have no interest in going again," she said. "Besides, I have to put Grandma Rose into the hospital. She is not doing well. Hospital food will kill her, so I'm bringing her food every day from home. That way I'll be sure she can keep up her strength."

From the Golan Heights to the Red Sea, climbing up to Masada and exploring the Jewish fortress, to the celebration of Sukkot, which honors joy and gratitude for the fall harvest, to bearing witness the Holocaust memorial, Yad Veshem, and partying into the night with Israelis who revere living in the present, I learned that Israeli Jews mix some secular elements into their lives unless they are Hasidic. Jewish secularism had less to do with ritual and more to do with being observant Jews – maybe not every Friday night Shabbat Jews, but the Jewish identification that has more to do with an intellectual and energetic connection to the tribe.

Israel was an exciting country, always displaying elements of the warrior mentality and people who were quick to make decisions and quick to display their passion for literature and theater. I met an actor from the Israeli Repertory Company who took me to see Isaac Bashevis Singer's *Yentl* in Hebrew. After the show, everyone congregated backstage to break bread. It was a blessing for the community. It was Israel's identity.

When I returned home, I immediately wanted to see my Grandma Rose. My mother joined me in the lobby of the hospital to hear my mother's assessment.

"She's not eating," said my mother with tears in her eyes. "And she won't know you, honey, but you can see her at peace. That woman is incredible. There's not a line in her face. She looks so young. She was a great woman, Joanie. I always admired her courage and the way she loved us. I'm glad we had these last years with her." I walked into grandma's hospital room and cried. I remembered how Grandma Rose had polished my black and white saddle shoes when she lived with our family in San Rafael for a time. I was grateful to be able to watch her at rest in her final peace. She died at eighty-nine.

On the day of Jonathan's bar mitzvah, my parents arrived at our synagogue, Temple Beth Shalom, and walked behind Jerry, Jonathan, and myself. My second son, Aaron, walked behind them with Lance and Carole. I turned around for no reason other than to see how my parents were doing – thinking my Mom would be proud. Her facial expression told me she wasn't. There was a scowl on her face, and she mouthed the words: I don't know why you have to do this. Then she pointed to the yarmulke on Jonathan's head, as if to say: Don't announce it! Don't point it out! Keep your identity behind the mirror so no one will know! Was her trauma going to last a lifetime?

It was hard for me to accept my mother on those terms – still the reluctant Jew.

You can run but you can't hide. In spite of my mother's resistance, she would always be my Jewish mother. She was raised by her Jewish mother, Rose, so my mother sat in temple as her mother would have done, perhaps gritting her teeth. Yet, I am convinced she was still proud of her first grandson.

As they grew older, my parents began to pull back on building and selling homes. My mother became less driven to succeed. My brother's sons came around frequently. The eldest son, Phillip, adored my Dad. They were quite a funny pair. My mother excelled at other activities. She taught senior aerobics, joined the Red Hat Society's tap group, and continued to create designer clothes. My father read history, listened to the news and walked the dog.

Almost immediately after my brother's youngest son, Matthew, graduated from high school, he had an accident in his family's garage. He was working under his car and the jack holding up the car gave out. This tragedy was to alter the fabric of our family significantly. There was an explosion of sadness and grief for the young life lost. Matthew was an exceptional young man and son. I think for those of us who are still alive his loss to us has never healed. The unpredictability of life is constant, and pain is part of our living experience. Carole experienced physical pain for several years. No doctor was able to discover the reason for her pain because it was located in her lower spine. In fact, it emanated from the vertebrae in her neck. It was cancer and spreading. Carole chose not to take a curative path. She was ready to meet Matthew somewhere in the universe. A soul never dies. Time transcends time. Jonathan married a Jewish girl and the lavish wedding was held in Santa Barbara. It was difficult for my mother to travel at that time. She declined to go. Jonathan and Carli were nevertheless close to my mother when they lived in Las Vegas, My mother enjoyed them both as a couple and the grandchildren that were to follow.

Aaron's wedding took place several years later in Santa Monica and was presided over by a female rabbi, a friend of both Aaron and his new wife. My mother could not have been more excited and happy to be in attendance. All the trauma, all the anger, all the resentment were gone. In those last decades, my mother had come to a determination, whether conscious or unconscious, that this was her Jewish family.

Recently, I sat in temple on the occasion of the bar mitzvah for Jude, my fourth grandson, and the third son of Jonathan and Carli. My mother had passed – and my Dad had passed ten years before – and it was a bittersweet moment for my family. I was filled with pride, surrounded by my Jewish family – my ex-husband, Jonathan and his two other sons, Aaron, his wife and their two children. I watched with joy as Jude moved with grace and dignity on the bimah. Jude exemplified an innate intelligence and an emotional connection to his ceremony as did his brothers before him. I was filled with gratitude. Being Jewish had come full circle in my family, and I was truly grateful for my mother's decision to reveal her secret to me so I could know her truth – our truth.

The essence of Estelle Moran is a constant in my life – she was a force of nature, an extraordinary being, an abiding presence who lived her life with grace and goodness, tenacity and curiosity. Although she did not believe in tradition, nor did she have faith in a God, nor did she stand by the full import of her ancestry, my mother carried the Jewish essence of her mother, Rose Rosenberg Lanch throughout her life. I now carry that lineage with love and compassion for those who suffered the trauma of discrimination. What keeps the Jewish connection alive is the beauty exemplified by love for family – the central value of Jewish life. My mother will always be my Jewish mother.

AN EXCERPT FROM JOAN'S BOOK
ONCE A HOMECOMING QUEEN

Carlos was working at the construction company for about two weeks when he was profiled by a local cop on his way to the church to close up. The fact that he was a U.S. citizen did not make a difference to the cop because Carlos had no papers on him. Carlos argued that he had a license, but the cop was unmoved. What Carlos did have was a rap sheet that showed he was previously incarcerated in Long Beach and Fort Collins. Carlos made a phone call to Francine to rescue him from jail. He had not been living with her for long, but he'd been good to her, and he hoped she had some mercy for him.

"Damnit, Carlos, you didn't have your papers with you?" she said when he called her from jail. "I thought you were smarter than that. Get a grip."

She picked up Ida and together they went to the jail to see what they could do. It was too late to get him out on bail or help him find his legal papers. Carlos had a swift hearing and was incarcerated for thirty days.

"Bad luck and lack of skills kept Carlos in bondage," said Francine.

Ida was holding Francine's arm as they walked down the stairs of the Grand Rapids Police Department. It was a bright, sunny afternoon with a bouncy blue and white sky that belonged in a watercolor painting by Joseph Turner.

"What are you saying, Francine? Because you picked this guy up on the street and he's living with you and you get him a job, you give him a get out of jail free card? Are you nuts?"

"He's a good guy, Ida, and I felt sorry for him."

"What is he, your boyfriend? Sex at your age is not an option. And besides, he's using you. And he could kill you when you turn your back or when you're sleeping in bed."

"Don't be so dramatic. Or a racist. Both attitudes are unbecoming a woman of your age. I'm not about being abused anyway. This guy is sweet like marshmallows. Let's go to our usual place. I'm starving. It's on me. I didn't thank you for taking care of my dogs last year when I landed in detox after the accident."

"Accident, my ass," said Ida. "You were drunk when you fell down the stairs. I don't know why you don't sleep on the couch like you're supposed to when you've had three too many."

Francine and Ida had been going to Chez Moi for decades. They knew the menu by heart and the waitress by name. It still retained its old musty smell after forty years in business. The furnishings had not been changed in twenty years. The brown leather sofas at the front entrance were falling apart. The leather was peeling off the sides like skin from a dead animal. But the menu was better than Applebee's. More important were the bartender's generous shots of bourbon in their drinks.

"Look, Ida, you're my oldest friend since I moved to Grand Rapids, and you need to be on my side with this Carlos business. Rachel already met him."

"I won't say anything to Rachel if she calls me, but you promise me you'll be careful. You never stayed sober when you got out of the hospital after your fall. So you'd better not drink so much while he's around. Things happen."

"Well, I kind of detoxed, but my physical therapist and I had a thing going on with the orderly. Not sexual, so get your mind out of the gutter. We laughed and played cards, and he brought me little booze bottles, like from the airplane, and a thermos of tequila. God, it was fun."

"You cheated through physical therapy, Francine. They could've expelled you."

"Oh, well yes and no. And you wouldn't have taken a drink or two if you'd had the opportunity?"

"Probably true, but luckily, I've never detoxed, so I can't relate. But we did make a promise after you got out of recovery that we would only drink after five in the afternoon."

"How's that going for us?" asked Francine.

"I'm no saint," said Ida. "But I don't drive at night when I drink. And I hope you don't because I don't know what I'd do without you."

"We don't have to drink today," said Francine. "Not even a glass of wine. God, I hate wine."

Jane, their favorite waitress, stood at the table listening to most of the conversation. A skinny, long-legged dirty-blonde woman in her fifties, she bore the marks of alcohol and cigarettes on her face. Lines pinched her eyes and exaggerated the abundance of fatigue she was obviously feeling.

"Let's have our usual, Jane, except no drinks," Ida said.

"You sure?" asked Jane as she glanced at Francine.

"For now," said Francine, glaring at Ida.

Jane nodded, smiled, and walked away to place the order.

"Jane looks like she had quite a night," said Ida. "Poor thing shackled to this job day in, day out. We're lucky we ended up on the right side of the coin. You more than me, Francine."

"It pretty much cost me my life. Remember my crazy third husband trying to light himself on fire with the oxygen pole? Third time was the charmer. Good old Peter."

"Good old Sam. He saved my life more times than I can remember. I shouldn't drink, Francine. I don't hold my liquor like I used to. Doesn't take much to make me feel dizzy."

"You keep talking like that and I'll order a drink."

"You crack me up, for sure." Ida giggled.

"Did I tell you Rachel announced that she hates her marketing job at Spectrum Healthcare? She wants to become a farmer?"

"What are you talking about? Why would anyone want that?"

"She wants to grow vegetables, have a garden, and sell them at Farmer's markets. And just when Mark is about ready to make partner in his exclusive downtown law firm."

"Could be a perfect life," said Ida. "At least, Rachel doesn't confront your drinking like my Karen did."

"I think Rachel went to Al-Anon."

"How do you know?"

"You know how you know. You just know."

"I went to AA for a year. Not a big deal. Rachel probably keeps her secrets just like Karen, and I'll make you a bet my daughter is angry. But I don't care what Rachel thinks, nor do I feel the need to explain my choices. I drink. So be it. I'm sure Rachel hates my drinking. I got balled out for missing Christmas dinner because I had a gorilla of a hangover. But she's my good girl and wouldn't walk out on me. We planned a trip in the spring to Louisiana on one of those gambling riverboats. I love hanging out with her."

"I'd rather travel to exotic places," said Ida. "I wish I could have done that with my daughter. I really screwed this life up, Francine."

"I don't know, Ida. Maybe we both did. But at least we did it together. Ida and Francine. Francine and Ida. Screw the world."

"We're in control, then. Right?" asked Ida.

"Let's renew our pact not to drink until five, but let's start that promise tomorrow. I mean, after all, we are at our favorite place to eat lunch."

"What about a bottle of Chardonnay?"

"Chardonnay tastes like piss, Ida. Let's go for a bottle of Merlot. If I have to drink wine, make it wine with teeth. Merlot is the only wine I can tolerate."

"Anything else?" Jane asked as she set down the food order.

"A bottle of your best Merlot," said Francine.

"Those are my girls," said Jane as she left the table.

They got drunk that afternoon and kept their promise not to drive while intoxicated. Jane called them a cab.

BOOKS AVAILABLE FROM JOAN MORAN ON AMAZON

Women Obsessed
Sixty, Sex & Tango: Confessions of a Beatnik Boomer
I'm the Boss of Me! Stay Sexy, Smart and Strong at Any Age
An Accidental Cuban
Once a Homecoming Queen
Suddenly Jewish: The Life and Times of My Jewish Mother

www.ingramcontent.com/pod-product-compliance
Lightning Source LLC
Chambersburg PA
CBHW051937290426
44110CB00015B/2014